THE RESTAURANT TRAINING PROGRAM

An Employee Training Guide for Managers

Karen Eich Drummond, F.M.P.

John Wiley & Sons, Inc.

New York • Chichester • Brisbane • Toronto • Singapore

This publication is designed to provide accurate and authoritative information in regard to the subject matter covered. It is sold with the understanding that the publisher is not engaged in rendering legal, accounting, or other professional service. If legal advice or other expert assistance is required, the services of a competent professional person should be sought. FROM A DECLARATION OF PRINCIPLES JOINTLY ADOPTED BY A COMMITTEE OF THE AMERICAN BAR ASSOCIATION AND A COMMITTEE OF PUBLISHERS.

Senior Editor: Claire Thompson
Managing Editor: Janice Weisner
Production Services: Crane Typesetting Service, Inc.

Library of Congress Cataloging-in-Publication Data

Drummond, Karen Eich.
    The restaurant training program : an employee training guide for managers / Karen Eich Drummond.
        p.   cm.
    Includes index.
    ISBN 0-471-55207-0
    1. Restaurants, lunch rooms, etc.—Employees—Training of.
    I. Title.
TX911.3.T73D78   1992
647.95′068′3—dc20   92-47
                                                            CIP

Printed in the United States of America

10 9 8 7 6 5 4 3

Acknowledgments

Selected On-the-Job Training Outlines and Group Training Outlines contain material from **The Health Care Food Service Training Manual**, Aspen Publishing (Gaithersburg, MD), 1990. Permission has been granted from the publisher to adapt this material.

Chapters 1 and 2 contain material from **Developing and Conducting Training for Foodservice Employees: A Guide for Trainers**, the American Dietetic Association (Chicago, IL), 1992. Permission has been granted from the publisher.

Contents

Chapter 4   Group Training Outlines   293

Appendix A   Training Resources   399
Appendix B   Training Forms   402

Preface

Training, in restaurants, simply means teaching employees how to do their jobs. It involves teaching the procedures to follow and helping employees to develop the skills they need to reach the standards required. Three kinds of training are needed in restaurants: new employee orientation, job training, and retraining. This book provides both guidance and ready-to-use materials to help you get off the dime and start conducting training for your staff.

Orientation is the initial introduction to the job. It sets the tone of what it is like to work for the company and explains the facility and the nitty-gritty of days and hours and rules and policies. It takes place at the beginning of Day One. Chapter 1 clearly explains how to set up and implement an orientation program for new hires and includes a sample Orientation Checklist.

Job training is instruction in what to do and how to do it for every detail of a given job in a given restaurant. It begins on Day One and may be spread in small doses over a number of days, depending on how much needs to be taught and the complexity of the job.

Retraining applies to current employees. It is necessary when workers are not measuring up to standards, whenever a new method or menu or piece of equipment is introduced, or when a worker asks for it. It takes place whenever it is needed.

Chapter 2 discusses how to develop and implement a job training/retraining program for hourly employees. It includes Job Training Checklists for five key restaurant jobs as well as on-the-job training information.

To help develop your own job training/retraining program, Chapter 3 gives you fifty On-the-Job Training Outlines in the following areas: sanitation and safety, service skills, and food production skills. The sanitation and safety outlines are primarily designed for back-of-the-house personnel, the service skills outlines for front-of-the-house personnel, and the production skills outlines for food preparation and cooking staff. Each On-the-Job Training Outline includes a Trainer's Outline, a step-by-step description of what the trainer is to do, and an Employee's Outline with exercises and key points to remember. The Employee's Outline, as well as any materials in this book, may be photocopied. In most cases, an Employee Quiz and Job Aids are also provided. Job Aids are large-print lists of important information, such as how to operate the dishmachine, that can be posted in your operation. Most On-the-Job Training Outlines are designed to be completed in 10 to 20 minutes, with some requiring up to 30 minutes. Trainers are asked at various points in the materials to customize the procedure to their own operations before conducting training.

Chapter 4 has eight Group Training Outlines designed to be used with your hourly foodservice employees in group classroom training. Each Group Training Outline explains what employees need to know, as well as how the trainer can get the content across to the employees. There are also ready-to-photocopy employee materials called Employee Guides that contain exercises, key points, and quizzes. In addition to the Group Training Outlines and Employee Guides, there are Teaching Aids that can be used to make posters or transparencies.

The Appendixes contain other useful material. Appendix A contains a listing of sources for training videotapes for restaurants. It is possible to use videotapes as part of any of the training offered in this program. Videotapes are an excellent means of training when you also provide an introduction, discussion of major points, summary, and evaluation, all of which are included here. Appendix B has an employee training record form, class evaluation form, and employee certificate of completion of training.

With this book, you can successfully implement a high-quality training program that will be reflected in heightened guest satisfaction, employee morale, productivity, and job performance.

CHAPTER 1

New Employee Orientation

Orientation Programs

Research increasingly indicates that no orientation or poor orientation contributes to new hires' dissatisfaction and turnover. For new hires, the first thirty days are likely to be the most crucial. Without an orientation, new employees take longer to get up to speed in their new positions and they make more mistakes. They also tend to experience more frustration and less commitment to the operation.

By providing an orientation program, you communicate to employees what is expected of them and how their job fits into the overall operation. It also helps employees to fit into their new jobs faster, be more productive and satisfied, and realize that you care about how they do their jobs.

Use your orientation program as a way to give a good first impression to new hires about your operation; remember, you may not get a second chance to make a favorable first impression. Also remember that how employees treat customers is often a reflection of how they are treated by management.

Orientation Checklist

An *Orientation Checklist*, as seen in Figure 1-1, is an excellent tool for conducting orientation. It lists sample topics covered during an orientation program such as how to request a day off. These topics are grouped into four categories: Introduction to the Restaurant, Pay and Benefits, Policies and Procedures, and The New Job. One benefit of using such a checklist is that it ensures consistency among managers and supervisors who are conducting orientation, and makes it unlikely that some topic will be forgotten.

Now let's discuss the steps to use when developing an orientation checklist. Choose the topics you feel need to be covered. Your *Policy and Procedure Manual* is a handy

FIGURE 1-1   Orientation Checklist

INTRODUCTION TO THE RESTAURANT

_____ Welcome the new employee.

_____ Describe restaurant briefly, including history, operation (type of menu, service, hours of operation), and goals.

_____ Show how restaurant is structured or organized.

PAY AND BENEFITS

_____ As applicable, explain benefits to which the employee is entitled, such as medical insurance.

_____ Review amount of sick time, holiday time, personal time, and vacation time allowed as applicable.

_____ Review the new employee's salary and when and where to pick up the paycheck, as well as who can pick up the employee's paycheck. If applicable, explain policy on overtime.

POLICIES AND PROCEDURES

_____ Explain dress code and who furnishes uniforms.

_____ Describe where to park.

_____ Explain how to sign in and out and when.

_____ Assign locker and explain its use.

_____ Explain how to call in if unable to come to work.

_____ Explain the procedure for requesting time off.

_____ Discuss the rules on personal telephone use.

_____ Explain the department's smoking policy.

_____ Explain the department's meal policy including when and where food can be eaten.

_____ Explain channels of communication such as meetings and bulletin boards.

_____ Review disciplinary guidelines.

_____ Review the teamwork policy.

_____ Explain the Equal Employment Opportunity policy.

_____ Discuss promotional and transfer opportunities.

_____ Explain the professional conduct policy.

_____ Explain requirements for giving notice if employee decides to leave the job.

FIGURE 1-1 Orientation Checklist (continued)

THE NEW JOB

_____ *Review the job description and standards of performance.

_____ *Review the daily work schedule including break times.

_____ *Review the hours of work and days off. Show where the schedule is posted.

_____ *Explain how and when the employee will be evaluated.

_____ Explain the probationary period.

_____ *Explain the training program including its length.

_____ Describe growth opportunities.

_____ Give tour of restaurant, including location of rest rooms, and introduce the new employee to other managers and co-workers.

*Handouts

The topics above have been reviewed.

_____   _____   _____
      Employee Signature   Date   Supervisor Signature

Source: Karen Eich Drummond, **Staffing Your Foodservice Operation**, New York: Van Nostrand Reinhold, 1991. Reprinted with the permission of the publisher.

reference here. Also, get feedback from managers and employees on what they feel is important. Their advice can be very useful.

Group the topics into headings such as The New Job or Policies and Procedures. Under each heading, place the topics in a logical order for presentation. Remember to begin with the most relevant and immediate kinds of information, because when new employees start work, they are normally quite anxious to become competent in doing their job.

Decide how much detail you want to provide for each topic. For example, when describing the restaurant, you may decide to include its history, size, types of services provided, goals, and organization.

Type up your Orientation Checklist, providing as much detail for each item as felt necessary by the trainers who will be using the checklist. Number each item and leave a space in front of it. At the end, provide a space for both the new employee and the trainer to sign and date the checklist, indicating that orientation was completed. This provides valuable training documentation.

Orientation Handbook

In addition to the checklist, it is a good idea to develop and hand out to new employees an *Orientation Handbook* (see Figure 1-2). The Orientation Handbook (sometimes

FIGURE 1-2 *Excerpt from an Orientation Booklet*

PERFORMANCE

Your supervisor will discuss with you both the general duties and expectations of your job (contained in the Job Description), as well as your daily assignments (contained in the Job Duty Schedule). Make sure you understand what we expect of you—this is vital for all of us. Your supervisor will also give you the Performance Evaluation form that will be used in three months to determine if you have completed your probationary period satisfactorily. This form is also used for your yearly evaluations. If you have any questions, please ask!

HOURS OF WORK

Your supervisor will give you a copy of your schedule. As a member of a team, it is important that you arrive in your assigned work area, ready for work, at the scheduled time. Since we serve meals every single day of the year, you do work some weekends and holidays.

You are entitled to one 15-minute scheduled work break for each 4 hours of work. Work breaks are paid time and are not guaranteed in length or frequency. They cannot be saved or added together. You receive 30 minutes (unpaid time) for lunch or dinner if you are a full-time employee.

called the Employee Handbook) is a written record of everything covered in orientation. Because employees are likely to forget much of what is said during orientation, particularly about policies and procedures, the orientation handbook is a wonderful reference for them to use later. Once the orientation handbook is written and typed, you can make it into a booklet by adding a cover and stapling.

Finally, it is a good idea to determine the following: who will do the orientation, how much time is needed, and when orientation can be done. Most often it is the employee's new supervisor who conducts orientation. This is advantageous as most new employees are anxious to know and feel comfortable with their new boss. Orientation is usually conducted within the first few days or first week of a new employee's arrival. Orientation is more effective when covered over several sessions, rather than completed in one session, so as not to overwhelm the employee.

In summary, your first step is to choose the topics to be covered and group them into headings such as The New Job or Policies and Procedures. Decide how much detail you want to provide for each topic. Now you should be ready to type up your Orientation Checklist. In addition to the checklist, it is a good idea to develop and hand out to new employees an orientation handbook. Finally, consider who will do the orientation, how much time will be needed, and when orientation will be done.

How to Orient New Employees

We will now discuss general guidelines for orienting new employees, whether orienting one or several employees. When doing orientation, do your best to find a place free from distractions. As much as possible, make arrangements to prevent being disturbed by phone calls and the like. When you don't give new employees your full attention, you give the message that they don't need to pay full attention to their job either. By asking frequent questions during orientation, you can turn what is often a one-way conversation into a mutual discussion. Once orientation is over, follow up with your new employees to see how they are doing and if they have any questions or concerns.

Now we are ready to discuss the actual steps you will use to perform orientation. First, get all your materials ready ahead of time, including copies of the Orientation Checklist and Orientation Handbook for yourself and the new employees. In addition, it is suggested to have these handouts for new employees: job description, daily work schedule, weekly schedule with days off, overview of training program, and performance appraisal or evaluation form. These handouts are starred on Figure 1-1.

Next, greet the new employees warmly, introduce yourself, and explain your role in the department and how you will interact with the employee. Briefly explain the purpose and scope of orientation. Give the employee a copy of the Orientation Checklist and the Orientation Handbook and explain the importance of asking questions at any time during orientation. Review each item, asking questions to ascertain the employee's understanding. Besides checking on the employee's comprehension, your questions also help the employee to retain the material reviewed. Be sure to ask the employee for any questions he or she may have.

Plan at some point to give the new employee a tour of the department and an opportunity to meet his or her peers. At the end of orientation, have the checklist signed off.

Figure 1-3 is a checklist for the trainer to use before and during orientation to help perform new employee orientation as described here.

FIGURE 1-3 *Trainer Checklist: Orientation*

Directions: Use this checklist to help you perform new employee orientation. Check off each item as it is used. Circle any item that you would like to work harder on next time you do orientation.

GENERAL GUIDELINES

1. Do orientation in an environment as free from distractions as possible. _____

2. Make sure orientation is more than just one-way communication by asking _____ questions of the new employee as much as possible.

3. After orientation is done, follow up with new employees to see how they are _____ doing and if they have any questions.

FIGURE 1-3 *Trainer Checklist: Orientation (continued)*

STEPS TO ORIENT NEW EMPLOYEES

1. Get all materials ready ahead of time. _____

2. Greet the new employee warmly, introduce yourself, and explain your role _____ in the department and how you will interact with the employee.

3. Briefly explain the purpose and scope of orientation. _____

4. Give the employee a copy of the Orientation Checklist and Orientation _____ Handbook.

5. Explain to the employee the importance of asking questions at any time _____ during orientation.

6. Review each item, asking questions to ascertain the employee's under- _____ standing.

7. Ask the employee for any questions he or she may have. _____

8. Be sure to give the new employee an appropriate tour and an opportunity _____ to meet peers.

9. Make sure the Orientation Checklist is signed properly at the end of orienta- _____ tion and filed.

Source: Karen Eich Drummond, **Developing and Conducting Training for Foodservice Employees** (audiocassette), 1992. Courtesy of The American Dietetic Association.

In many cases, orientation is accomplished in short daily segments, such as 30–45 minutes, over a period of several days or up to one week. The length will depend largely on how much material needs to be covered. The remaining time is spent in job training. This approach is beneficial because new employees are normally quite anxious to fit into the new job and work group.

This chapter was adapted from Karen Eich Drummond, **Developing and Conducting Training for Foodservice Employees** (audiocassette), 1992. Courtesy of The American Dietetic Association.

CHAPTER 2

Job Training

Job Training Programs

A *job training program* teaches new employees how to do their jobs and retrains current employees. Retraining is necessary when an employee is having difficulty meeting job standards, when procedures are going to change such as a new menu is being introduced, or when an employee asks for it.

Job training and retraining can be accomplished by using individualized or group training. Examples of individualized job teaching methods include *on-the-job training* and *self-study*. An advantage of individualized training is that it can be personalized, in most cases, to the learner. Group training refers mainly to training groups of employees, usually small groups with two to ten employees, in a classroom situation. Groups of employees can also be trained in on-the-job settings, such as showing a small group how to set up the dishmachine. Group training is advantageous when you need to relay information to more than one person.

On-the-job training is the most widely used method of job training and retraining. In this method, the employee is placed into the real work situation and trained to do the various parts of his or her job by an experienced employee or supervisor who uses the tell/show/do/review teaching method. In brief, there are four steps in this method: tell or lecture the employee about what he or she is going to learn, show or demonstrate it to the employee, let the employee do it, and review what has been taught.

One benefit of on-the-job training is that it provides immediate application and satisfaction for the new employee who is often anxious. Also, fellow employees can help the trainee, which enhances teamwork and the integration of the new employee into the work group. On-the-job training, when done correctly, can be very effective.

Job Training Checklist

With a *Job Training Checklist* (see Figures 2-1 to 2-5) and a good trainer, job training can be very productive. The first step is to list the job duties. The job description is a good resource for this information. Next, arrange the job duties in a logical order for

FIGURE 2-1 Sample On-the-Job Training Checklist for a Host/Hostess

OJT CHECKLIST: HOST/HOSTESS

Name of Trainee: _____

Date Starting Training: _____

Trainer(s): _____

Directions: *Write the date in the blank space next to each task when you feel the trainee has mastered it.*

Dining Room Operation

_____ Supervising opening duties and sidework, serving (including responsible service of alcohol), handling the guest check, and closing duties and sidework

_____ Taking reservations

_____ Conducting daily meeting with staff

_____ Greeting guests at door and seating them

_____ Directing service of guests as needed to meet service standards

_____ Answering guest questions on menu, wine, cocktails, and liquor served

_____ Handling guest complaints

_____ Checking on responsible service of alcohol

Supervision of Staff

_____ Reviewing all job descriptions

_____ Calculating payroll hours

_____ Scheduling staff

_____ Coaching staff

_____ Filling out yearly performance appraisals forms

_____ Holding weekly meetings

_____ Disciplining staff when needed

_____ Interviewing applicants

_____ Selecting and hiring staff

_____ Orienting and training new employees

FIGURE 2-1   Sample On-the-Job Training Checklist for a Host/Hostess (continued)

Dining Room Maintenance

_____ Checking on completion of sidework assignments

_____ Completing orders for dining room supplies

_____ Reporting dining room repairs

Cost Control

_____ Planning dining room budget

_____ Checking dining room payroll costs against budget and explaining any variances

_____ Checking dining room supply costs against budget and explaining any variances

General

_____ Dresses according to dress code

_____ Is hospitable and courteous toward guests

_____ Comes to work and is on time

_____ Works as a team member

Please sign below upon completion of training. Both the Employee and the Trainer certify by their signatures that the training has been adequate to prepare the new employee to function in his/her new position.

_____   _____

Signature/Date—Employee   Signature/Date—Trainer

Source: Karen Eich Drummond, Staffing Your Foodservice Operation, New York: Van Nostrand Reinhold, 1991. Reprinted with the permission of the publisher.

FIGURE 2-2   Sample On-the-Job Training Checklist for a Server

OJT CHECKLIST: SERVER

Name of Trainee: _____

Date Starting Training: _____

Trainer(s): _____

Directions: *Write the date in the blank space next to each task when you feel the trainee has mastered it.*

FIGURE 2-2   Sample On-the-Job Training Checklist for a Server (continued)

Serves Guests

_____ Greets guest cordially within 5 minutes

_____ Explains menu and specials to guests and answers questions

_____ Takes food, wine, and beverage orders

_____ Recommends wines appropriate to menu items

_____ Picks up orders and completes plate preparation

_____ Serves and clears

_____ Accepts and processes payment

_____ Uses suggestive selling techniques

_____ Serves alcohol responsibly

_____ Handles guest complaints

Sidework

_____ Performs opening duties

_____ Sets tables

_____ Stocks server station

_____ Performs closing duties

General

_____ Dresses according to dress code

_____ Is hospitable and courteous toward guests

_____ Comes to work and is on time

_____ Works as a team member

Please sign below upon completion of training. Both the Employee and the Trainer certify by their signatures that the training has been adequate to prepare the new employee to function in his/her new position.

_____   _____

Signature/Date—Employee   Signature/Date—Trainer

Source: Karen Eich Drummond, **Staffing Your Foodservice Operation**, New York: Van Nostrand Reinhold, 1991. Reprinted with the permission of the publisher.

FIGURE 2-3 *Sample On-the-Job Training Checklist for a Dining Room Attendant*

OJT CHECKLIST: DINING ROOM ATTENDANT

Name of Trainee: _____

Date Starting Training: _____

Trainer(s): _____

Directions: *Write the date in the blank space next to each task when you feel the trainee has mastered it.*

Assists Servers

_____ Setting tables

_____ Folding napkins

_____ Clearing a table

_____ Stacking and carrying a bus pan

_____ Pouring water

_____ Serving bread and butter

_____ Serving coffee and tea

_____ Changing an ashtray

_____ Doing sidework

General

_____ Dresses according to dress code

_____ Is hospitable and courteous toward guests

_____ Comes to work and is on time

_____ Works as a team member

Please sign below upon completion of training. Both the Employee and the Trainer certify by their signatures that the training has been adequate to prepare the new employee to function in his/her new position.

_____   _____

Signature/Date—Employee   Signature/Date—Trainer

Source: Karen Eich Drummond, **Staffing Your Foodservice Operation**, New York: Van Nostrand Reinhold, 1991. Reprinted with the permission of the publisher.

FIGURE 2-4 Sample On-the-Job Training Checklist for a Cook

OJT CHECKLIST: COOK

Name of Trainee: _____

Date Starting Training: _____

Trainer(s): _____

Directions: *Write the date in the blank space next to each task when you feel the trainee has mastered it.*

Prepares Food

_____ Using production sheet

_____ Locating and using recipes

_____ Adjusting recipes

_____ Gathering necessary supplies

_____ Operating kitchen equipment

_____ Timing food preparation

_____ Portioning food

_____ Garnishing food

_____ Evaluating product

_____ Keeping written records of all food produced and left over

_____ Following safe food handling guidelines

_____ Handling leftovers

_____ Cleaning and sanitizing work area using cleaning schedule

General

_____ Dresses according to dress code

_____ Is hospitable and courteous toward guests

_____ Comes to work and is on time

_____ Works as a team member

Please sign below upon completion of training. Both the Employee and the Trainer certify by their signatures that the training has been adequate to prepare the new employee to function in his/her new position.

_____   _____
Signature/Date—Employee   Signature/Date—Trainer

Source: Karen Eich Drummond, **Staffing Your Foodservice Operation**, New York: Van Nostrand Reinhold, 1991. Reprinted with the permission of the publisher.

FIGURE 2-5 Sample On-the-Job Training Checklist for a Storekeeper

OJT CHECKLIST: STOREKEEPER

Name of Trainee: _____

Date Starting Training: _____

Trainer(s): _____

Directions: *Write the date in the blank space next to each task when you feel the trainee has mastered it.*

Receiving

_____ Verifying actual quantity received against vendor's invoice and purchase order

_____ Verifying price

_____ Spot checking quality of incoming goods

_____ Discussing with chef any receiving problems immediately

Storing

_____ Storing foods in appropriate locations

_____ Storing frozen and refrigerated food quickly

_____ Rotating stock

_____ Cleaning storage areas according to cleaning schedule

Record Keeping

_____ Taking physical inventory using inventory book

_____ Issuing stock

General

_____ Dresses according to dress code

_____ Is hospitable and courteous toward guests

_____ Comes to work and is on time

_____ Works as a team member

Please sign below upon completion of training. Both the Employee and the Trainer certify by their signatures that the training has been adequate to prepare the new employee to function in his/her new position.

_____   _____

Signature/Date—Employee   Signature/Date—Trainer

Source: Karen Eich Drummond, **Staffing Your Foodservice Operation**, New York: Van Nostrand Reinhold, 1991. Reprinted with the permission of the publisher.

teaching a new employee. Try to start with easier duties and work up to the more difficult and complex ones.

You can now determine which training method is best for teaching each job duty. To guide trainees toward learning basic information, such as on sanitation and safety, classroom training works very well. To guide trainees toward learning specific skills, especially manual skills such as mopping floors, on-the-job training is a good choice. To guide trainees toward improving attitudes, classroom training is an excellent choice.

Some job training topics, such as converting recipes, can be taught using either classroom training or on-the-job training. Other topics work better using one method or the other. For example, if you want to review basic cooking terms with your new cooks, classroom training is the ideal choice. However, if you want to review how to use a French knife, on-the-job training is the best choice.

After deciding on training methods, you can determine how much time it will take to train a new employee on each job duty. This is normally accomplished by looking at the steps involved in completing each job duty and asking current employees and other managers for their input. It is a good idea to mark the training time required on the checklist. With some positions, you may want to develop a training schedule that shows exactly which duties will be covered during each day of training.

On-the-Job Trainers

Even with a good job training checklist, your efforts at on-the-job training can falter without a good trainer. Ideally, a manager or a supervisor is the best choice for training. Although in many cases an hourly employee can assist in training a new employee, it is very important to consider that many of your employees may not be suitable trainers.

There are a number of qualities to look for when choosing a trainer. The individual should like and want to train, perform his or her own job well, be respected and get along well with others, demonstrate a positive attitude toward his or her job, and communicate well.

If a competent hourly employee can train, be sure he or she goes beyond simply working with the new employee, and actually trains this individual. The magic apron method of training, in which employees are thought to be trained by just being put to work, should be avoided. It is also advisable to compensate the employee who helps train others because the employee is being asked to take on a significant responsibility. While training is usually a job duty for managers, it is rarely a job duty for hourly employees. Examples of rewards for trainers include pay increases, a bonus, a new title at a higher level, or some mark of distinction such as a pin.

How to Conduct On-the-Job Training

On-the-job training consists of four steps: telling, showing, doing, and reviewing. Start by telling the employee, "The job duty you are going to learn is how to set up a three-compartment sink." Then find out what the employee already knows as it may reveal prior experience to which new learning can be related or it may interfere with new learning. Explain the steps involved in the job duty. For example, to set up a three-compartment sink the steps are to fill each sink with enough water to cover the largest pot or pan, use the proper amount of detergent and sanitizer, and check the water temperatures. Also explain the overall purpose of the procedure. In this case, the purpose is to clean and sanitize in order to prevent foodborne illness.

Next, show or demonstrate how to set up a three-compartment sink, explaining what, when, why, and how well to do the steps. Instruct at a rate that allows the employee to understand the task. Instruct clearly, completely, and not too fast. Ask for questions from the employee.

Now let the employee set up the sink. Give frequent, specific, and accurate feedback and correct in a calm, positive, and friendly way. Praise and give encouragement. Ask questions to assess the employee's understanding, get him or her thinking, and increase retention. Examples of questions include: "Why did you check the water temperatures?" "What would happen if you did not use the chemical sanitizer?" "What do you do if you run out of detergent?" "How will you measure the proper amount of sanitizer?"

In the final step, review the what, how, how well, and why of the job duty, continuing to ask questions of the employee as well as encouraging further questions. When felt appropriate, put the employee on his or her own and coach the performance.

Some general guidelines for conducting on-the-job training include avoiding training of new job duties at very busy times and making sure the work area is ready. Don't forget to present the big picture so the employee understands how his or her job contributes to the department. Also, provide the employee with a written copy of what he or she is being trained to do.

Figure 2-6 is a checklist of the above steps and guidelines for the trainer to use.

FIGURE 2-6 *Trainer Checklist: On-the-Job Training*

TRAINER CHECKLIST: ON-THE-JOB TRAINING

Directions: *Use this checklist to help you perform on-the-job training. Check off each item as it is used. Circle any item that you would like to work harder on next time you do on-the-job training.*

General Guidelines

1. Avoid training of new job duties at very busy times. _____

2. Have the work area ready. _____

3. Present the big picture. _____

4. Provide the employee with a written copy of what he or she is being trained _____ to do.

How to Use the Tell/Show/Do/Review Method

1. Tell (lecture)
   a. Tell the employee: "The job duty you are going to learn is . . . ." _____

FIGURE 2-6 **Trainer Checklist: On-the-Job Training**
(continued)

---

    b. Find out what the employee already knows about the duty as it may reveal _____
       prior experience to which new learning can be related or it may interfere
       with new learning.

    c. Explain the steps involved in the job duty and the overall purpose.   _____

2. Show (demonstrate)

    a. Demonstrate the procedure in order, explaining what, when, why, and _____
       how well to do the steps.

    b. Instruct at a rate that allows the employee to understand the task.   _____

    c. Instruct clearly, completely, and not too fast.   _____

    d. Ask for questions from the employee.   _____

3. Do (application)

    a. Let the employee do the job.   _____

    b. Give frequent, specific, and accurate feedback.   _____

    c. Correct in a calm, positive, and friendly way.   _____

    d. Praise and give encouragement.   _____

    e. Ask questions to assess the employee's understanding, get him or her _____
       thinking, and increase retention.

       "Why did you . . . ?"   _____

       "What would happen if . . . ?"

       "What do you do if . . . ?

       "How will you . . . ?"

    f. Ask the employee, "How do you think you are doing?"   _____

4. Review (lecture, coach)

    a. Review the what, how, how well, and why of the job duty, continuing to _____
       ask questions.

    b. Encourage further questions from the employee.   _____

    c. Put the employee on his/her own and coach.   _____

How to Conduct Group Training

Before actually conducting class, you need to do some preparation. First, set up a training policy, if you don't have one, including an attendance policy and classroom ground rules (see Figure 2-7). Ground rules might include that employees are expected to get to class on time, participate in class, and ask questions and make comments. Next, pick an appropriate date and time, and post the class at least one week ahead of time. Before class, review the entire training outline, including which training methods

FIGURE 2-7 *Training Policy and Procedure*

TRAINING POLICY AND PROCEDURE

Policy: *Current and new employees will complete relevant and up-to-date job training to enable them to do their jobs well.*

Procedures

1. All new employees will be given an appropriate Orientation utilizing the Orientation Checklist (for the Manager) and the Orientation Handbook (for the employee).

2. All new employees will be trained in their new positions by both managers and hourly employees designated as Team Leaders. An On-the-Job Training Checklist will be utilized. Although most training will be on-the-job, there are selected topics that will be taught using videotape programs and group training.

3. Once a new employee has completed training in his or her new position, he or she will be evaluated within 30 days by the Supervisor.

4. Periodically, the restaurant will provide group training sessions on diverse topics in the dining room during off hours. Employees will be expected to attend these sessions and will be paid for their time.

5. During any training, employees are expected to participate, make comments, and ask questions.

---

are to be used (see Table 2-1). Get your materials together, such as handouts, pencils, audiovisual aids, and demonstration materials. On the day of the class, set up any audiovisual or visual aids and test them out.

When teaching a group, be aware of and use appropriate body language and speech. Show you are comfortable with the group through natural, positive body language including good posture and keeping your hands away from your face. Make good eye contact with everyone in your group. Pay close attention to the pace, volume, and tone of your voice. The pace should be neither too fast nor too slow, and the volume should be at an appropriate level for everyone to hear you. Vary the tone of your voice to avoid sounding boring. Avoid speech habits such as "um" or "you know." Smile and nod to employees frequently to show positive reinforcement.

The way you talk to employees greatly influences how receptive they are to your leadership. Convey respect and appreciation by making statements such as, "Thanks for taking the time from your busy jobs to be here today." Share what you have in common with the employees such as certain knowledge, skills, and frustrations. Use informal, familiar language and phrase your directives gently, as in "I guess we could start today's class by doing an exercise." Encourage employee comments, both positive and negative, and give your employees lots of praise and support. When employees bring up different points of view, make a positive statement about this, such as "It's always interesting to hear several points of view." Lastly, correct in a calm, positive, and friendly manner.

TABLE 2-1   Teaching Methods

1. LECTURE

A lecture is a presentation given by the trainer with minimal or no learner involvement. It is useful in the early stages of learning, when time is short and many ideas must be presented, or when you want to give the same information to many people. Because lecturing does not involve the learner, retention of content is not as good as with a participative method. In addition, the learner's attention and interest may wander.

Almost any topic can be covered using the lecture method. Some examples include cooking methods and terminology and kitchen safety rules.

Guidelines for Use:

1. Know the material to be covered.
2. Use visual aids to increase learning and focus attention.
3. Allow time periodically for questions and answers.
4. Try to use this method with other teaching methods.

2. GUIDED DISCUSSION

This method involves interaction between the instructor and the employees by the instructor posing questions for the employees to answer. It allows employees to participate and be recognized for knowledge of certain topics. Although this method requires more time than lecture, it is well worth it because the employees become involved in their own learning, which will increase retention.

Guided discussion can be useful to cover many different topics. For example, when explaining the rules of personal hygiene to employees, you could ask why each rule is important.

Guidelines for Use:

1. Plan to use guided discussions with smaller groups.
2. Arrange seating so that learners can see and hear each other easily, such as in a horseshoe or circle pattern.
3. Avoid questions with yes-no answers or real easy questions.
4. Always reinforce when an employee gives a correct answer by saying something like "That's right!" or "Thank you for the correct answer."
5. Be tactful when an employee gives you the wrong answer. Never tell an employee in front of a class that his or her answer was wrong. Instead, give encouraging feedback such as "Almost!" or "You're very close."
6. Be patient with employee answers.
7. Know your material since employees will be more apt to ask their own questions.
8. Try to avoid wandering to other topics.

TABLE 2-1 *Teaching Methods (continued)*

3. DEMONSTRATION

In a demonstration the trainer skillfully performs a skill or procedure showing precisely how it would be done on the job. For example, you can demonstrate how to use a fire extinguisher or poach eggs. It is useful to teach manual skills particularly when employees are allowed to practice the skill after or during the demonstration. Demonstrations can be used to focus attention on basic procedures and to demonstrate certain standards of performance for these procedures.

Guidelines for Use:

1. Use with small groups so that each person can see and hear the demonstration.
2. Run through the demonstration beforehand and make sure you are totally comfortable and competent at doing it.
3. Set up your demonstration ahead of time and try to remove any distractions from the area. Check the operation of all equipment just before you do the demonstration.
4. First perform the skill at normal speed and then more slowly.
5. Explain why each step is done as you do it.
6. Point out critical parts of the procedure including safety precautions.
7. Ask questions of the learners during the demonstration to ascertain understanding.
8. Follow with supervised practice by employees. Coach.

4. TELL/SHOW/DO/REVIEW

This method has 4 components: lecture (tell), demonstration (show), do (employee practice), and lecture (review). It is an excellent method for teaching a new skill or procedure. Employees practice and apply the knowledge and skills under controlled conditions after the trainer has explained and demonstrated the procedure.

Guidelines for Use:

1. Employees should have listing of procedures either in hand or posted so they can follow them during practice.
2. Small groups are best.
3. Supervise closely and correct employees quickly.
4. Be sure all safety aspects of the process have been thoroughly discussed and demonstrated.
5. Give employees enough practice time in order to be proficient.
6. Allow enough time for this method as it is quite time-consuming.

TABLE 2-1   Teaching Methods (continued)

5. QUIZ

A quiz, such as a set of matching questions, can be given to employees as an in-class exercise with each employee correcting his or her own paper. The quiz is usually not handed in, but is kept by each employee. Quizzes can use any type of test question such as true/false, multiple choice, and matching.

Guidelines for Use:

1. Read the instructions to the employees so you are sure they understand what to do.
2. Explain to the employees that the quiz will not be handed in or graded.
3. Make sure all employees have completed the quiz by checking to see if anyone is still writing before going over the answers.
4. Always review answers promptly. You may ask employees to volunteer their answers first before giving the correct answer so as to involve them.
5. Bring extra pens or pencils to class when there is a quiz.

6. GAME

Games are structured competitions designed to provide opportunities to bring out specific knowledge. They might be board games or any situation in which employees work alone or usually in teams and compete with each other for a prize of some type. The contest is governed by a set of rules. Games, when well designed, are very participative, are well accepted by employees, and represent a change of pace. A disadvantage of games is that they are difficult to develop.

Guidelines for Use:

1. Make sure the rules are explicit and communicated well.
2. Have a prize that is desired by most of the employees playing the game and that is of appropriate value.
3. When employees pick their own teams, make sure everyone has a team.
4. Make sure there is enough time to complete the game once it is started.

7. BUZZ GROUPS

In a buzz group, employees split into small groups of two to four people to discuss a specific topic, and are then asked to report the key discussion points back to the larger group. The instructor then may write down these points on a board or easel pad.

Buzz groups can be used successfully when employees can develop their own set of answers to a question. For example, instead of lecturing about sanitation guidelines, ask employees to develop them.

TABLE 2-1   Teaching Methods (continued)

Guidelines for Use:

1. As with all group discussions, monitor the groups to make sure they have not wandered off track.

2. If any members of groups are not participating at all in the group discussion, ask them a question to get them involved in the discussion.

3. Make sure each group has a person recording the discussion.

4. When writing down each group's key discussion points, either write each group's points separately or put them all together. When putting together all their responses, do not write down the same response twice. If a group gives you a response that is just worded differently than one written down, explain that they say the same thing.

5. Give adequate time for all groups to respond.

8. CASE STUDY

These are descriptions of a real-life situation, event, or incident that the employee or groups of employees analyze and discuss usually through answering specific questions. They allow for analysis of information and an opportunity to use newly acquired skills and knowledge. The answers to the questions should be discussed in class.

Areas in which use of case studies would be appropriate include sanitation and guest relations. A case study about sanitation could describe what took place in the kitchen on the day before there was an outbreak of foodborne illness. Employees would be asked to figure out what caused the problem.

Guidelines for Use:

1. Make sure your case study is real enough to be taken seriously.

2. If you ask groups of employees to develop answers to the case study questions, follow the guidelines for group discussion found in #7.

9. ROLE-PLAY

In role-play, employees simulate or act out a real or hypothetical situation in order to acquire the skills needed to manage the interpersonal dynamics of that situation. This technique can be used to examine current behaviors or try out new ones to build skill and confidence. It is usually followed by discussion and analysis among its participants.

Role-play has several advantages: learners are directly involved in the learning process, it can change attitudes by putting the learner into a new situation, and it teaches learners what to be aware of and to understand other people's feelings.

A popular area for role-playing is guest relations. Employees can role-play many of the different situations in which they interact with guests, such as handling guest complaints.

TABLE 2-1 Teaching Methods (continued)

Guidelines for Use:

1. Keep class size small.

2. Make sure you plan for enough time.

3. Introduce the role-play at a point when the employees' knowledge of the subject will make success probable. Explain the purpose of the role-play and what your expectations are for the role-play and the role-players.

4. Thoroughly explain the situation to be role-played and each of the roles.

5. Always demonstrate a role-play first before employees try it. Keep a serious, but not too serious, tone so the role-play does not become silly or turn into a play.

6. Ask the learners to become the role, improvise within the confines of the role, and allow themselves to change their attitude during role-play.

7. Coach closely. Give lots of positive reinforcement and correct tactfully.

Handle problem behaviors in an effective manner. For example, when an employee disagrees, complains, or argues, don't take it personally and don't let it ruffle your feathers. Say "You've got a good point" even if you disagree with the employee, or ask the employee to discuss the matter with you after class. Make sure you use a warm but businesslike tone of voice. In this type of situation, you may also want to use some humor, as long as you are not being sarcastic or patronizing to the employee. When an employee seems to be monopolizing the class, summarize what he or she has said and move on to the next topic. Another technique is to ask other employees to participate. When employees are having private conversations during your class, try making eye contact, moving closer, and asking one of them a question. These techniques are often helpful in ending distracting conversations.

Avoid time wasters. Always start on time and stay on track. Classes sometimes get off track and, when this happens, it is important to redirect the group back to your outline. Another time waster is when you pass out handouts during class. This can be easily avoided by passing out handouts either as employees come in or leave. If your handout is a summary of the class, it is better to give it at the end of class so employees aren't distracted by it during class. If you must give out handouts before class, focus employees' attention on a visual aid of some type during class.

Facilitate employee participation and discussions by asking questions that are not too easy or too hard for the employees to answer. Express appreciation to participants who ask questions or make comments, especially those that are interesting or insightful. Make a comment, such as "Thank you for bringing that to my attention." Never criticize anyone for contributing. Paraphrase what someone has said so the employee knows he or she has been understood and the other employees get a short summary. Bring into discussions employees who are not participating. Energize a discussion by being funny or asking the group for more participation. These two techniques work best when you have close working relationships with the employees. Ask employees to clarify their comments when you or the employees are not sure of their meaning. Summarize the major points or different viewpoints being discussed.

Use visual aids to avoid constantly referring to your notes. Don't block the visual aid, and don't put your back to the employees when using the visual aid. Talk to the employees, not to the visual. Do not read your visual; paraphrase what it says. After you have explained a visual's message, remove it from view. When using an overhead projector, turn the lamp off when not in use, use a pen to direct attention to one part of the transparency, and place a sheet of paper under the transparency to show information a little at a time. When using a flip chart, face the audience and turn pages with the hand nearest the flip chart. Flip to a blank page when not in use.

Figure 2-8 is a checklist of the above steps and guidelines for the trainer to use.

FIGURE 2-8 Trainer Checklist: Group Training

TRAINER CHECKLIST: GROUP TRAINING

Directions: *Use this checklist to help you perform group training. Check off each item as it is used. Circle any item that you would like to work harder on next time you do in-service training.*

Preparation

1. Set up training policy including attendance and classroom ground rules. _____

2. Pick appropriate date and time. _____

3. Post class at least one week ahead of time. _____

4. Review entire training outline and get materials together—handouts, _____
   pencils, audiovisual aids, demonstration materials, employee attendance
   sheet, and so on.

5. Be sure training room has enough chairs, is at a good temperature, _____
   and is otherwise ready.

6. Set up any audiovisual and visual aids and test. _____

Classroom Teaching Skills

1. Be aware of and use appropriate body language and speech.
   a. Show you are comfortable with the group through natural, _____
      positive body language.
   b. Make eye contact. _____
   c. Pay attention to the pace, volume, and tone of your voice. _____
   d. Avoid speech habits such as "um" or "you know." _____
   e. Smile and nod to employees to show positive reinforcement. _____

FIGURE 2-8   Trainer Checklist: Group Training (continued)

2. The way you talk to employees greatly influences how receptive they are to your leadership, so:

   a. Convey respect and appreciation. _____

   b. Share what you have in common with the employees. _____

   c. Use informal, familiar language. _____

   d. Phrase your directives gently. _____

   e. Encourage employee comments. _____

   f. Praise and give encouragement. _____

   g. State what's positive about different points of view. _____

   h. Correct in a calm, positive, and friendly way. _____

3. Handle problem behaviors in an effective manner.

   a. When an employee disagrees, complains, or argues: _____

      1. Don't take problem behaviors personally and don't let them get to you. _____

      2. Say "You've got a good point" even if you disagree with the employee, _____ or ask the employee to discuss the matter with you after class; use a warm but businesslike tone of voice.

      3. Humor the employee without being sarcastic or patronizing. _____

   b. When an employee monopolizes the class: _____

      1. Summarize what the employee has said and move on to your next _____ topic.

      2. Ask other employees for input. _____

   c. When employees are talking during class: _____

      1. Make eye contact with them. _____

      2. Move closer. _____

      3. Ask one of the employees a question. _____

4. Avoid time wasters.

   a. Start on time. _____

   b. Pass out handouts either as employees come in or leave. _____

   c. Stay on track and redirect the group when needed. _____

5. Facilitate employee participation and discussion.

   a. Ask questions that are not too easy or too hard. _____

   b. Express appreciation to participants who ask questions or make _____ comments, especially those that are interesting or insightful; never criticize anyone for contributing.

   c. Paraphrase what someone has said so the employee knows he/she _____ has been understood and the other employees get a short summary.

   d. Bring into discussions employees who are not participating. _____

FIGURE 2-8 *Trainer Checklist: Group Training (continued)*

    e. Energize a discussion by being funny or asking the group for more _____
       participation.

    f. Ask employees to clarify their comments when necessary.   _____

    g. Summarize the major points or different viewpoints being discussed. _____

6. Use visual aids effectively.

    a. Don't block the visual aid, and don't turn your back to the employees. _____

    b. Talk to the employees, not the visual.   _____

    c. Do not read your visual; paraphrase what it says.   _____

    d. After a visual's message has been explained, remove it from view. _____

    e. When using an overhead projector, turn the lamp off when not in use; use _____
       a pen to direct attention to one part of the transparency, and place a sheet
       of paper under the transparency to show information a little at a time.

    f. When using a flip chart, face the audience and turn pages with the hand _____
       nearest the flip chart; flip to a blank page when not in use.

Nonideal Training Situations

When training employees, there are always situations that are especially trying. Let's take a look at a few of them.

It is not unusual to have employees in your department who, for whatever reason, have problems with literacy. Literacy means the ability to read and write, do basic arithmetic, communicate orally, and speak English (in the United States). The best approach to take with these employees is to find out if there is a literacy or basic skills program available. More and more employers are making these types of programs available to their employees generally through an outside provider. Another way to overcome this problem is to utilize, when appropriate, training materials written or spoken in the native language. Many training materials are available in several languages.

Another situation that occurs frequently enough is the employee who has "heard it all before." You probably have employees who have been attending sanitation in-services at least once a year for many years. The best way to handle these employees is to use a participative teaching method, such as a short case study, in which the employees develop the content of the training session. Another way to handle this situation is to vary your teaching method from year to year so employees are not bored.

Another problem develops when your new hire is surrounded by unhappy and unproductive employees. One way to avoid having the new employee influenced is to team up the new employee with one of your better employees. In this manner, the employee provides a good role model. Of course, managers and supervisors should also work hard at being good role models.

Coaching[1]

Whether your job training program uses on-the-job training or group training, or both, the most important component of your program is not the actual training, but what happens after the training is completed. *Through coaching your employees and setting the right example, you can make their training stick.*

So what is coaching? Coaching is a two-part process involving observation of employee performance and conversation between the manager and employee that focuses on job performance. The overall goals of the conversation are to evaluate work performance, and then encourage optimum work performance by either reinforcing good performance or confronting and redirecting poor performance. Coaching therefore provides employees with regular feedback and support about their job performance, and lets managers know exactly what their employees need to know.

If coaching employees is so beneficial, why do managers often avoid it? Following are some possible reasons:

- Lack of time
- Fear of confronting an employee with a performance concern
- Assumption that the employee already knows he or she is doing a good job
- Little experience either doing or observing coaching
- Assumption that the employee will ask questions when appropriate and does not need feedback

The first step of coaching is to observe employees doing their jobs. If the employee is doing the job well, don't hesitate to tell the employee. Everyone likes to be told that they are doing a good job, so praise employees as often as you can. Work on catching your employees doing things right, and then use these steps:

1. Describe the specific action you are praising.
2. Explain the results or effects of the actions.
3. State your appreciation.
4. Ask the employees how they feel about doing a good job.
5. Say thank-you.
6. Write a letter of thanks and make sure a copy goes into the employee's personnel file.

---

[1] This section was adapted from: Karen Eich Drummond, **Retaining Your Foodservice Employees**, New York: Van Nostrand Reinhold, 1991. Reprinted with the permission of the publisher.

If there appears to be a problem with some aspect of the employee's performance, answer the following questions before talking with the employee:

1. What is the difference between the employee's performance level and the performance standard? Is it significant?
2. Is the performance standard realistic?
3. Does the employee know what is supposed to be done?
4. Does the employee understand why it is supposed to be done?
5. Does the employee know how it is supposed to be done?
6. Are there any hindrances to the employee's performance that the employee can't control, such as inadequate equipment?
7. Has the employee received feedback on this before or has this problem been ignored?

The next step is to confront, not criticize, the employee's poor performance. Confronting is a positive process used to correct performance problems, gain the employee's commitment to improvement, and maintain a constructive supervisor-employee relationship. Criticism, on the other hand, is a negative process that, instead of concentrating on performance, blames the employee personally for not doing a job properly. It tends to be general, rather than specific, in nature, and generates excuses, blaming of others, and guilt on the employee's part. Managers who confront employees are more interested in helping them feel confident about improving future performance, rather than making them feel inadequate and guilty about past performance.

When confronting an employee with what is perceived to be a performance problem, follow these steps:

1. Speak in private with the employee without any interruptions or distractions. Make the atmosphere as relaxed and friendly as possible.
2. Explain the reason for the meeting and express in a calm manner your concern about the specific aspect of job performance you feel needs to be improved. Describe the job performance concern in behavioral terms and explain its effect. Also, explain that you have not made up your mind yet as to the cause of the performance problem.
3. Ask the employee for his or her thoughts and opinions, using the seven questions just listed as a starting point to get employee feedback.
4. If the employee is the cause of the performance problem, work on getting his or her agreement that the problem exists. Next, ask the employee for some solutions to the problem. Discuss together some possible solutions and mutually agree on a course of action and time frame. Ask the employee to restate what has been agreed upon to check on understanding. State your confidence in the employee's ability to turn the situation around.
5. Lastly, schedule a follow-up meeting to check on progress.

Following are general coaching guidelines:

1. Be specific about the job performance.

2. Actively listen to the employee. Be supportive. Don't let the conversation drift away to other issues or other employees. If the conversation starts to drift, make a statement such as "Let's get back to the issue at hand."

3. Focus on the employee's behavior, not the employee. Always maintain the self-respect and self-esteem of the employee. To reduce employee defensiveness, use "I" statements rather than "you" statements.

4. Reinforce or confront job performance as soon as possible after observing it. However, if you are at all angry or upset, don't confront the employee until you have cooled down.

5. Praise in public; correct in private. Employees are very sensitive about being told they are doing something wrong in front of their peers. Unless the error could have grave consequences, wait until you can at least pull the employee aside long enough to tell him or her how to correct it.

6. Explain the impact of the employee's job performance, whether satisfactory or unsatisfactory, on the work group and operation.

7. Be a coach, not a drill sergeant. Don't stay constantly on someone's back and watch everything they do.

Some sections of this chapter were adapted from Karen Eich Drummond, **Developing and Conducting Training for Foodservice Employees** (audiocassette), 1992. Courtesy of The American Dietetic Association.

CHAPTER 3

On-the-Job Training Outlines

How to Use the On-the-Job Training Outlines

This chapter contains fifty ready-to-use *On-the-Job Training Outlines* in the following areas:

* Sanitation and Safety
* Service Skills
* Food Production Skills

The sanitation and safety outlines are primarily designed for back-of-the-house personnel, the service skills outlines for front-of-the-house personnel, and the production skills outlines for food preparation and cooking staff. Figure 3-1 shows which outlines are best suited to specific positions in your restaurants.

Each On-the-Job Training Outline is designed to help you do on-the-job training of new employees, as well as retraining of current employees, and contains these four sections (although some may not have a quiz or job aid, depending on the topic):

* Trainer's Outline (for the trainer's use)
* Employee's Outline (for the employee's use)
* Employee Quiz
* Job Aid(s)

The *Trainer's Outline* is the trainer's set of directions and it uses the following headings:

- Time Required—An estimate is given of the time required to do the training. Training sessions are kept short, mostly 10 to 20 minutes, with none running longer than 30 minutes.

- Materials Needed—All materials needed to do the training are specified.

- Steps—Each step that the trainer will use during the training is given. There are usually two to three steps per outline. For each step, a two-column format is used to help the trainer proceed. The left column, Key Concepts, contains what the trainer must teach the employee. The right column, Trainer's Directions, gives explicit instructions on how to get this information across to the employee.

The *Employee's Outline* contains all the Key Concepts covered in the Trainer's Outline and can be photocopied for use. It is frequently referred to during training.

Most, but not all, On-the-Job Training Outlines contain an *Employee Quiz* and *Job Aids*, both of which can also be photocopied for use. The Employee Quiz is typically given at the end of the training session and the correct answers are reviewed immediately. Each quiz has spaces for the employee to write down the correct answers as they are reviewed.

The important points covered in a training session are summarized on one or more pages referred to as Job Aids. For example, in the training session on hand washing, there is a job aid listing the steps involved in hand washing. This job aid can be posted by the hand-washing sink and used during and after training to reinforce the training message.

Standard industry practices and procedures are given, and trainers are instructed at many points to customize the procedures to their own operations.

FIGURE 3-1 **Training Guide: On-the-Job Training Outlines**

	1: Personal Hygiene	2: Hand Washing	3: Serving Safe Food	4: Using the Three-Compartment Sink	5: Operating the Dishmachine	6: Cleaning Stationary Equipment	7: Kitchen Safety Rules	8: Back Safety	9: Handling Hazardous Chemicals	10: Quality Service
Cooks	✓	✓	✓			✓	✓	✓	✓	
Bakers	✓	✓	✓			✓	✓	✓	✓	
Salads/Cold Food Preparation	✓	✓	✓			✓	✓	✓	✓	
Storeroom	✓	✓	✓			✓	✓	✓		
Dishroom	✓	✓	✓	✓	✓	✓	✓	✓	✓	
Pot and Pan Washer	✓	✓	✓	✓	✓	✓	✓	✓	✓	
Porter-Utility-Cleaning Personnel	✓	✓	✓	✓	✓	✓	✓	✓	✓	
Host/Hostess	✓	✓						✓	✓	✓
Server	✓	✓						✓	✓	✓
Busperson	✓	✓						✓	✓	✓
Bartender	✓	✓						✓	✓	✓
Beverage Server	✓	✓						✓	✓	✓

FIGURE 3-1 Training Guide: On-the-Job Training Outlines (continued)

	11: Dining Room Stations & Sidework	12: How to Set Tables	13: How to Load and Lift a Food Tray	14: How to Serve and Clear	15: Steps of American-Style Service: 1	16: Steps of American-Style Service: 2	17: Steps of American-Style Service: 3	18: Steps of American-Style Service: 4	19: Steps of American-Style Service: 5	20: Steps of American-Style Service: 6
Cooks										
Bakers										
Salads/Cold Food Preparation										
Storeroom										
Dishroom										
Pot and Pan Washer										
Porter-Utility-Cleaning Personnel										
Host/Hostess	✓	✓	✓	✓	✓	✓	✓	✓	✓	✓
Server	✓	✓	✓	✓	✓	✓	✓	✓	✓	✓
Busperson	✓	✓	✓	✓						
Bartender				✓						
Beverage Server				✓						

FIGURE 3-1 Training Guide: On-the-Job Training Outlines (continued)

	21: Steps of American-Style Service: 7	22: Steps of American-Style Service: 8	23: Learning the Menu	24: Serving Safe Food	25: Suggestive Selling	26: How to Listen to Guests	27: How to Handle Complaints	28: Serving Alcohol Responsibly	29: Safely Operating Equipment	30: How to Operate the Range
Cooks									✓	✓
Bakers									✓	✓
Salads/Cold Food Preparation									✓	✓
Storeroom										
Dishroom									✓	
Pot and Pan Washer									✓	
Porter-Utility-Cleaning Personnel									✓	
Host/Hostess	✓	✓	✓	✓	✓	✓	✓	✓		
Server	✓	✓	✓	✓	✓	✓	✓	✓		
Busperson				✓		✓	✓	✓		
Bartender				✓	✓	✓	✓	✓		
Beverage Server				✓	✓	✓	✓	✓		

FIGURE 3-1 Training Guide: On-the-Job Training Outlines (continued)

	31: How to Operate a Conventional Oven	32: How to Operate a Convection Oven	33: How to Operate a Microwave Oven	34: How to Operate the Broiler	35: How to Operate the Grill	36: How to Operate the Steamer	37: How to Operate the Steam-Jacketed Kettle	38: How to Operate the Deep-Fat Fryer	39: How to Operate the Tilt Skillet	40: How to Operate the Slicer
Cooks	√	√	√	√	√	√	√	√	√	√
Bakers	√	√	√				√			√
Salads/Cold Food Preparation	√	√	√	√						√
Storeroom										
Dishroom										
Pot and Pan Washer										
Porter-Utility-Cleaning Personnel										
Host/Hostess										
Server										
Busperson										
Bartender										
Beverage Server										

FIGURE 3-1 Training Guide: On-the-Job Training Outlines (continued)

	41: How to Operate the Mixer	42: How to Operate the Food Chopper	43: Measuring	44: Portion Control	45: Converting Recipe Yields	46: Knife Safety	47: Types of Knives	48: Cutting Terms	49: How to Use a Chef's Knife	50: How to Sharpen and True a Blade
Cooks	√	√	√	√	√	√	√	√	√	√
Bakers	√	√	√	√	√	√	√	√	√	√
Salads/Cold Food Preparation	√	√	√	√	√	√	√	√	√	√
Storeroom										
Dishroom										
Pot and Pan Washer										
Porter-Utility-Cleaning Personnel										
Host/Hostess										
Server										
Busperson										
Bartender			√							
Beverage Server			√							

Trainer's Outline

■ **STEPS:**

1. Define personal hygiene and explain its importance.

2. Discuss good personal hygiene practices when working in a restaurant.

3. Give quiz.

■ **TIME REQUIRED:** 20–30 minutes

■ **MATERIALS NEEDED:** Employee's Outline, Employee Quiz, and Job Aids. Plate, cup, bowl, fork, knife, and spoon.

■ **AHEAD OF TIME:** You may want to post Job Aids 1-1 to 1-5 on Positive Personal Hygiene Tips in a visible location for employees.

STEP 1. *Define personal hygiene and explain its importance.*

KEY CONCEPTS	TRAINER'S DIRECTIONS
• *Personal hygiene* refers to those actions we take to promote our health and cleanliness, such as eating right and taking a daily shower.	• Ask the employee what he/she thinks personal hygiene is. Asking the employee to follow along in the Employee Outline, define personal hygiene.
• *Personal hygiene is important* because poor personal hygiene practices, such as coughing over food, may result in customers becoming ill with foodborne illness.	• Explain why personal hygiene is important. Explain that foodborne illness is a disease carried to people by food and, in most cases, is preventable.

STEP 2. *Discuss good personal hygiene practices when working in a restaurant.*

KEY CONCEPTS	TRAINER'S DIRECTIONS
	• Asking the employee to follow along in the Employee Outline, review the *Positive Personal Hygiene Tips*, asking the employee why each one is important.
Positive Personal Hygiene Tips	
• Take a daily shower or bath and use deodorant.	• Ask: "Why?" Showering helps wash away harmful germs and keeps you smelling good too!
• Wash your hair as needed.	• Ask: "Why?" Oily, dirty hair is attractive to germs, and dandruff can flake into food.

- Brush your teeth often.

- Clip fingernails short.

- Do not use nail polish.

- Wear a clean and pressed uniform and apron.

- Wash your hands often.

- Do not use your apron as a hand towel.

- Wear a hair restraint or covering.

- Avoid excessive makeup, cologne, and jewelry.

- Cover all coughs and sneezes.

- Don't touch your face or other parts of your body while handling food.

- Taste food properly. Don't use your fingers or a spoon that is reused. Use a plastic spoon or the two-spoon method, that is, use one spoon to dip into the food and the other to eat from.

- If feeling sick, even with a minor cold, speak to your supervisor immediately.

- Cover all cuts, burns, and boils with a bandage and plastic glove, and report to your supervisor immediately.

- Wear plastic gloves as directed.

- Ask: "Why?" Brushing reduces the number of germs in your mouth.

- Ask: "Why?" Long fingernails provide hiding places for dirt and germs.

- Ask: "Why?" It may chip into food.

- Ask: "Why?" Soiled clothing harbors germs, which may be transferred to food.

- Ask: "Why?" Dirty hands will contaminate food with germs.

- Ask: "Why?" The apron will be contaminated and possibly transfer germs to food.

- Ask: "Why?" You lose about 50 strands of hair daily. A hair restraint keeps hair from falling into food.

- Ask: "Why?" They may get into food. Jewelry is a place where germs grow and jewelry is hard to keep clean.

- Ask: "Why?" They send germs far and wide. Wash your hands after coughing and sneezing.

- Ask: "Why?" Germs are on your skin and can be introduced into food by your hands.

- Ask: "Why?" Germs on your hands or in your mouth are directly transferred into the food.

- Ask: "Why?" You might contaminate food. Explain that you may temporarily assign a sick employee to a job that doesn't involve food handling.

- Ask: "Why?" There are many germs in cuts, burns, and boils, and they can easily find their way into food when not covered.

- Ask: "Why?" Food must be protected from germs on skin. However, gloves get contaminated just like hands, so they must be changed frequently.

- Use utensils such as tongs and spoons to handle food.

- Avoid touching food-contact surfaces of dishes, utensils, etc.

- Smoke and eat only in designated areas.

- No gum chewing.

- Ask: "Why?" Germs from your hands could contaminate food.

- Explain that the food-contact surface is the surface that will be touched by food or drink. Show employee how to:
  - handle glasses, bowls, and cups by the bottom.
  - handle plates by the bottom or edge.
  - handle forks, knives, and spoons by the handle.

- Ask: "Why?" Hands that contact your mouth when smoking or eating should not touch the food.

- Ask: "Why?" Gum can contaminate food when blowing bubbles.

STEP 3. Give quiz.

KEY CONCEPTS	TRAINER'S DIRECTIONS

- Ask the employee to complete *Employee Quiz* and then review the answers (given at left).

Employee Quiz Answer Key   Check off in the space provided when the incident described is a *poor* personal hygiene practice.

__X__	1. Dipping your finger into food to taste it.	__X__	9. Smoking or eating in a food preparation area.
__X__	2. Wiping your hands on your apron.	__X__	10. Tossing or mixing foods with your bare hands.
_____	3. Wearing a hair restraint.	_____	11. Reporting to work after taking a shower and brushing your teeth.
__X__	4. Having long fingernails.		
__X__	5. Showing up at work when you are sick.	__X__	12. Coughing over food.
__X__	6. Touching your face or hair and then handling food.	__X__	13. Holding a cup by the bottom or the handle.
_____	7. Using scoops and tongs to handle food.	__X__	14. Working with an open, unbandaged cut on your hand.
__X__	8. Starting work with a dirty apron or uniform.	__X__	15. Chewing gum.

Employee's Outline

■ KEY POINTS TO REMEMBER

Personal hygiene refers to those actions we take to promote our health and cleanliness, such as eating right and taking a daily shower. Personal hygiene is important because poor personal hygiene practices, such as coughing over food, may result in customers becoming ill.

Following are examples of good personal hygiene practices to use when working in a restaurant.

Positive Personal Hygiene Tips

- Take a daily shower or bath and use deodorant. Showering helps wash away harmful germs and keeps you smelling good too!
- Wash your hair as needed because oily, dirty hair is attractive to germs, and dandruff can flake into food.
- Brush your teeth often. Brushing reduces the number of germs in your mouth.
- Clip fingernails short. Long fingernails provide hiding places for dirt and germs.
- Do not use nail polish as it may chip into the food.
- Wear a clean and pressed uniform and apron because soiled clothing harbors germs that may be transferred to food.
- Wash your hands often to prevent contaminating foods.
- Do not use your apron as a hand towel because the apron will become contaminated and possibly transfer germs to food.
- Wear a hair restraint or covering because you lose about 50 strands of hair daily.
- Avoid excessive makeup, cologne, and jewelry as they may get into the food. Also, jewelry is a place where germs grow and jewelry is hard to keep clean.
- Cover all coughs and sneezes as germs are sent far and wide. Wash your hands after coughing and sneezing.
- Don't touch your face or other parts of your body while handling food because germs on your skin can then be introduced into food.
- Taste food properly. Don't use your fingers or a spoon that is reused. Use a plastic spoon or the two-spoon method, that is, use one spoon to dip into the food and the other to eat from.
- If feeling sick, even with a minor cold, speak to your supervisor immediately so you do not contaminate the food. You may be temporarily assigned to a job that doesn't require handling food.
- Cover all cuts, burns, and boils with a bandage and plastic glove, and report to your supervisor immediately.

- Wear plastic gloves as directed.
- Use utensils such as tongs and spoons to handle food so germs from your hands will not contaminate the food.
- Avoid touching food-contact surfaces of dishes, utensils, and so on. The food-contact surface is the surface that will be touched by food or drink.
  - Handle glasses, bowls, and cups by the bottom.
  - Handle plates by the bottom or edge.
  - Handle forks, knives, and spoons by the handle.
- Smoke and eat only in designated areas. When you smoke or eat, your hands come in contact with your mouth.
- Do not chew gum because you can contaminate food when blowing bubbles.

Employee Quiz

Name: _____

Job Title: _____

Date: _____

Directions: *Check off in the space provided when the incident described is a* poor *personal hygiene practice.*

Your Answer   *Correct Answer*

_____   _____   **1.** Dipping your finger into food to taste it.

_____   _____   **2.** Wiping your hands on your apron.

_____   _____   **3.** Wearing a hair restraint.

_____   _____   **4.** Having long fingernails.

_____   _____   **5.** Showing up at work when you are sick.

_____   _____   **6.** Touching your face or hair and then handling food.

_____   _____   **7.** Using scoops and tongs to handle food.

_____   _____   **8.** Starting work with a dirty apron or uniform.

_____   _____   **9.** Smoking or eating in a food preparation area.

_____   _____   **10.** Tossing or mixing foods with your bare hands.

_____   _____   **11.** Reporting to work after taking a shower and brushing your teeth.

_____   _____   **12.** Coughing over food.

_____   _____   **13.** Holding a cup by the bottom or the handle.

_____   _____   **14.** Working with an open, unbandaged cut on your hand.

_____   _____   **15.** Chewing gum.

POSITIVE PERSONAL HYGIENE TIPS

- Take a daily shower or bath and use deodorant. Showering helps wash away harmful germs and keeps you smelling good too!

- Wash your hair as needed because oily, dirty hair is attractive to germs, and dandruff can flake into food.

- Brush your teeth often. Brushing reduces the number of germs in your mouth.

- Clip fingernails short. Long fingernails provide hiding places for dirt and germs.

- Do not use nail polish as it may chip into the food.

- Wear a clean and pressed uniform and apron because soiled clothing harbors germs that may be transferred to food.

- Wash your hands often to prevent contaminating foods.

- Do not use your apron as a hand towel because the apron will become contaminated and possibly transfer germs to food.

- Wear a hair restraint or covering because you lose about 50 strands of hair daily.

continued

- Avoid excessive makeup, cologne, and jewelry as they may get into the food. Also, jewelry is a place where germs grow and jewelry is hard to keep clean.

- Cover all coughs and sneezes as germs are sent far and wide. Wash your hands after coughing and sneezing.

- Don't touch your face or other parts of your body while handling food because germs on your skin can then be introduced into food.

- Taste food properly. Don't use your fingers or a spoon that is reused. Use a plastic spoon or the two-spoon method, that is, use one spoon to dip into the food and the other to eat from.

- If feeling sick, even with a minor cold, speak to your supervisor immediately so you do not contaminate food. You may be temporarily assigned to a job that doesn't require handling food.

- Cover all cuts, burns, and boils with a bandage and plastic glove, and report to your supervisor immediately.

- Wear plastic gloves as directed.

continued

- Use utensils such as tongs and spoons to handle food so germs from your hands will not contaminate the food.

- Avoid touching food-contact surfaces of dishes, utensils, and so on. The food-contact surface is the surface that will be touched by food or drink.

  Handle glasses, bowls, and cups by the bottom.

  Handle plates by the bottom or edge.

  Handle forks, knives, and spoons by the handle.

- Smoke and eat only in designated areas. When you smoke or eat, your hands come in contact with your mouth.

- No gum chewing.

Trainer's Outline

■ **STEPS:**

1. Explain why clean hands are so vital in foodservice.
2. Review when it is necessary to wash hands.
3. Demonstrate how to wash hands and let the employee practice.
4. Give quiz.

■ **TIME REQUIRED:**   15–25 minutes

■ **MATERIALS NEEDED:**   Employee's Outline, Employee Quiz, Job Aids, handwashing sink with soap and paper towels

■ **AHEAD OF TIME:**   You may want to post Job Aid 2-2 next to your handwashing sink(s).

STEP 1. Explain why clean hands are so vital in foodservice.

KEY CONCEPTS	TRAINER'S DIRECTIONS
Hand Washing: Why? • Hand washing removes dirt and grime from your hands that you do not want in the food or on the dishes. • Hand washing reduces the number of bacteria on your hands so you are less likely to contaminate foods or dishes.	• Asking the employee to follow along in the Employee's Outline, explain the two reasons why hand washing is so important.

STEP 2. Review when it is necessary to wash hands.

KEY CONCEPTS	TRAINER'S DIRECTIONS
	• Asking the employee to follow in the Employee's Outline, explain when you should wash your hands. Ask the employee "Why?" as directed below.
Wash Your Hands After You: 1. Smoke	• Ask: "Why?" When smoking, your fingers come in contact with saliva in your mouth.
2. Eat	• Ask: "Why?" Same as #1.

3. Use the rest room

4. Touch money

5. Touch raw foods

6. Touch your face, hair, or skin

7. Cough, sneeze, or blow your nose

8. Comb your hair

9. Handle anything dirty (including your apron)

10. You take a break (and also before)

- Ask: "Why?" Your body, feces, and urine are full of germs.
- Ask: "Why?" Money is very dirty.
- Ask: "Why?" They may contain harmful germs.
- Ask: "Why?" Germs are all over your body.
- Ask: "Why?" These actions spread germs.
- Ask: "Why?" Your hair is full of germs.
- Ask: "Why?" Dirt and grime get on your hands.

STEP 3. Demonstrate how to wash hands and let the employee practice.

KEY CONCEPTS	**TRAINER'S DIRECTIONS**
	• Ask the employee what he/she knows about hand washing.
	• Asking the employee to follow along in the Employee's outline; review how to wash hands properly.
	• Demonstrate how to wash your hands, then let the employee practice. Coach.

How to Wash Hands

1. First, pick a handwashing sink.

2. If wearing a watch, remove it.

3. Turn water to as hot as you can stand.

4. Moisten hands and exposed forearms. Soap thoroughly and lather.

5. Wash for 20 seconds by rubbing hands and wash between fingers, under rings and nails, and up forearms. Use brush for nails if provided.

6. Rinse hands and forearms well with hot water.

7. Dry hands and forearms thoroughly.

8. Turn water off, preferably with a paper towel.

9. Tell your supervisor if there is no soap or paper towels.

STEP 4.   Give quiz.

KEY CONCEPTS	TRAINER'S DIRECTIONS
	• Ask the employee to complete Employee Quiz and then review the answers (given at left).

Employee Quiz Answer Key

Directions: *Check the appropriate answers.*

You should wash your hands after you:

__X__	**1.**	Smoke
__X__	**2.**	Eat
__X__	**3.**	Use the rest room
__X__	**4.**	Touch money
__X__	**5.**	Touch raw foods
_____	**6.**	Talk to a friend
__X__	**7.**	Touch a dirty uniform or apron
__X__	**8.**	Blow your nose
__X__	**9.**	Comb your hair
_____	**10.**	Check your schedule

Employee's Outline

■ **KEY POINTS TO REMEMBER**

Let's take a look at why we wash our hands, when we need to do it, and how.

Why? Hand washing removes dirt and grime from your hands that you do not want in food or on dishes. Hand washing also reduces the number of bacteria on your hands so you are less likely to contaminate foods or dishes.

When? You should wash your hands after you:

- Smoke (when smoking, your fingers come in contact with the saliva in your mouth).
- Eat (when eating, your fingers come in contact with the saliva in your mouth).
- Use the rest room (your body, feces, and urine contain germs).
- Touch money (money is very dirty—it never gets washed!).
- Touch raw foods (they may contain harmful germs).
- Touch your face, hair, or skin (germs are all over your body).
- Cough, sneeze, or blow your nose (these actions spread germs).
- Comb your hair (your hair is full of germs!).
- Handle anything dirty (including your apron).
- Take a break (wash both before and after).

How? Following are the steps for washing your hands correctly.

1. First, pick a handwashing sink.
2. If wearing a watch, remove it.
3. Turn water to as hot as you can stand.
4. Moisten hands and exposed forearms. Soap thoroughly and lather.
5. Wash for 20 seconds by rubbing hands and wash between fingers, under rings and nails, and up forearms. Use a brush for your nails if provided.
6. Rinse hands and forearms well with hot water.
7. Dry hands and forearms thoroughly.
8. Turn water off, preferably with a paper towel.
9. Tell your supervisor if there is no soap or paper towels.

Employee Quiz

Name: _____

Job Title: _____

Date: _____

Directions: *Check the appropriate answers.*

You should wash my hands after you:

Your Answer	*Correct Answer*	
_____	_____	**1.** Smoke
_____	_____	**2.** Eat
_____	_____	**3.** Use the rest room
_____	_____	**4.** Touch money
_____	_____	**5.** Touch raw foods
_____	_____	**6.** Talk to a friend
_____	_____	**7.** Touch a dirty uniform or apron
_____	_____	**8.** Blow your nose
_____	_____	**9.** Comb your hair
_____	_____	**10.** Check your schedule

WASH YOUR HANDS AFTER YOU:

1. Smoke.
2. Eat.
3. Use the rest room.
4. Touch money.
5. Touch raw foods.
6. Touch your face, hair, or skin.
7. Cough, sneeze, or blow your nose.
8. Comb your hair.
9. Handle anything dirty (including your apron).
10. Take a break (and also before).

1. First, pick a handwashing sink.

2. If wearing a watch, remove it.

3. Turn water to as hot as you can stand.

4. Moisten hands and exposed forearms. Soap thoroughly and lather.

5. Wash for 20 seconds by rubbing hands and wash between fingers, under rings and nails, and up forearms. Use a brush for your nails if provided.

6. Rinse hands and forearms well with hot water.

7. Dry hands and forearms thoroughly.

8. Turn water off, preferably with a paper towel.

9. Tell your supervisor if there is no soap or paper towels.

Trainer's Outline

■ **STEPS:**

1. Explain the major causes of foodborne illness.
2. Explain the Requirements for Serving Safe Food.
3. Give quiz.

■ **TIME REQUIRED:**   20–30 minutes

■ **MATERIALS NEEDED:**   Employee's Outline, Employee Quiz, Job Aids. As appropriate: ice bath, thermometer, alcohol swab or sanitizing solution, plate, cup, bowl, fork, knife, and spoon.

■ **AHEAD OF TIME:**   On the Employee's Outline, check off the examples under each of the Requirements for Serving Safe Food that apply to the employee being trained (some examples may not be relevant to certain jobs).

STEP 1. Explain the major causes of foodborne illness.

KEY CONCEPTS	TRAINER'S DIRECTIONS
	• Ask the employee what he/she thinks foodborne illness is (a disease carried to people by food that causes upset stomach, vomiting, etc. for one or more days). Explain that foodborne illness is preventable.
	• Asking the employee to follow along in the Employee's Outline, review the major causes of foodborne illness.
Major Causes of Foodborne Illness	
1. Food left in the Danger Zone (45–140 degrees F) for 4 or more hours, such as hot foods that are not chilled rapidly	• Explain that room temperature is normally 70 degrees F and refrigerators run below 45 degrees F, so room temperature is right in the Danger Zone.
2. An employee with sloppy personal hygiene habits	
3. Preparing food a day or more before serving	
4. Food that is served when it is not completely cooked	

STEP 2. Explain the Requirements for Serving Safe Food.

KEY CONCEPTS	TRAINER'S DIRECTIONS
	• Asking the employee to follow along in the Employee Outline, explain the Requirements for Serving Safe Food, and review the examples that apply to his/her job.

Requirements for Serving Safe Food

1. Keep foods out of the danger zone (45–140 degrees F).

Examples

a. Keep hot foods hot and cold foods cold.

b. Handle foods quickly during delivery and put refrigerated and frozen foods away as soon as possible.

c. Thaw foods in refrigerator, microwave, or under cold running water for not more than 2 hours (followed immediately by cooking).

       • Emphasize never to thaw foods at room temperature.

d. Handle foods quickly during preparation. Only handle enough food that can be either cooked or refrigerated in 1 hour or less.

e. Don't use hot food holding equipment such as a steam table to heat or reheat food.

f. Cook and serve foods at a temperature of at least 140 degrees F. Heat leftovers to 165 degrees F. and pork to 150 degrees F.

g. To cool down hot foods, use shallow pans and an ice bath. Stir hot foods to remove heat. Cut large pieces of meat, fish, and so forth into smaller pieces to allow heat loss. Cool foods to 45 degrees F or less in less than 4 hours.

       • You may want to show the employee some shallow pans and/or demonstrate an ice bath (placing pans of hot food into a larger container of cold water and ice).

h. Use thermometers to check food temperature during storing, cooking, serving, cooling, and reheating.

- You may want to demonstrate how to use a thermometer by putting it into the thickest part of the product. Show that the thermometer must be immersed up to the dimple on the stem in order to get an accurate reading.

2. Inspect foods thoroughly for freshness and wholesomeness upon receipt and before cooking and serving.

Examples

a. Check incoming canned goods for rust, dents, and bulges.

- Ask: "Why?" They may indicate the presence of a bacteria in the can that causes a deadly disease known as botulism.

b. Be sure to first use the foods in storage that have been there the longest.

c. Check that foods are not outdated.

d. Check for off-colors and odors.

e. Do not use eggs that are cracked.

- Ask: "Why?" They may contain significant amounts of a bacteria that can cause foodborne illness.

f. Wash thoroughly raw foods such as fruits and vegetables before use.

g. When in doubt, throw it out.

3. Store foods and equipment properly.

Examples

a. Cover, label, and date foods in storage.

- Explain your policy.

b. Do not store food in open cans.

c. Store new foods behind old ones.

d. Store food off the floor and away from the wall.

- Ask: "Why?" It helps prevent pests and animals from getting a free meal.

e. Check temperatures of refrigerators and freezers daily.

f. Defrost freezers as necessary. Frost buildup causes freezers to warm up.

g. Dry goods storage areas should be cool and dry for good food quality.

h. Do not store food or equipment under exposed sewer or water lines.

i. Keep storage areas clean.

j. Store all equipment so dust can't settle on it.

k. Store chemicals and pesticides separately from food.

4. Only use sanitized equipment and table surfaces.

Examples

a. Clean and sanitize all equipment, tools, tables, dishes, and so forth after each use.

b. Store wiping cloths in sanitizing solution.

5. Avoid letting the microorganisms from one food contaminate another food.

Examples

a. Keep separate cutting boards for raw and cooked foods.

b. Never mix leftovers with fresh food.

c. Store fresh raw meats, poultry, and fish on lowest racks.

d. Sanitize thermometers after each use.

e. When thawing raw foods in the refrigerator, place them on the lowest shelf.

6. Observe good grooming and hygiene practices including frequent hand washing.

7. Avoid preparing food further in advance than absolutely necessary.

8. Dispose of waste properly.

- Ask: "Why?" To prevent contamination of the food.

- Ask "Why?" To prevent them from dripping onto other foods.
- You may want to demonstrate by using an alcohol swab or a sanitizing solution.
- Ask: "Why?" To avoid cross-contamination of foods.

- This is covered in detail in On-the-Job Training Outline 1.

Examples

a. Cover garbage cans as much as possible.

b. Remove garbage regularly.

c. Clean and sanitize garbage cans regularly.

d. Keep outside garbage containers closed with tight-fitting lids.

e. Throw out food that was served but not eaten (unless it is wrapped), falls on the floor, is outdated, does not meet quality standards, was exposed to hazardous chemicals, was in the Danger Zone over 4 hours, or was otherwise mishandled.

f. Store soiled linen in a laundry bag or nonabsorbent container.

- Ask: "Why?" To prevent contamination.
- Ask: "Why?" To prevent odors, bugs, and animals.
- Review your policy. Mention the importance of washing cans in areas away from any food, equipment, or tableware.

9. Keep insects and animals out.

Examples

a. Keep doors closed.

b. Take garbage out frequently.

c. Keep garbage areas clean and garbage sealed.

d. Report any holes where an animal could enter.

e. Don't provide a free meal.

f. Keep work areas clean and uncluttered.

10. Handle ice and tableware properly.

Examples

a. Use clean scoops or tongs to pick up ice. Don't use hands or a glass.

b. Store scoops or tongs in a clean container, not in the ice.

c. Don't store any food or beverage in the ice.

- Ask: "Why?" Hands carry bacteria and a glass might chip in the ice.
- Ask: "Why?" To minimize contamination.
- Ask: "Why?" To prevent contamination of the ice.

d. Avoid touching food-contact surfaces of dishes, utensils, and so on.

- Explain that the food-contact surface is the surface that will be touched by food or drink. Show employee how to:

  - handle glasses, bowls, and cups by the bottom.
  - handle plates by the bottom or edge.
  - handle forks, knives, and spoons by the handle.

STEP 3. *Give quiz.*

KEY CONCEPTS	TRAINER'S DIRECTIONS

- Ask the employee to complete the Employee Quiz and then review the answers (given at left).

Employee Quiz Answer Key

Directions: *Check off in the space provided when the incident described could result in unsafe food being served.*

   X   **1.** Thawing frozen ground beef in a pan on a table in the preparation area

           2. Using a sanitized thermometer to test if meat is done

           3. Cooling down hot foods quickly (within 3 hours)

   X   **4.** Preparing and serving a leftover that has a strange color but smells okay

           5. Using only clean and sanitized equipment

   X   **6.** Storing raw meats above cooked meats in the refrigerator

   X   **7.** Serving a piece of toast that fell on the floor

           8. Handling dishes by the bottom or edge

_____**X**_____ **9.** Using a glass to scoop out ice

_____ **10.** Keeping work areas clean and uncluttered

Employee's Outline

■ KEY POINTS TO REMEMBER

In most cases, foodborne illness is a preventable disease carried to people through food. It makes you sick to your stomach and may cause vomiting, stomach cramps, and diarrhea for one or more days.

Major Causes of Foodborne Illness

1. Food left in the Danger Zone (45–140 degrees F) for 4 or more hours, such as hot foods that are not chilled rapidly enough
2. An employee with sloppy personal hygiene habits
3. Preparing food a day or more before serving
4. Food that is served when it is not completely cooked

The following list explains what you can do to prevent foodborne illness in your restaurant.

Requirements for Serving Safe Food

(The items that are checked off are the most important to you.)

1. Keep foods out of the danger zone (45–140 degrees F).

Examples

_____ a. Keep hot foods hot and cold foods cold.

_____ b. Handle foods quickly during delivery and put refrigerated and frozen foods away as soon as possible.

_____ c. Thaw foods in refrigerator, microwave, or under cold running water for not more than 2 hours (followed immediately by cooking). Never thaw at room temperature.

_____ d. Handle foods quickly during preparation. Only handle enough food that can be either cooked or refrigerated in 1 hour or less.

_____ e. Don't use hot food holding equipment such as a steam table to heat or reheat food.

_____ f. Cook and serve foods at a temperature of at least 140 degrees F. Heat leftovers to 165 degrees F. and pork to at least 150 degrees F.

_____ g. To cool down hot foods, use shallow pans and an ice bath. To make an ice bath, place the container holding the hot food into a larger container filled with ice and cold water. Stir hot foods to remove heat. Cut large pieces of meat, fish, and so forth into smaller pieces to allow heat loss. Cool foods to 45 degrees F or less in less than 4 hours.

_____ h. Use thermometers to check food temperature during storing, cooking, serving, cooling, and reheating.

_____ i. Place the thermometer into the center, or thickest, part of the food and make sure it is immersed up to the dimple on the stem in order to get an accurate reading.

2. Inspect foods thoroughly for freshness and wholesomeness upon receipt and before cooking and serving.

Examples

_____ a. Check incoming canned goods for rusted, dented, and bulging cans. They may indicate the growth of bacteria in the can, which causes a deadly disease called botulism. Also check for leaking.

_____ b. Be sure to first use foods in storage that have been there the longest.

_____ c. Check that foods are not outdated.

_____ d. Check for off-colors and odors.

_____ e. Do not use eggs that are cracked because they may contain significant amounts of a bacteria that can cause foodborne illness.

_____ f. Wash thoroughly raw foods such as fruits and vegetables before use.

_____ g. When in doubt, throw it out.

3. Store foods and equipment properly.

Examples

_____ a. Cover, label, and date foods in storage.

_____ b. Do not store food in open cans.

_____ c. Store new foods behind older ones.

_____ d. Store food off the floor and away from the wall to help prevent pests and animals from getting a free meal.

_____ e. Check temperatures of refrigerators and freezers daily.

_____ f. Defrost freezers as necessary. Frost buildup causes freezers to warm up.

_____ g. Dry goods storage areas should be cool and dry for good food quality.

_____ h. Do not store food or equipment under exposed sewer or water lines.

_____ i. Keep storage areas clean.

_____ j. Store all equipment so dust can't settle on it.

_____ k. Store chemicals and pesticides separately from food to avoid contamination.

4. Only use sanitized equipment and table surfaces.

   Examples

   _____ a. Clean and sanitize all equipment, tools, tables, dishes, and so forth after each use.

   _____ b. Store wiping cloths in a sanitizing solution.

5. Avoid letting the microorganisms from one food contaminate another food.

   Examples

   _____ a. Keep separate cutting boards for raw and cooked foods.

   _____ b. Never mix leftovers with fresh food.

   _____ c. Store fresh raw meats, poultry, and fish on lowest racks so they don't drip into cooked foods.

   _____ d. Sanitize thermometers after each use.

   _____ e. When thawing raw foods in the refrigerator, place them on the lowest shelf so they don't drip into cooked foods.

6. Observe good grooming and hygiene practices including frequent handwashing.

7. Avoid preparing food further in advance than absolutely necessary.

8. Dispose of waste properly.

   Examples

   _____ a. Cover garbage cans as much as possible to avoid contamination.

   _____ b. Remove garbage promptly to prevent odors, bugs, and animals.

   _____ c. Clean and sanitize garbage cans regularly. Wash cans in areas away from any food, equipment, or tableware.

   _____ d. Keep outside garbage containers closed with tight-fitting lids.

   _____ e. Throw out food that was served but not eaten (unless it is wrapped), falls on the floor, is outdated, does not meet quality standards, was exposed to hazardous chemicals, was in the Danger Zone over 4 hours, or was otherwise mishandled.

   _____ f. Store soiled linen in a laundry bag or nonabsorbent container.

9. Keep insects and animals out.

   Examples

   _____ a. Keep doors closed.

   _____ b. Take garbage out frequently.

_____ c. Keep garbage areas clean and garbage sealed.

_____ d. Report any holes where an animal could enter.

_____ e. Don't provide a free meal.

_____ f. Keep work areas clean and uncluttered.

10. Handle ice and tableware properly.

Examples

_____ a. Use clean scoops or tongs to pick up ice. Don't use hands (they're contaminated) or a glass (it could chip and leave glass fragments in the ice).

_____ b. Store scoops or tongs in a clean container, not in the ice.

_____ c. Don't store any food or beverage in the ice because it could contaminate the ice.

_____ d. Avoid touching food-contact surfaces of dishes, utensils, and so on. The food-contact surface is the surface that will be touched by food or drink.

- Handle glasses, bowls, and cups by the bottom.
- Handle plates by the bottom or edge.
- Handle forks, knives, and spoons by the handle.

Employee Quiz

Name: _____

Job Title: _____

Date: _____

Directions: *Check off in the space provided when the incident described could result in unsafe food being served.*

Your Answer   *Correct Answer*

_____   _____   **1.** Thawing frozen ground beef in a pan on a table in the preparation area

_____   _____   **2.** Using a thermometer to test if meat is done

_____   _____   **3.** Cooling down hot foods quickly (within 3 hours)

_____   _____   **4.** Preparing and serving a leftover that has a strange color but smells okay

_____   _____   **5.** Using only clean and sanitized equipment

_____   _____   **6.** Storing raw meats above cooked meats in the refrigerator

_____   _____   **7.** Serving a piece of toast that fell on the floor

_____   _____   **8.** Handling dishes by the bottom or edge

_____   _____   **9.** Using a glass to scoop out ice

_____   _____   **10.** Keeping work areas clean and uncluttered

1. Keep foods out of the danger zone (45–140 degrees F).

2. Inspect foods thoroughly for freshness and wholesomeness upon receipt and before cooking and serving.

3. Store foods and equipment properly.

4. Only use sanitized equipment and table surfaces.

5. Avoid letting the microorganisms from one food contaminate another food.

6. Observe good grooming and hygiene practices including frequent hand washing.

7. Avoid preparing food further in advance than absolutely necessary.

8. Dispose of waste properly.

9. Keep insects and animals out.

10. Handle ice and tableware properly.

Trainer's Outline

■ **STEPS:**

1. Demonstrate how to set up a three-compartment sink and let the employee practice.
2. Demonstrate how to use the three-compartment sink and let the employee practice.
3. Give quiz.

■ **TIME REQUIRED:**   20–30 minutes

■ **MATERIALS NEEDED:**   Employee's Outline, Employee Quiz, Job Aids, three-compartment sink

■ **AHEAD OF TIME:**   You may want to post Job Aids 4-1 and 4-2 by the three-compartment sink.

STEP 1. Demonstrate how to set up a three-compartment sink and let the employee practice.

KEY CONCEPTS	TRAINER'S DIRECTIONS
	• Ask the employee if he/she has ever set up and used a three-compartment sink.
	• Demonstrate how to set up a three-compartment sink, then let the employee do it. Coach.

How to Set Up a Three-Compartment Sink

1. Fill each sink with enough water to cover the largest pot or pan, using the following water temperatures:
   • wash—120 degrees F
   • rinse—120–140 degrees F
   • sanitize—75 degrees F or higher, unless using hot water to sanitize, then use 170 degrees F
   • Explain that sanitizing reduces the number of germs to an acceptable level.

2. Put the proper amount of detergent in the wash sink.

3. If using a chemical sanitizer, properly mix it in the last sink.

4. Check water temperatures with thermometer and test concentration of chemical sanitizer, if used, with chemical test kit.

STEP 2. *Demonstrate how to use the three-compartment sink and let the employee practice.*

KEY CONCEPTS	TRAINER'S DIRECTIONS
	• Demonstrate how to use the three-compartment sink, then let the employee do it. Coach.

Using a Three-Compartment Sink

KEY CONCEPTS	TRAINER'S DIRECTIONS
1. Scrape food.	
2. Sort pots.	
3. Prerinse to further remove food.	
4. Wash in hot water.	
5. Rinse well in clean, hot water.	• Explain that the purpose of rinsing is to remove any soil or detergent because it will interfere with the action of the sanitizer.
6. Sanitize for 1 minute in chemical sanitizer or 30 seconds in 170-degree F water.	• Mention to use a basket to lower items into 170-degree F water—it's too hot for hands.
7. Drain and air dry.	• Ask: "Why?" Because drying with towels could contaminate the equipment.
8. Store.	• Emphasize to store equipment only when it is dry so as to prevent the bacteria in water from causing contamination. Also protect equipment from dust, which also contains bacteria and other contamination.
9. Change water as needed in sinks and check the concentration of the sanitizer frequently.	

STEP 3. *Give quiz.*

KEY CONCEPTS	TRAINER'S DIRECTIONS
	• Ask the employee to complete the Employee Quiz and then review the answers (given at left).

Employee Quiz Answer Key

Directions: *Following are the steps for cleaning and sanitizing using a three-compartment sink. Number them according to the order in which they are done.*

___5___ Rinse

___8___ Store

___1___ Scrape

___7___ Drain and air dry

___6___ Sanitize

___2___ Sort

___4___ Wash

___3___ Prerinse

Employee's Outline

■ **KEY POINTS TO REMEMBER**

Setting Up and Using a Three-Compartment Sink

Cleaning and sanitizing of pots, pans, and so forth typically occurs in a three-compartment sink. The three compartments are essential to perform the functions of washing, rinsing (removing the soap), and sanitizing (reducing the number of germs to a safe level).

How to Set Up a Three-Compartment Sink

1. Fill each sink with enough water to cover the largest pot or pan, using the following water temperatures:
   • wash—120 degrees F
   • rinse—120–140 degrees F
   • sanitize—75 degrees F or higher, unless using hot water to sanitize, then use 170-degree F water
2. Put the proper amount of detergent in the wash sink.
3. If using a chemical sanitizer, properly mix it in the last sink.
4. Check water temperatures with a thermometer and test concentration of chemical sanitizer, if used, with a chemical test kit.

Following are the steps for using the three-compartment sink to clean and sanitize.

How to Use the Three-Compartment Sink

1. Scrape surfaces of large particles of food, bones, and so forth into garbage can or disposal.
2. Sort pots and pans.
3. Prerinse to further remove food.
4. Wash in first compartment with detergent and hot water.
5. In middle compartment, rinse with clean, hot water. It is very important to do a good job of rinsing because any soil or detergent left on the item will interfere with the next step of sanitizing.
6. Sanitize in third compartment for 30 seconds at 170 degrees F (you can't touch water this hot—you have to use a basket) or for 1 minute in a chemical sanitizer such as bleach.
7. Drain and air dry.
8. Store dry equipment so that the food-contact surface does not accumulate dust, which contains bacteria.
9. Change water as needed and test the concentration or temperature of the sanitizing solution from time to time.

Copyright © 1992 by John Wiley & Sons, Inc.

Employee Quiz

Name: _____

Job Title: _____

Date: _____

Directions: *Following are the steps for cleaning and sanitizing using a three-compartment sink. Number them according to the order in which they are done.*

Your Answer	*Correct Answer*	
_____	_____	Rinse
_____	_____	Store
_____	_____	Scrape
_____	_____	Drain and air dry
_____	_____	Sanitize
_____	_____	Separate
_____	_____	Wash
_____	_____	Prerinse

1. Fill each sink with enough water to cover the largest pot or pan, using the following water temperatures:

   wash—120 degrees F

   rinse—120–140 degrees F

   sanitize—75 degrees F or higher, unless using hot water to sanitize, then use 170-degree F water

2. Put the proper amount of detergent in the wash sink.

3. If using a chemical sanitizer, properly mix it in the last sink.

4. Check water temperatures with a thermometer and test concentration of chemical sanitizer, if used, with a chemical test kit.

1. Scrape surfaces of large particles of food, bones, and so forth into garbage can or disposal.

2. Sort pots and pans.

3. Prerinse to further remove food.

4. Wash in first compartment with detergent and hot water.

5. In middle compartment, rinse with clean, hot water. It is very important to do a good job of rinsing because any soil or detergent left on the item will interfere with the next step of sanitizing.

6. Sanitize in third compartment for 30 seconds at 170 degrees F (you can't touch water this hot— you have to use a basket) or for 1 minute in a chemical sanitizer such as bleach.

7. Drain and air dry.

8. Store dry equipment so that the food-contact surface does not accumulate dust, which contains bacteria.

9. Change water as needed and test the concentration or temperature of the sanitizing solution from time to time.

Trainer's Outline

■ **STEPS:**

1. Demonstrate how to operate the dishmachine and let the employee practice.
2. Give quiz.

■ **TIME REQUIRED:**   15–25 minutes

■ **MATERIALS REQUIRED:** Employee's Outline, Employee Quiz, Job Aid

■ **AHEAD OF TIME:**   You may want to post Job Aid 5-1 by the dishmachine.

STEP 1. Demonstrate how to operate the dishmachine and let the employee practice.

KEY CONCEPTS	TRAINER'S DIRECTIONS
	• Ask the employee if he/she has ever operated the dishmachine before.
	• Demonstrate how to operate the dishmachine, then let the employee do it. Coach.
How to Operate the Dishmachine	
1. Scrape items.	• Ask: "Why?" It makes it easier for the dishmachine to do its job.
2. Separate dishes, glasses, trays, etc.	• Ask: "Why?" To fit more in a rack or on the conveyor, and to make it easier to put them away.
3. Rack items or put them on the conveyor belt and be sure to: put dishes of the same type and size together in straight rows.	
place cups, bowls, and glasses upside down.	• Ask: "Why?" So spray hits inside them.
avoid stacking or overlapping dishes. put food-contact surfaces of dishes toward exit of machine.	• Ask: "Why?" So spray hits them directly.
4. Prerinse all items with overhead spray.	• Ask "Why?" To keep the wash water cleaner and let the detergent do its job.

5. Remove items without touching food-contact surfaces. Check for cleanliness and chipping. If using racks, tilt them to allow water to run off from recessed surfaces.

- Demonstrate how to hold plates and bowls by the bottom, hold cups by the handle or bottom, and hold silverware by the handles.

6. Store items when dry in a clean area where they are protected from dust and other contamination.

7. Check temperature gauges, detergent, and rinse additive frequently:

   prewash—80–110 degrees F

   wash—140–160 degrees F

   rinse—170–180 degrees F

   final rinse—180 degrees F

8. Change water in tanks as needed.

9. Clean flatware appropriately.

- Discuss your operation's policy on cleaning flatware. Be sure to mention to store silverware with the handles up.

10. Tell your supervisor if there are problems with dishmachine temperatures or if dishes are coming out dirty, spotted, streaked, filmy, or stained (such as coffee stains).

STEP 2. Give quiz.

KEY CONCEPTS	TRAINER'S DIRECTIONS
	• Ask the employee to complete Employee Quiz and then review the answers (given at left).

Employee Quiz Answer Key

Directions: *Following are the steps for operating the dishmachine. Number them according to the order in which they are done.*

____6____ Store items when dry in a place where they won't be contaminated.

____4____ Rack items or put them on a conveyor belt.

____1____ Scrape items.

_____5_____ Remove items without touching food-contact surfaces.

_____2_____ Separate dishes, glasses, trays, etc.

_____3_____ Prerinse all items with overhead spray.

7 & 8. When operating the dishmachine, name two things you need to check on frequently.

    7. __**detergent**__

    8. __**temperature**__

       also, the sanitizer

Employee's Outline

■ KEY POINTS TO REMEMBER

How to Operate the Dishmachine

1. Scrape dishes well so the dishmachine can do a good job.

2. Separate items so they fit better and are easier to put away.

3. Rack or put items on a conveyor belt. Put dishes of same type and size together. Place cups, bowls, and glasses upside down. Only one layer of dishes is allowed. Put food-contact surfaces of dishes toward exit end of machine to allow spray to clean them well.

4. Prerinse all items with overhead spray to keep the dish water cleaner and so the detergent wash will do a better job.

5. Remove items. If using racks, tilt them to allow water to run off from recessed surfaces. When handling dishes, don't touch the food-contact surfaces. Hold tableware by the bottoms or handles. Check dishes and silverware for cleanliness, chipping, and breakage.

6. Store items when dry in a clean area where dust won't accumulate on the food-contact surfaces.

7. Check temperature gauges frequently, add chemicals, and change the water in the tanks as needed:

   prewash—80–110 degrees F

   wash—140–160 degrees F

   rinse—170–180 degrees F

   final rinse—180 degrees F (for machines using hot water to sanitize)

8. Change water in tanks as needed.

9. Clean flatware appropriately.

10. Tell your supervisor if there are problems with temperatures or if the dishes are coming out dirty, spotted, streaked, filmy, or stained.

Employee Quiz

Name: _____

Job Title: _____

Date: _____

Directions: *Following are the steps to operate the dishmachine. Number them according to the order in which they are done.*

Your Answer	*Correct Answer*	
_____	_____	Store items when dry in a place where they won't be contaminated.
_____	_____	Rack items or put them on a conveyor belt.
_____	_____	Scrape items.
_____	_____	Remove items without touching food-contact surfaces.
_____	_____	Separate dishes, glasses, trays, etc.
_____	_____	Prerinse all items with overhead spray.

7 & 8. When operating the dishmachine, name two things you need to check on frequently.

7. _____

8. _____

1. Scrape dishes well so the dishmachine can do a good job.

2. Separate items so they fit better and are easier to put away.

3. Rack or put items on a conveyor belt. Put dishes of same type and size together. Place cups, bowls, and glasses upside down. Only one layer of dishes is allowed. Put food-contact surfaces of dishes toward exit of machine to allow spray to clean them well.

4. Prerinse all items with overhead spray to keep the dish water cleaner and so the detergent will do a better job.

5. Remove items. If using racks, tilt them to allow water to run off from recessed surfaces. When handling dishes, don't touch the food-contact surfaces. Hold tableware by the bottoms or handles. Check dishes and silverware for cleanliness, chipping, and breakage.

6. Store items when dry in a clean area where dust won't accumulate on the food-contact surfaces.

continued

7. Check temperature gauges frequently; add chemicals and change the water in the tanks as needed:

   prewash—80–110 degrees F

   wash—140–160 degrees F

   rinse—170–180 degrees F

   final rinse—180 degrees F (for machines using hot water to sanitize)

8. Change water in tanks as needed.

9. Clean flatware appropriately.

10. Tell your supervisor if there are problems with temperatures or if the dishes are coming out dirty, spotted, streaked, filmy, or stained.

Trainer's Outline

■ **STEPS:**

1. Demonstrate how to clean stationary equipment and let the employee practice.
2. Give quiz.

■ **TIME REQUIRED:** 15–20 minutes

■ **MATERIALS REQUIRED:** Employee's Outline, Employee Quiz, Job Aid

■ **AHEAD OF TIME:** You may want to post Job Aid 6-1.

STEP 1. Demonstrate how to clean stationary equipment and let the employee practice.

KEY CONCEPTS	TRAINER'S DIRECTIONS
	• Ask the employee if he/she has ever cleaned stationary equipment before.
	• Demonstrate how to clean a piece of stationary equipment, such as a slicer, then let the employee do it. Coach.
How to Clean Stationary Equipment	
1. Unplug equipment. Make sure your hands are dry.	
2. Disassemble.	
3. Wash removable parts in dishmachine or three-compartment sink.	
4. Wash and rinse stationary parts.	
5. Sanitize food-contact surfaces with a sanitizer mixed to twice its strength.	
6. Air dry before reassembling without touching food-contact surfaces.	

STEP 2. Give quiz.

KEY CONCEPTS	TRAINER'S DIRECTIONS
	• Ask the employee to complete Employee Quiz and then review the following answers.

Employee Quiz Answer Key

Directions: *Following are the steps for cleaning stationary equipment. Number them according to the order in which they are done.*

___4___ Wash and rinse stationary parts.

___2___ Disassemble.

___5___ Sanitize food-contact surfaces with a sanitizer mixed to twice its strength.

___1___ Unplug equipment.

___6___ Air dry.

___3___ Wash removable parts.

Employee's Outline

■ **KEY POINTS TO REMEMBER**

If equipment is stationary, and can't be moved to a sink, it is necessary to clean it in place using the following steps.

How to Clean Stationary Equipment

1. Unplug equipment, making sure your hands are dry.
2. Disassemble.
3. Wash removable parts in dishmachine or three-compartment sink.
4. Wash and rinse stationary parts.
5. Sanitize food-contact surfaces with a sanitizer mixed to twice its strength.
6. Air dry before reassembling without touching food-contact surfaces.

Employee Quiz

Name: _____

Job Title: _____

Date: _____

Directions: *Following are the steps for cleaning and sanitizing stationary equipment. Number them according to the order in which they are done.*

Your Answer	*Correct Answer*	
_____	_____	Wash and rinse stationary parts.
_____	_____	Disassemble.
_____	_____	Sanitize food-contact surfaces with a sanitizer mixed to twice its strength.
_____	_____	Unplug equipment.
_____	_____	Air dry.
_____	_____	Wash removable parts.

1. Unplug equipment. Make sure your hands are dry.

2. Disassemble.

3. Wash removable parts in dishmachine or three-compartment sink.

4. Wash and rinse stationary parts.

5. Sanitize food-contact surfaces with a sanitizer mixed to twice its strength.

6. Air dry before reassembling without touching food-contact surfaces.

Trainer's Outline

■ **STEPS:**

1. Discuss how to prevent each of the following: cuts, burns, fires, falls, and electric shock.
2. Give quiz.

■ **TIME REQUIRED:**   15–25 minutes

■ **MATERIALS NEEDED:**   Employee's Outline, Employee Quiz, Job Aids

■ **AHEAD OF TIME:**   On the Employee's Outline, check off the numbers on the Kitchen Safety Checklist that apply to the employee being trained (some examples may not be relevant to certain jobs).

STEP 1. Discuss how to prevent each of the following: cuts, burns, fires, falls, and electric shock.

KEY CONCEPTS	TRAINER'S DIRECTIONS
	• Ask the employee if he or she was ever hurt working in a kitchen. If so, ask the employee to describe what happened.
Why Accidents Occur	• Ask the employee why accidents occur in a kitchen. Review some of the reasons and explain that employees can prevent most accidents and should try to because accidents often cause pain, cost money, and lower morale.
• Fooling around	
• Rushing	
• Being careless	
• Working under the influence of drugs or alcohol	
• Not paying attention	
• Overdoing it	
• Ignorance	
• Feeling they are bound to happen	
	• Asking the employee to follow along in the Employee Outline, explain the Kitchen Safety Checklist, and review the examples that apply to his/her job.

Kitchen Safety Checklist
Preventing Cuts

1. Know how to operate equipment.

2. Pay attention when using sharp equipment.
   - Ask employee to name any sharp equipment he/she works with.

3. Use guards when provided on equipment.

4. Use tampers to push food into equipment, not your hands!

5. Turn equipment off before adjusting.
   - Ask: "Why?" You could be hurt by moving gears and/or blades.

6. No loose sleeves, ties or dangling jewelry should be by equipment.
   - Ask: "Why?" They can get caught in equipment and also pull in your arm, for example.

7. Use knives carefully.
   - This is covered more in Training Outline 24.

8. Carry dishes and glassware carefully.
   - Ask: "Why?" They break easily and shatter.

9. Sweep up broken glass.
   - Emphasize not to use your hands to pick up broken glass.

10. Use a special container to dispose of broken glass, dishes, and other sharp objects.
    - Ask: "Why?" Sharp items can cut through bags and cut the person removing the trash.

11. Remove nails and staples in shipping cartons and crates, and wear gloves.

12. Remove can lids entirely from cans and put back into empty cans for disposal.

Preventing Burns

1. Pay attention when working around hot equipment.
   - Ask employee which equipment they need to be cautious about in their work areas.

2. Use dry potholders.
   - Explain that wet potholders conduct heat to your hands.

3. Keep pot handles turned in from the edge of the range and away from open flames.
   - Ask: "Why?" Otherwise they may be hit by someone, causing hot foods to spill.

4. Avoid overfilling containers with hot foods.
   - Ask: "Why?" They may spill and cause burns.

5. Get help lifting heavy pots of food.
   - Ask: "Why?" To avoid spills and burns.

6. Open lids of pots and doors of steamers away from you, and do so slowly.

- Ask: "Why?" To avoid steam burns, which are worse than burns from boiling water. You may want to demonstrate with a pot and lid.

7. Stir foods with long-handled spoons.

8. Warn others of hot surfaces.

- Ask the employee what phrases to use to warn others of hot surfaces, such as "Coming through!"

9. Let equipment cool before cleaning. Don't use wet rags to clean hot equipment.

10. Don't put icy frozen foods into the fryer. Put foods slowly into the fryer and stand back.

- Ask: "Why?" Grease may splatter.

11. Strike match before turning on gas equipment.

- Ask: "Why?" Otherwise you risk a flare-up or large flame.

12. Wear closed-toe and closed-heel shoes that don't absorb liquids.

- Ask: "Why?" They protect your feet in case of a spill.

13. Warn guests of hot dishes.

Preventing Fires

1. Smoke only where allowed.

- Mention also the importance of using and having available ashtrays in smoking areas.

2. Don't turn your back on hot fat.

- Ask: "Why?" It may burst into flames.

3. Keep equipment and hoods free from grease buildup.

- Emphasize that grease causes many fires. Ask employee where he/she needs to pay attention to grease buildup in the kitchen.

4. Don't set the fryer at too high a temperature.

- Ask: "Why?" Overheated grease can burst into flames.

5. Store matches in a covered container away from heat.

6. Keep garbage in covered containers.

7. Store chemicals away from heat.

- Ask: "Why?" Many chemicals are flammable.

Preventing Falls

1. Wipe up spills immediately.

2. Use "Wet Floor" signs.

3. Wear shoes with nonskid soles and heels.

4. Keep aisles and stairs clear.

5. Walk, don't run.

6. Follow established traffic patterns.

7. Don't carry anything that blocks your vision.

8. Keep drawers closed.

9. Use ladders properly. Never stand on a chair, table, or box.

• Mention not to stand on the top rung of a ladder and do not overreach.

10. Use handrails on stairs.

11. Turn lights on to see.

Preventing Electric Shock

1. Never touch electrical equipment or outlets with wet hands or while standing in water.

2. Unplug equipment before cleaning or disassembling.

• Ask: "Why?" A damp cloth on a piece of equipment that is plugged in can cause shocks.

3. Do not yank plugs out by the cord.

• Ask: "Why?" It may damage the cord, which may then cause shocks.

4. Report damaged and worn plugs and cords to your supervisor.

STEP 2. Give quiz.

KEY CONCEPTS	TRAINER'S DIRECTIONS
	• Ask the employee to complete Employee Quiz and then review the answers (given at left).

Employee Quiz Answer Key

Directions: Check off in the space provided whether the practice described is safe or unsafe.

Safe	Unsafe	
X		1. Remove can lids and put them back into the empty container for disposal.
	X	2. Use a damp potholder.
	X	3. Strike match after turning on gas equipment.

Safe	Unsafe	
X		**4.** Open lids of pots away from you.
	X	**5.** While deep-fat frying chicken, leave to go to the bathroom.
	X	**6.** Stand on a chair to reach supplies.
	X	**7.** Yank a plug out by the cord.
X		**8.** Unplug equipment before cleaning.
	X	**9.** Wipe up spills when you get the chance.
X		**10.** Know how to operate equipment before doing so.

Employee's Outline

■ **KEY POINTS TO REMEMBER**

Accidents all have one thing in common: a human being. We cause accidents by fooling or clowning around, rushing, being careless, not paying attention, overdoing it, or simply not knowing what we are doing. Accidents also occur when we accept wrongly that they are a part of life, or when we are working under the influence of drugs or alcohol. Unfortunately accidents cause many kinds of problems. To begin with, accidents usually cause pain and discomfort to those who get hurt. Besides being painful, work time may be lost, and medical bills are expensive. Accidents can also lower morale and damage reputations.

Kitchen Safety Checklist

Preventing Cuts

_____ 1. Know how to operate equipment.

_____ 2. Pay attention when using sharp equipment. Never touch edges of sharp blades, and wipe away from sharp edges when cleaning.

_____ 3. Use guards when provided on equipment.

_____ 4. Use tampers to push food into equipment.

_____ 5. Turn equipment off before adjusting to avoid being cut by moving gears and/ or blades.

_____ 6. No loose sleeves, ties, or dangling jewelry should be by equipment because they may get caught and pull in your arm, for example.

_____ 7. Use knives carefully.

_____ 8. Carry dishes and glassware carefully.

_____ 9. Sweep up broken glass; use a broom, not your hands.

_____ 10. Use a special container to dispose of broken glass, dishes, and other sharp objects because they tend to cut through bags and cut the person removing the trash.

_____ 11. Remove nails and staples in shipping cartons and crates, and wear gloves.

_____ 12. Remove can lids entirely from cans and put them back into empty cans for disposal.

EMPLOYEE'S OUTLINE (continued)

Preventing Burns

————————— 1. Pay attention when working around hot equipment.

————————— 2. Use dry potholders. Wet potholders conduct heat to your hands.

————————— 3. Keep pot handles turned in from the edge of the range so they are not accidentally knocked. Keep pot handles away from open flames because the flame will heat them up.

————————— 4. Avoid overfilling containers with hot foods.

————————— 5. Get help lifting heavy pots of food.

————————— 6. Open lids of pots and doors of steamers away from you, and do so slowly to avoid a steam burn. Steam burns are worse than burns from boiling water.

————————— 7. Stir foods with long-handled spoons.

————————— 8. Warn others of hot surfaces.

————————— 9. Let equipment cool before cleaning. Don't use wet rags to clean hot equipment.

————————— 10. Don't put icy frozen foods into the fryer. Put foods slowly into the fryer and stand back to avoid being splattered with grease.

————————— 11. Strike match before turning on gas equipment to avoid a flare-up or large flame.

————————— 12. Wear closed-toe and closed-heel shoes that don't absorb liquids.

————————— 13. Warn guests of hot dishes.

Preventing Fires

————————— 1. Smoke only where allowed.

————————— 2. Don't turn your back on hot fat as it may burst into flames.

————————— 3. Keep equipment and hoods free from grease buildup because grease causes many foodservice fires.

————————— 4. Don't set the fryer at too high a temperature.

————————— 5. Store matches in a covered container away from heat.

————————— 6. Keep garbage in covered containers.

————————— 7. Store chemicals away from heat because many chemicals are flammable.

Preventing Falls

————————— 1. Wipe up spills immediately.

————————— 2. Use "Wet Floor" signs.

EMPLOYEE'S OUTLINE (continued)

_____ 3. Wear shoes with nonskid soles and heels.

_____ 4. Keep aisles and stairs clear.

_____ 5. Walk, don't run.

_____ 6. Follow established traffic patterns.

_____ 7. Don't carry anything that blocks your vision.

_____ 8. Keep drawers closed.

_____ 9. Use ladders properly. Never stand on a chair, table, or box. Don't stand on the top rung of a ladder and do not overreach.

_____ 10. Use handrails on stairs.

_____ 11. Turn lights on to see.

Preventing Electric Shock

_____ 1. Never touch electrical equipment or outlets with wet hands or while standing in water.

_____ 2. Unplug equipment before cleaning or disassembling to avoid shocks.

_____ 3. Do not yank plugs out by the cord because it can cause damage to the cords, which may then cause shocks.

_____ 4. Report damaged and worn plugs and cords to your supervisor.

Employee Quiz

Name: _____

Job Title: _____

Date: _____

Directions: *Check off in the space provided whether the practice described is safe or unsafe.*

Safe	**Unsafe**	
_____	_____	1. Remove can lids and put them back into the empty container for disposal. Correct Answer: _____
_____	_____	2. Use a damp potholder. Correct Answer: _____
_____	_____	3. Strike match after turning on gas equipment. Correct Answer: _____
_____	_____	4. Open lids of pots away from you. Correct Answer: _____
_____	_____	5. While deep-fat frying chicken, leave to go to the bathroom. Correct Answer: _____
_____	_____	6. Stand on a chair to reach supplies. Correct Answer: _____
_____	_____	7. Yank a plug out by the cord. Correct Answer: _____
_____	_____	8. Unplug equipment before cleaning. Correct Answer: _____
_____	_____	9. Wipe up spills when you get the chance. Correct Answer: _____
_____	_____	10. Know how to operate equipment before doing so. Correct Answer: _____

PREVENTING CUTS

_____ **1.** Know how to operate equipment.

_____ **2.** Pay attention when using sharp equipment. Never touch edges of sharp blades, and wipe away from sharp edges when cleaning.

_____ **3.** Use guards when provided on equipment.

_____ **4.** Use tampers to push food into equipment.

_____ **5.** Turn equipment off before adjusting to avoid being cut by moving gears and/or blades.

_____ **6.** No loose sleeves, ties, or dangling jewelry should be by equipment because they may get caught and pull in your arm, for example.

_____ **7.** Use knives carefully.

_____ **8.** Carry dishes and glassware carefully.

_____ **9.** Sweep up broken glass; don't use your hands.

continued

_____ **10.** Use a special container to dispose of broken glass, dishes, and other sharp objects because they tend to cut through bags and cut the person removing the trash.

_____ **11.** Remove nails and staples in shipping cartons and crates, and wear gloves.

_____ **12.** Remove can lids entirely from cans and put them back into empty cans for disposal.

PREVENTING BURNS

____ **1.** Pay attention when working around hot equipment.

____ **2.** Use dry potholders. Wet potholders conduct heat to your hands.

____ **3.** Keep pot handles turned in from the edge of the range so they are not accidentally knocked. Keep pot handles away from open flames because the flame will heat them up.

____ **4.** Avoid overfilling containers with hot foods.

____ **5.** Get help lifting heavy pots of food.

____ **6.** Open lids of pots and doors of steamers away from you, and do so slowly to avoid a steam burn. Steam burns are worse than burns from boiling water.

____ **7.** Stir foods with long-handled spoons.

____ **8.** Warn others of hot surfaces.

____ **9.** Let equipment cool before cleaning. Don't use wet rags to clean hot equipment.

continued

_____ **10.** Don't put icy frozen foods into the fryer. Put foods slowly into the fryer and stand back to avoid being splattered with grease.

_____ **11.** Strike match before turning on gas equipment to avoid a flare-up or large flame.

_____ **12.** Wear closed-toe and closed-heel shoes that don't absorb liquids.

_____ **13.** Warn guests of hot dishes.

PREVENTING FIRES

____ **1.** Smoke only where allowed.

____ **2.** Don't turn your back on hot fat as it may burst into flames.

____ **3.** Keep equipment and hoods free from grease buildup because grease causes many foodservice fires.

____ **4.** Don't set the fryer at too high a temperature.

____ **5.** Store matches in a covered container away from heat.

____ **6.** Keep garbage in covered containers.

____ **7.** Store chemicals away from heat because many chemicals are flammable.

PREVENTING FALLS

____ **1.** Wipe up spills immediately.

____ **2.** Use "Wet Floor" signs.

____ **3.** Wear shoes with nonskid soles and heels.

____ **4.** Keep aisles and stairs clear.

____ **5.** Walk, don't run.

____ **6.** Follow established traffic patterns.

____ **7.** Don't carry anything that blocks your vision.

____ **8.** Keep drawers closed.

____ **9.** Use ladders properly. Never stand on a chair, table, or box. Don't stand on the top rung of a ladder and do not overreach.

____ **10.** Use handrails on stairs.

____ **11.** Turn lights on to see.

PREVENTING ELECTRIC SHOCK

_____ **1.** Never touch electrical equipment or outlets with wet hands or while standing in water.

_____ **2.** Unplug equipment before cleaning or disassembling to avoid shocks.

_____ **3.** Do not yank plugs out by the cord because it can cause damage to the cords, which may then cause shocks.

_____ **4.** Report damaged and worn plugs and cords to your supervisor.

Trainer's Outline

■ **STEPS:**

1. Have employee complete Warmup Exercise and review answers.

2. Demonstrate how to lift properly and let the employee practice.

3. Demonstrate how to properly move a cart or truck and let the employee practice.

4. Give quiz.

■ **TIME REQUIRED:**   15–25 minutes

■ **MATERIALS NEEDED:**   Employee's Outline, Employee Quiz, Job Aids

■ **AHEAD OF TIME:**   You can post Job Aids 8-1 and 8-2 in visible areas for employees and trainees to use.

STEP 1.   Have employee complete Warmup Exercise and review answers.

KEY CONCEPTS	TRAINER'S DIRECTIONS
	• Ask employee to complete the Warmup Exercise in the Employee's Outline and review answers.

Warmup Exercise

Circle True or False.

1. Back injuries are the most common on-the-job accident.

   A. True

2. Back injuries are the most costly on-the-job accident.

   A. True

3. Back injuries are rarely preventable.

   B. False

   Explain that most back injuries can be prevented when employees know how to lift and move equipment, boxes, etc. properly.

4. When lifting, use your legs, not your back.

   A. True

Explain that your leg muscles are quite strong and should be used in lifting.

5. It is better and easier to pull, rather than push, a cart.

B. False

Explain that it is easier to push.

STEP 2. *Demonstrate how to lift properly and let the employee practice.*

KEY CONCEPTS	TRAINER'S DIRECTIONS
	• Ask the employee what he/she knows about lifting properly in order to avoid hurting his/her back.
	• Asking the employee to follow along in the Employee's Outline, review Lifting Properly.
	• Next, demonstrate how to lift properly, then let the employee practice. Coach.
Lifting Properly	
1. Plan it!	
Do you need help?	
Could you use a cart?	
Where is it going?	
Which route is best?	
2. Get ready!	
Spread your feet shoulder width apart.	
Put one foot slightly in front of the other for a good support base.	
Squat down with back straight and head up. Don't bend over from the waist!	• Emphasize using your leg muscles to lift, not your back muscles, because back muscles become injured much more easily.
Grip the object firmly with both hands. Keep elbows and arms close to body. Tuck in chin.	
If lifting a tray, squat down alongside the tray stand and slide the tray onto your shoulder and hand.	

3. Lift it!

Straighten your knees slowly and smoothly to a stand. Avoid doing this in a quick or jerky manner.

Don't lift and twist at the same time.

- This is the cause of most back injuries and it puts undue stress on your lower back. Instead of twisting, stand up straight and move your feet to change position.

4. Move it!

Keep object close to you.

- Explain this gives you more control and lessens the pressure.

To change position, move your feet and entire body. Don't twist from the waist!

Look where you are going.

Call out "Coming through" as needed.

5. Set it down!

Bend your knees slowly and smoothly.

Slide load into place—watch your fingers and toes!

STEP 3. *Demonstrate how to properly move a cart or truck and let the employee practice.*

KEY CONCEPTS	**TRAINER'S DIRECTIONS**
	• Ask the employee what he/she knows about moving a cart or truck to avoid hurting his/her back.
	• Asking the employee to follow along in the Employee's Outline, review Moving a Cart or Truck Properly.
	• Next, demonstrate how to move a cart or truck, then let the employee practice. Coach.

Moving a Cart or Truck Properly

How to Move a Cart or Truck

1. Push rather than pull.

2. Spread your feet wide, one in front of the other, with your front knee bent.

3. Keep back straight.

4. Slowly push into the cart with your body weight, using your leg muscles to do much of the pushing.

5. Push slowly and smoothly. Avoid sudden motions or twisting your back.

STEP 4.   Give quiz.

KEY CONCEPTS	**TRAINER'S DIRECTIONS**
	• Ask the employee to complete Employee Quiz and then review the answers (given at left).

Employee Quiz Answer Key

Directions: *Circle either True or False.*

1. When lifting, you should use your back muscles.

   B. False

   Explain you should use your leg muscles.

2. Instead of twisting your back when lifting, you should wait until you are standing up and then move your feet into the desired position.

   A. True

3. Push, don't pull, trucks.

   A. True

4. When lifting, do it quickly.

   B. False

   Explain that quick, jerky movements may damage your back.

5. Keep your back straight when moving a cart.

   A. True

6. Squat down and get your shoulder under a tray before lifting it.

   A. True

Employee's Outline

■ **WARMUP EXERCISE**

Directions: *Circle the correct answer.*

1. Back injuries are the most common on-the-job accident.
   A. True
   B. False

   Correct Answer: _____

2. Back injuries are the most costly on-the-job accident.
   A. True
   B. False

   Correct Answer: _____

3. Back injuries are rarely preventable.
   A. True
   B. False

   Correct Answer: _____

4. When lifting, use your legs, not your back.
   A. True
   B. False

   Correct Answer: _____

5. It is better and easier to pull, rather than push, a cart.
   A. True
   B. False

   Correct Answer: _____

■ **KEY POINTS TO REMEMBER**

Back safety is a topic of crucial importance to foodservice employees because almost everybody does some lifting in their jobs, and when done improperly, lifting can cause serious back problems. The bad news is that the most common, as well as the most costly, type of accident involves an employee's back. The good news is that hurting your back is preventable if you follow these steps when lifting or moving a cart or truck.

EMPLOYEE'S OUTLINE (continued)

Lifting Properly

1. Plan it!

   Do you need help?

   Could you use a cart?

   Where is it going?

   Which route is best?

2. Get ready!

   Spread your feet shoulder width apart.

   Put one foot slightly in front of the other for a good support base.

   Squat down with back straight and head up. Don't bend over from the waist!

   Grip the object firmly with both hands. Keep elbows and arms close to the body. Tuck in chin.

   If lifting a tray, squat down alongside the tray stand and slide the tray onto your shoulder and hand.

3. Lift it!

   Straighten your knees slowly and smoothly to a stand. Avoid doing this in a quick or jerky manner.

   Don't lift and twist at the same time.

4. Move it!

   Keep object close to you.

   To change position, move your feet and entire body. Don't twist from the waist!

   Look where you are going.

   Call out "Coming through" as needed.

5. Set it down!

   Bend your knees slowly and smoothly.

   Slide load into place—watch your fingers and toes!

Moving a Cart or Truck Properly

1. Push rather than pull.
2. Spread your feet wide, one in front of the other, with your front knee bent.
3. Keep back straight.
4. Slowly push into the cart with your body weight, using your leg muscles to do much of the pushing.
5. Push slowly and smoothly. Avoid sudden motions or twisting your back.

Employee Quiz

Name: _____

Job Title: _____

Date: _____

Directions: *Circle the appropriate answer.*

1. When lifting, you should use your back muscles.
   A. True
   B. False

   Correct Answer: _____

2. Instead of twisting your back when lifting, you should wait until you are standing up and then move your feet into the desired position.
   A. True
   B. False

   Correct Answer: _____

3. Push, don't pull, trucks.
   A. True
   B. False

   Correct Answer: _____

4. When lifting, do it quickly.
   A. True
   B. False

   Correct Answer: _____

5. Keep your back straight when moving a cart.
   A. True
   B. False

   Correct Answer: _____

6. Squat down and get your shoulder under a tray before lifting it.
   A. True
   B. False

   Correct Answer: _____

1. Plan it!

Do you need help?

Could you use a cart?

Where is it going?

Which route is best?

2. Get ready!

Spread your feet shoulder width apart.

Put one foot slightly in front of the other for a good support base.

Squat down with back straight and head up. Don't bend over from the waist!

Grip the object firmly with both hands. Keep elbows and arms close to body. Tuck in chin.

If lifting a tray, squat down alongside the tray stand and slide the tray onto your shoulder and hand.

3. Lift it!

Straighten your knees slowly and smoothly to a stand. Avoid doing this in a quick or jerky manner.

Don't lift and twist at the same time.

continued

4. Move it!

   Keep object close to you.

   To change position, move your feet and entire body. Don't twist from the waist!

   Look where you are going.

   Call out "Coming through" as needed.

5. Set it down!

   Bend your knees slowly and smoothly.

   Slide load into place—watch your fingers and toes!

1. Push rather than pull.

2. Spread your feet wide, one in front of the other, with your front knee bent.

3. Keep back straight.

4. Slowly push into the cart with your body weight, using your leg muscles to do much of the pushing.

5. Push slowly and smoothly. Avoid sudden motions or twisting your back.

Trainer's Outline

■ **STEPS:**

1. Explain the do's and don'ts of safe chemical handling.

2. Demonstrate how to read instructions and warnings on Material Safety Data Sheets and let employee practice.

3. Demonstrate how to read instructions and warnings on product labels and let employee practice.

4. Give quiz.

■ **TIME REQUIRED:**   20–30 minutes

■ **MATERIALS NEEDED:**   Employee's Outline, Employee Quiz, Job Aids

STEP 1.   Explain the do's and don'ts of safe chemical handling.

KEY CONCEPTS	TRAINER'S DIRECTIONS
	• Ask the employee to identify any hazardous chemicals in his/her work area such as detergent, all-purpose cleaner, and oven cleaner.
	• Explain that many of the cleaning agents we use are hazardous—that is, they can cause burns, skin irritations, and other health problems.
	• Asking the employee to follow along in the Employee Outline, review the Do's and Don'ts of Safe Chemical Handling.

Do's and Don'ts of Safe Chemical Handling

Do's

1. Do know where the Material Safety Data Sheets are posted and read them.

2. Do read the labels of all products *before* you use them.

3. Do follow the directions for proper storage, handling, and use of all chemicals.

4. Do ask your supervisor any question or concern you may have about using a certain product.

5. Do know how to call for medical help in case of an emergency.

- Review how to do so.

Don'ts

1. Don't ever mix chemicals together.

- Explain that when certain chemicals are mixed together, such as bleach and ammonia, they produce a deadly gas.

2. Don't store chemicals in unmarked containers.

3. Don't store chemicals in or close to food storage, preparation, or serving areas.

- Ask: "Why?" To prevent contamination of food.

4. Don't leave aerosol spray containers near heat or spray close to an open flame.

- Ask: "Why?" They could explode.

5. Don't dispose of any empty chemical container until you have checked the label instructions for how to do so.

STEP 2. Demonstrate how to read instructions and warnings on Material Safety Data Sheets and let employee practice.

KEY CONCEPTS	TRAINER'S DIRECTIONS
	• Asking the employee to follow along in the Outline, explain the six sections of the Material Safety Data Sheet (MSDS) that give important handling and safety information to the employee.

Reading the MSDS

1. Product name

2. Fire hazard

explains if the product can catch fire or explode

3. Health hazards

explains effects of overexposure

explains emergency and first aid procedures

4. Spill precautions

explains steps to take in case of spill

5. Special protection

describes any special measures, such as goggles and rubber gloves, to use to decrease exposure and risk

6. Special precautions

tells precautions when handling and storing

- Next give the employee a copy of an MSDS for a product used in your operation. Point out each of the six sections just discussed.

- Give the employee the MSDS for a product he/she uses and ask him/her to tell you the important information it contains.

STEP 3. ***Demonstrate how to read instructions and warnings on product labels and let employee practice.***

KEY CONCEPTS	TRAINER'S DIRECTIONS
	• Asking the employee to follow along in the Outline, explain the types of information given on product labels that will help him/her use these products safely.

Reading Product Labels

1. Name

2. Physical and health hazards

3. Instructions for storing, handling, and use

4. Instructions on what to do in case of an emergency

- Next give employee a copy of a label for a product used in your operation. Point out each of the four sections just discussed.

- Give the employee the label of a product he/she uses and ask him/her to tell you the important information it contains.

STEP 4. *Give quiz.*

KEY CONCEPTS	TRAINER'S DIRECTIONS
	• Ask the employee to complete Employee Quiz and then review the answers (given at left).

Employee Quiz Answer Key

Directions: *Check either "Do" or "Don't" as appropriate to complete the sentence.*

Do	Don't	
X		1. ask your supervisor any question or concern you may have on using a certain product.
	X	2. store chemicals in or close to food storage, preparation, or serving areas.
X		3. follow the directions for proper storage, handling, and use for all chemicals you use.
	X	4. leave aerosol spray containers near heat or spray close to an open flame or your eyes.
	X	5. store chemicals in unmarked containers.
X		6. know how to call for medical help in case of an emergency.
	X	7. mix together any chemicals.
X		8. read the labels of all products *before* you use them.
	X	9. dispose of any empty chemical container until you have checked on the label for how to do so.
X		10. know where the Material Safety Data Sheets are posted and read them.

Employee's Outline

■ KEY POINTS TO REMEMBER

As you probably know, there are a number of hazardous materials in your workplace, including all-purpose cleaners, detergents, oven cleaners, degreasers, and pesticides. These materials often present hazards such as irritating skin or burning skin or eyes.

Do's and Don'ts of Safe Chemical Handling

1. Do know where the Material Safety Data Sheets are posted and read them.
2. Do read the labels of all products *before* you use them.
3. Do follow the directions for proper storage, handling, and use for all chemicals you use.
4. Do ask your supervisor any question or concern you may have about using a certain product.
5. Do know how to call for medical help in case of an emergency.
6. Don't ever mix chemicals together.
7. Don't store chemicals in unmarked containers.
8. Don't store chemicals in or close to food storage, preparation, or serving areas.
9. Don't leave aerosol spray containers near heat or spray close to an open flame.
10. Don't dispose of any empty chemical container until you have checked on the label for how to do so.

Reading Material Safety Data Sheets

Both the Material Safety Data Sheet (MSDS) and product labels are valuable sources of information on the correct use and storage of hazardous materials. Following are listed the sections of both the MSDS and product labels that contain this information.

Reading the MSDS

1. Product name
2. Fire hazard

   explains if the product can catch fire or explode
3. Health hazards

   explains effects of overexposure

   also explains emergency and first aid procedures
4. Spill precautions

   explains steps to take in case of spill

5. Special protection

describes any special measures, such as goggles and rubber gloves, used to decrease exposure and risk

Reading Product Labels

1. Name

2. Physical and health hazards

3. Instructions for storing, handling, and use

4. Instructions on what to do in case of an emergency

Employee Quiz

Name: _____

Job Title: _____

Date: _____

Directions: *Check either "Do" or "Don't" as appropriate to complete the sentence.*

Do	Don't	
_____	_____	**1.** ask your supervisor any question or concern you may have about using a certain product. Correct Answer: _____
_____	_____	**2.** store chemicals in or close to food storage, preparation, or serving areas. Correct Answer: _____
_____	_____	**3.** follow the directions for proper storage, handling, and use for all chemicals you use. Correct Answer: _____
_____	_____	**4.** leave aerosol spray containers near heat or spray close to an open flame. Correct Answer: _____
_____	_____	**5.** store chemicals in unmarked containers. Correct Answer: _____
_____	_____	**6.** know how to call for medical help in case of an emergency. Correct Answer: _____
_____	_____	**7.** mix together any chemicals. Correct Answer: _____
_____	_____	**8.** read the labels of all products *before* you use them. Correct Answer: _____
_____	_____	**9.** dispose of any empty chemical container until you have checked on the label for how to do so. Correct Answer: _____
_____	_____	**10.** know where the Material Safety Data Sheets are posted and read them. Correct Answer: _____

1. Do know where the Material Safety Data Sheets are posted and read them.

2. Do read the labels of all products *before* you use them.

3. Do follow the directions for proper storage, handling, and use for all chemicals you use.

4. Do ask your supervisor any question or concern you may have about using a certain product.

5. Do know how to call for medical help in case of an emergency.

6. Don't ever mix chemicals together.

7. Don't store chemicals in unmarked containers.

8. Don't store chemicals in or close to food storage, preparation, or serving areas.

9. Don't leave aerosol spray containers near heat or spray close to an open flame.

10. Don't dispose of any empty chemical container until you have checked on the label for how to do so.

1. Product name

2. Fire hazard

   explains if the product can catch fire or explode

3. Health hazards

   explains effects of overexposure

   also explains emergency and first aid procedures

4. Spill precautions

   explains steps to take in case of a spill

5. Special protection

   describes any special measures, such as goggles
   and rubber gloves, used to decrease exposure
   and risk

1. Name

2. Physical and health hazards

3. Instructions for storing, handling, and use

4. Instructions on what to do in case of an emergency

Trainer's Outline

■ **STEPS:**

1. Explain the Quality Service Checklist.
2. Give quiz.

■ **TIME REQUIRED:**　　　　10–20 minutes

■ **MATERIALS NEEDED:**　　　Employee's Outline, Employee Quiz, Job Aid

STEP 1.　Explain the Quality Service Checklist.

KEY CONCEPTS	TRAINER'S DIRECTIONS
	• Asking the employee to follow along in the Employee's Outline, discuss each of the 12 items on the Quality Service Checklist.

Quality Service Checklist

You are providing quality service when you:

1. Report to your station on time, appropriately uniformed, well-groomed, and with your problems left at home.

2. Are friendly and courteous with guests and co-workers.

3. Cooperate with and assist your guests and co-workers.

4. Talk quietly and briefly with co-workers when necessary.

5. Actively listen to guests and co-workers and make eye contact.

6. Say "please," "thank you," and "come back again" often and greet guests and co-workers by name whenever possible.

7. Don't let the hustle-bustle or the occasional complaining guest ruin your day.

8. Know all aspects of your job and work in an organized manner.

9. Try to meet your guest's needs before they have to ask you.

10. Provide service in a timely manner.

11. Respond quickly and courteously to guest requests and complaints without making judgment.

12. Try to meet the needs of special guests (handicapped, special diets, celebrations).

STEP 2. Give quiz.

KEY CONCEPTS	TRAINER'S DIRECTIONS
	• Ask the employee to complete the Employee Quiz and then review the answers (given at left).

Employee Quiz Answer Key

Directions: *Circle either True or False.*

1. Your job is to serve food, not guests.
   A. True
   B. False
   Correct Answer: ___**B**___
   Explain that the server's job is, first and foremost, to serve guests.

2. Even when you may be having personal problems, it is important to take an interest in and work with, not against, your co-workers.
   A. True
   B. False
   Correct Answer: ___**A**___

3. By coming to work properly groomed and dressed, you are taking pride in yourself and your job.
   A. True
   B. False
   Correct Answer: ___**A**___

4. Cooperating with your co-workers can make your job much more pleasant.

   A. True

   B. False

   Correct Answer: ___**A**___

5. Learning to listen to guests is a worthwhile skill.

   A. True

   B. False

   Correct Answer: ___**A**___

   Explain that listening is a skill that does not come naturally to most people, but actually has to be learned.

6. If you know a guest's name, use it.

   A. True

   B. False

   Correct Answer: ___**A**___

   Explain that guests enjoy when you use their names; it makes them feel more welcome and comfortable.

7. You don't need to say "please" and "thank you" if you know your guests.

   A. True

   B. False

   Correct Answer: ___**B**___

   Even when you know your guests, you need to be polite.

8. During service, the dining room is not the place to catch up on what your co-workers did after work the previous night.

   A. True

   B. False

   Correct Answer: ___**A**___

   Explain that conversations in the dining room should be limited to business, not personal, matters.

9. Guests will complain from time to time and it is a good idea not to let it get you down.

A. True

B. False

Correct Answer: ___A___

10. Before your guest's coffee cup is empty is a good time to suggest a refill.

    A. True

    B. False

    Correct Answer: ___A___

Employee's Outline

■ **KEY POINTS TO REMEMBER**

Quality Service Checklist

You are providing quality service when you:

_____ 1. Report to your station on time, appropriately uniformed, well-groomed, and with your problems left at home.

_____ 2. Are friendly and courteous with guests and co-workers.

_____ 3. Cooperate with and assist your guests and co-workers.

_____ 4. Talk quietly and briefly with co-workers when necessary.

_____ 5. Actively listen to guests and co-workers and make eye contact.

_____ 6. Say "please," "thank you," and "come back again," often and greet guests and co-workers by name whenever possible.

_____ 7. Don't let the hustle-bustle or the occasional complaining guest ruin your day.

_____ 8. Know all aspects of your job and work in an organized manner.

_____ 9. Try to meet your guests' needs before they have to ask you.

_____ 10. Provide service in a timely manner.

_____ 11. Respond quickly and courteously to guest requests and complaints without making judgment.

_____ 12. Try to meet the needs of special guests (handicapped, special diets, celebrations).

Employee Quiz

Name: _____

Job Title: _____

Date: _____

Directions: *Circle the appropriate answer.*

1. Your job is to serve food, not guests.

   A. True

   B. False

   Correct Answer: _____

2. Even when you may be having personal problems, it is important to take an interest in and work with, not against, your co-workers.

   A. True

   B. False

   Correct Answer: _____

3. By coming to work properly groomed and dressed, you are taking pride in yourself and your job.

   A. True

   B. False

   Correct Answer: _____

4. Cooperating with your co-workers can make your job much more pleasant.

   A. True

   B. False

   Correct Answer: _____

5. Learning to listen to guests is a worthwhile skill.

   A. True

   B. False

   Correct Answer: _____

6. If you know a guest's name, use it.

   A. True

   B. False

   Correct Answer: _____

7. You don't need to say "please" and "thank you" if you know your guests.

    A. True

    B. False

    Correct Answer: _____

8. During service, the dining room is not the place to catch up on what your co-workers did after work the previous night.

    A. True

    B. False

    Correct Answer: _____

9. Guests will complain from time to time and it is a good idea not to let it get you down.

    A. True

    B. False

    Correct Answer: _____

10. Before your guest's coffee cup is empty is a good time to suggest a refill.

    A. True

    B. False

    Correct Answer: _____

You are providing quality service when you:

_____ 1. Report to your station on time, appropriately uniformed, well-groomed, and with your problems left at home.

_____ 2. Are friendly and courteous with guests and co-workers.

_____ 3. Cooperate with and assist your guests and co-workers.

_____ 4. Talk quietly and briefly with co-workers when necessary.

_____ 5. Actively listen to guests and co-workers and make eye contact.

_____ 6. Say "please," "thank you," and "come back again" often and greet guests and co-workers by name whenever possible.

_____ 7. Don't let the hustle-bustle or the occasional complaining guest ruin your day.

_____ 8. Know all aspects of your job and work in an organized manner.

_____ 9. Try to meet your guests' needs before they have to ask you.

continued

_____ **10.** Provide service in a timely manner.

_____ **11.** Respond quickly and courteously to guest requests and complaints without making judgment.

_____ **12.** Try to meet the needs of special guests (handicapped, special diets, celebrations).

Trainer's Outline

- **STEPS:**

    1. Explain how dining room stations are set up.

    2. Explain all sidework duties that must be performed, including how and when.

- **TIME REQUIRED:**   15–25 minutes

- **MATERIALS NEEDED:**   Employee's Outline, floor plan for server stations, sidework duties sheet

STEP 1.   Explain how dining room stations are set up.

KEY CONCEPTS	TRAINER'S DIRECTIONS
A *dining room station* is a section of the dining room that is assigned as a server's work area.	• Explain what a dining room station is, then show the employee the floor plan for your dining room stations.
	• Walk through the dining room and show where each station is.
	• Give employee a copy of your floor plan or ask him/her to draw one in the Employee's Outline.

STEP 2.   Explain all sidework duties that must be performed, including how and when.

KEY CONCEPTS	TRAINER'S DIRECTIONS

Sidework refers to all the duties a server performs other than directly serving the guest.
 	
Sidework duties may include:
    opening duties.
    stocking server station.
    closing duties.
	• Ask the employee if he/she has ever performed sidework duties before. Explain what sidework is.
	
	• Explain to employees what sidework duties they are expected to perform. If this is written, make copies, hand out, and review. If not, review the sidework duties while the employee makes notes in the Employee's Outline. Be specific about what duties are to be performed, how, and when.

Employee's Outline

■ **KEY POINTS TO REMEMBER**

Dining Room Station

A dining room station is a section of the dining room that is assigned as a server's work area. Draw below the floor plan, including stations, for your dining room.

Sidework

Sidework refers to all the duties a server performs other than directly serving the guest. Your sidework duties may include opening duties, stocking the server station, and closing duties. Describe them below.

_____
_____
_____
_____
_____
_____
_____
_____
_____
_____
_____
_____

Trainer's Outline

■ **STEPS:**

1. Demonstrate how to set a table and let the employee practice.

■ **TIME REQUIRED:** 15–30 minutes

■ **MATERIAL NEEDED:** Employee's Outline, tableware to set tables

■ **AHEAD OF TIME:** The guidelines presented under Key Concepts below are general in nature. Be sure to read them ahead of time to check if they are applicable to your restaurant. Revise and make additions as necessary. There is space on the Employee's Outline for Additional Instructions.

STEP 1. Demonstrate how to set a table and let the employee practice.

KEY CONCEPTS	TRAINER'S DIRECTIONS
Laying a Tablecloth • Place a centerfold on the center of the table, then open the cloth, being sure the hem edges are facing the table. • Check that the tablecloth hangs evenly, with edges parallel to the floor. • The edges of the tablecloth should just touch the chairs.	• Explain and demonstrate how to lay a tablecloth, and silence cloth, if used. • Let employee practice. Coach.
General Table-Setting Guidelines 1. Fork is to the left of where entree plate will go. 2. Knife is to the right of plate, with the blade facing where the entree plate will go. 3. Teaspoon is to the right of the knife. 4. Water glass is above the knife. 5. Bread-and-butter plate is above the fork. Butter spreader is placed across the top edge or on the right side of the plate.	• Ask the employee what he/she knows about general table-setting guidelines, such as where the fork belongs. • As necessary, explain the General Table-Setting Guidelines while the employee follows along in the Employee's Outline. • Demonstrate how to set the table according to your rules. • Let the employee practice setting up another table. • Ask the employee to draw how a table setting appears in the Employee's Outline.

6. Coffee cup and saucer are to the right of the teaspoon.

7. Salad plate is to the left of the fork.

8. Set flatware 1 inch from the edge of the table at right angles to the edge.

9. Place covers so they face each other across the table when possible.

Employee's Outline

■ **KEY POINTS TO REMEMBER**

Laying a Tablecloth

• Place a centerfold on the center of the table, then open the cloth, being sure the hem edges are facing the table.

• Check that the tablecloth hangs evenly, with edges parallel to the floor.

• The edges of the tablecloth should just touch the chairs.

Additional Instructions:

_____

_____

_____

General Table-Setting Guidelines

1. Fork is to the left of where entree plate will go.
2. Knife is to the right of plate, with the blade facing where the entree plate will go.
3. Teaspoon is to the right of the knife.
4. Water glass is above the knife.
5. Bread-and-butter plate is above the fork. Butter spreader is placed across the top edge or on the right side of the plate.
6. Coffee cup and saucer are to the right of the teaspoon.
7. Salad plate is to the left of the fork.
8. Set flatware 1 inch from the edge of the table at right angles to the edge.
9. Place covers so they face each other across the table when possible.

Draw below the table setting or cover you are to use.

EMPLOYEE'S OUTLINE *(continued)*

Additional Instructions:

_____

_____

_____

Trainer's Outline

■ **STEPS:**

1. Demonstrate how to load food on a tray and let the employee practice.

2. Demonstrate how to lift a food tray and let the employee practice.

■ **TIME REQUIRED:**   15–25 minutes

■ **MATERIALS NEEDED:**   Employee's Outline, food trays, tableware to practice loading and lifting

■ **AHEAD OF TIME:**   The guidelines presented under Key Concepts below are general in nature. Be sure to read them ahead of time to check if they are applicable to your restaurant. Revise and make additions as necessary. There is space on the Employee's Outline for Additional Instructions.

STEP 1.   Demonstrate how to load food on a tray and let the employee practice.

KEY CONCEPTS	TRAINER'S DIRECTIONS
Rules for Loading Food on Trays	• Ask the employee if he/she has experience loading a food tray.
1. Check that tray is clean.	
2. Place a damp service towel on the tray if it does not have a nonskid surface.	• As necessary explain the Rules for Loading Food on Trays while the employee follows along in the Employee's Outline.
3. Load heavier, larger items in center of tray.	• Demonstrate how to load food on a tray.
4. Load lighter, smaller items around edges.	• Let the employee practice and coach.
5. Do not place cups on saucers; do not place soup bowls on underliners. Stack saucers and underliners.	
6. When stacking dishes with covers, don't stack more than four high.	
7. Balance the load as best as possible and don't overload the tray.	
8. Keep hot and cold foods separate as much as possible.	

STEP 2. *Demonstrate how to lift a food tray and let the employee practice.*

KEY CONCEPTS	TRAINER'S DIRECTIONS

How to Lift a Food Tray

1. Once you are sure the tray is loaded properly, position the tray so it extends about 6 inches from where it is resting.

2. Squat down with your back straight and position your left (or right) shoulder under the tray.

3. Pull the tray slowly onto your left shoulder with your right hand, while placing your left hand in the middle of the tray. Use the flat of the palm of your left hand for support and your right hand to steady the tray. (Left-handed employees can use opposite shoulder and hands.)

4. Using your leg muscles, stand up straight.

5. If the tray is very heavy, you can rest it somewhat on your shoulder.

- Ask the employee if he/she has lifted a loaded food tray.

- As necessary, explain How to Lift a Food Tray while the employee follows along in the Employee's Outline.

- Demonstrate how to lift a tray.

- Let the employee practice and coach.

Employee's Outline

■ **KEY POINTS TO REMEMBER**

Rules for Loading Food on a Tray

1. Check that tray is clean.
2. Place a damp service towel on the tray if it does not have a nonskid surface.
3. Load heavier, larger items in center of tray.
4. Load lighter, smaller items around edges.
5. Do not place cups on saucers and do not place soup bowls on underliners. Stack saucers and underliners.
6. When stacking dishes with covers, don't stack more than four high.
7. Balance the load as best as possible and don't overload the tray.
8. Keep hot and cold foods separate as much as possible.

Additional Instructions:

_____

_____

_____

How to Lift a Food Tray

1. Once you are sure the tray is loaded properly, position the tray so it extends about 6 inches from where it is resting.
2. Squat down with your back straight and position your left (or right) shoulder under the tray.
3. Pull the tray slowly onto your shoulder with your right hand, while placing your left hand in the middle of the tray. Use the flat of the palm of your left hand for support and your right hand to steady the tray. (Left-handed employees can use opposite shoulder and hand.)
4. Using your leg muscles, stand up straight.
5. If the tray is very heavy, you can rest it somewhat on your shoulder.

Additional Instructions:

_____

_____

_____

Copyright © 1992 by John Wiley & Sons, Inc.

Trainer's Outline

■ **STEPS:**

  1. Demonstrate how to serve a table and let the employee practice.

  2. Demonstrate how to clear a table and let the employee practice.

■ **TIME REQUIRED:**   20–30 minutes

■ **MATERIALS NEEDED:**   Employee's Outline, trays and tableware to practice serving and clearing

■ **AHEAD OF TIME:**   The guidelines presented under Key Concepts below are general in nature. Be sure to read them ahead of time to check if they are applicable to your restaurant. Revise and make additions as necessary. There is space on the Employee's Outline for Additional Instructions.

STEP 1. Demonstrate how to serve a table and let the employee practice.

KEY CONCEPTS	TRAINER'S DIRECTIONS
Serving Rules	• Ask the employee what he/she knows about serving rules.
1. Food is served from the left of the guest with the left hand.	• As necessary, explain the Serving Rules, as well as any additional rules you have.
2. Beverages are served from the right of the guest with the right hand.	• Demonstrate how to serve.
3. When pouring beverages, leave the glass or cup on the table.	• Let the employee practice and coach.

STEP 2. Demonstrate how to clear a table and let the employee practice.

KEY CONCEPTS	TRAINER'S DIRECTIONS
How to Clear a Table	• Ask the employee if he/she has ever cleared a table.
1. Clear when all guests have finished the course.	• As necessary, explain How to Clear a Table while the employee follows along in the Employee's Outline.
2. When in doubt if a guest is finished, ask.	• Demonstrate how to clear a table.
3. Clear from the right of the guest with the right hand.	• Let the employee practice and coach.
4. Move from guest to guest in a counterclockwise direction.	

5. Clear all soiled tableware before serving next course.

6. Before dessert remove all dishes except water glasses and coffee cups.

7. Stack big plates in an area where you will be giving the most support to the tray.

8. Stack plates with only one size per stack.

9. Put flatware in the middle of the tray with the handles in the same direction.

10. Put glasses and cups away from plates and put handles of cups facing inward.

11. Don't make your tray too heavy or unbalanced.

Employee's Outline

■ **KEY POINTS TO REMEMBER**

Serving Rules

1. Food is served from the left of the guest with the left hand.
2. Beverages are served from the right of the guest with the right hand.
3. When pouring beverages, leave the glass or cup on the table.

Additional Instructions:

_____

_____

_____

How to Clear a Table

1. Clear when all guests have finished the course.
2. When in doubt if a guest is finished, ask.
3. Clear from the right of the guest with the right hand.
4. Move from guest to guest in a counterclockwise direction.
5. Clear all soiled tableware before serving next course.
6. Before dessert remove all dishes except water glasses and coffee cups.
7. Stack big plates in an area where you will be giving the most support to the tray.
8. Stack plates with only one size per stack.
9. Put flatware in the middle of the tray with the handles in the same direction.
10. Put glasses and cups away from plates and put handles of cups facing inward.
11. Don't make your tray too heavy or unbalanced.

Additional Instructions:

_____

Trainer's Outline

■ **STEPS:**

1. Explain the steps involved in greeting the guests and presenting the menu.
2. Demonstrate how to greet guests and present the menu.
   Let the employee practice and coach.

■ **TIME REQUIRED:** 10–15 minutes

■ **MATERIALS NEEDED:** Employee's Outline

■ **AHEAD OF TIME:** The guidelines presented under Key Concepts below are general in nature. Be sure to read them ahead of time to see how well they apply to your restaurant. Revise and make additions and deletions as necessary. The employee can make changes in spaces provided in the Employee's Outline.

STEP 1. Explain the steps involved in greeting the guests and presenting the menu.

KEY CONCEPTS	TRAINER'S DIRECTIONS
1. Greeting the Guests and Presenting the Menu Greet guests quickly and welcome with a genuine smile. Make an appropriate verbal greeting, such as "Good evening. Welcome to . . . ." If you know the guest's name, use it. You may want to introduce yourself. Follow house procedures. Check for any special needs such as room to put away packages or coats, or a highchair for a baby. Present a menu to each guest, ladies first. Make sure menus are right side up. You may describe daily specials at this point. Pour ice water for each guest.	• Explain the guidelines given for Greeting the Guests and Presenting the Menu.

STEP 2. Demonstrate how to greet guests and present the menu. Let the employee practice and coach.

Employee's Outline

■ KEY POINTS TO REMEMBER

1. Greeting the Guests and Presenting the Menu

- Greet guests quickly and welcome with a genuine smile.
- Make an appropriate verbal greeting, such as "Good evening. Welcome to . . . ."
- If you know the guest's name, use it.
- You may want to introduce yourself. Follow house procedures.
- Check for any special needs such as a room to put away packages or coats, or a highchair for a baby.
- Present a menu to each guest, ladies first. Make sure menus are right side up.
- You may describe daily specials at this point.
- Pour ice water for each guest.

Additional Instructions:

_____

_____

_____

_____

Trainer's Outline

- **STEPS:**

  1. Explain the steps involved in taking and serving the beverage order.
  2. Demonstrate how to take and serve the beverage order. Let the employee practice and coach.

- **TIME REQUIRED:** 10–15 minutes
- **MATERIALS NEEDED:** Employee's Outline
- **AHEAD OF TIME:** The guidelines presented under Key Concepts below are general in nature. Be sure to read them ahead of time to see how well they apply to your restaurant. Revise and make additions and deletions as necessary. The employee can make changes in spaces provided in the Employee's Outline.

STEP 1. Explain the steps involved in taking and serving the beverage order.

KEY CONCEPTS	TRAINER'S DIRECTIONS
2. Taking and Serving the Beverage Order	• Explain the guidelines given for Taking and Serving the Beverage Order.
Suggest a cocktail, wine, or other beverage. Indicate where the wine list is located and describe some special cocktails or other drinks listed on the menu. Ask guests already with drinks if they would like refills.	
Record the beverage order. So you don't forget who ordered which drink, always stand at the same spot and number the seats in a clockwise fashion starting at your left, or use another seat designation system.	
Place and pick up the beverage order.	
While carrying your tray in your left hand, serve beverages from the right with your right hand. Place a cocktail napkin down first.	
Serve ladies first and hold glasses by the base or stem.	
Ask if the group is ready to order or if they would like a few more minutes.	

STEP 2. Demonstrate how to take and serve the beverage order. Let the employee practice and coach.

Employee's Outline

■ **KEY POINTS TO REMEMBER**

2. Taking and Serving the Beverage Order

• Suggest a cocktail, wine, or other beverage. Indicate where the wine list is located and describe some special cocktails or other drinks listed on the menu. Ask guests already with drinks if they would like refills.

• Record the beverage order. So you don't forget who ordered which drink, always stand at the same spot and number the seats in a clockwise fashion starting at your left (or use another seat designation system).

• Place and pick up the beverage order.

• While carrying your tray in your left hand, serve beverages from the right with your right hand. Place a cocktail napkin down first.

• Serve ladies first and hold glasses by the base or stem.

• Ask if the group is ready to order or if they would like a few more minutes.

Additional Instructions:

_____

_____

_____

_____

Trainer's Outline

■ **STEPS:**

1. Explain the steps involved in taking and placing the food order.
2. Demonstrate how to take and place the food order.
   Let the employee practice and coach.

■ **TIME REQUIRED:**   10–15 minutes

■ **MATERIALS NEEDED:**   Employee's Outline

■ **AHEAD OF TIME:**   The guidelines presented under Key Concepts below are general in nature. Be sure to read them ahead of time to see how well they apply to your restaurant. Revise and make additions and deletions as necessary. The employee can make changes in spaces provided in the Employee's Outline.

STEP 1.   Explain the steps involved in taking and placing the food order.

KEY CONCEPTS	TRAINER'S DIRECTIONS
3. Taking and Placing the Food Order Ask ladies and children for their orders first. Circle the table, standing to the right of the guest ordering. Suggest specific appetizers and a wine with dinner. Write clearly, neatly, and legibly. Again note who gets what. Follow house procedures. Make sure you get the order complete—types of salad dressings, how the meat should be cooked, condiments needed, and so on. Be courteous, quick, and relaxed. Answer guests' questions about the menu honestly. Help guests who need assistance by finding out what they want and making appropriate suggestions and recommendations. Once the order is complete, remove the menus and tell the guests their appetizers will be served shortly.	• Explain the guidelines given for Taking and Placing the Food Order.

Place the order in the kitchen
according to house procedures.

STEP 2. *Demonstrate how to take and place the food order. Let the employee practice and coach.*

Employee's Outline

■ **KEY POINTS TO REMEMBER**

3. Taking and Placing the Order

- Ask ladies for their orders first. Circle the table, standing to the right of the guest ordering.
- Suggest specific appetizers and a wine with dinner.
- Write clearly, neatly, and legibly. Again note who gets what. Follow house procedures.
- Make sure you get the order complete—types of salad dressings, how the meat should be cooked, condiments needed, and so on.
- Be courteous, quick, and relaxed.
- Answer guests' questions about the menu honestly. Help guests who need assistance by finding out what they want and making appropriate suggestions and recommendations.
- Once the order is complete, remove the menus and tell the guests their appetizers will be served shortly.
- Place the order in the kitchen according to house procedures.

Additional Instructions:

_____

_____

_____

_____

Trainer's Outline

■ **STEPS:**

1. Explain the steps involved in picking up the order from the kitchen.
2. Demonstrate how to pick up the order from the kitchen.
   Let the employee practice and coach.

■ **TIME REQUIRED:**   10–15 minutes

■ **MATERIALS NEEDED:**   Employee's Outline

■ **AHEAD OF TIME:**   The guidelines presented under Key Concepts below are general in nature. Be sure to read them ahead of time to see how well they apply to your restaurant. Revise and make additions and deletions as necessary. The employee can make changes in spaces provided in the Employee's Outline.

STEP 1.   Explain the steps involved in picking up the order from the kitchen.

KEY CONCEPTS	TRAINER'S DIRECTIONS
4. Picking Up the Order from the Kitchen Time it properly so that guests are ready and all the food items are ready as well. Pick up cold items first, then hot foods. Load in order of service as much as possible. Make sure each dish is complete. When picking up food in the kitchen, be as quiet as possible, talking only to the chef or expediter as needed about your order.	• Explain the guidelines given for Picking Up the Order from the Kitchen.

STEP 2.   Demonstrate how to pick up the order from the kitchen. Let the employee practice and coach.

Employee's Outline

■ **KEY POINTS TO REMEMBER**

4. Picking up the Order from the Kitchen

* Time it properly so that guests are ready and all the food items are ready as well.

* Pick up cold items first, then hot foods. Load in order of service as much as possible. Make sure each dish is complete.

* When picking up food in the kitchen, be as quiet as possible, talking only to the chef or expediter as needed about your order.

Additional Instructions:

_____

_____

_____

_____

Trainer's Outline

■ **STEPS:**

1. Explain the steps involved in serving each course.
2. Demonstrate how to serve each course.
   Let the employee practice and coach.

■ **TIME REQUIRED:** 10–15 minutes

■ **MATERIALS NEEDED:** Employee's Outline

■ **AHEAD OF TIME:** The guidelines presented under "Key Concepts" below are general in nature. Be sure to read them ahead of time to see how well they apply to your restaurant. Revise and make additions and deletions as necessary. The employee can make changes in spaces provided in the Employee's Outline

STEP 1. ***Explain the steps involved in serving each course.***

KEY CONCEPTS	TRAINER'S DIRECTIONS
5. Serving Each Course Serve everyone at the same time, starting with ladies and children. When serving entree plates, make sure the entree faces the guest, and side dishes are placed to the guest's left. Ask the guests for anything else.	• Explain the guidelines given for Serving Each Course.

STEP 2. ***Demonstrate how to serve each course. Let the employee practice and coach.***

Employee's Outline

■ **KEY POINTS TO REMEMBER**

5. *Serving Each Course*

• Serve everyone at the same time, starting with ladies and children.

• When serving entree plates, make sure the entree faces the guest, and side dishes are placed to the guest's left.

• Ask the guests for anything else.

Additional Instructions:

_____

_____

_____

_____

Trainer's Outline

■ **STEPS:**

1. Explain the steps involved in checking on the table.
2. Demonstrate how to check on the table.
   Let the employee practice and coach.

■ **TIME REQUIRED:**   10–15 minutes

■ **MATERIALS NEEDED:**   Employee's Outline

■ **AHEAD OF TIME:**   The guidelines presented under Key Concepts below are general in nature. Be sure to read them ahead of time to see how well they apply to your restaurant. Revise and make additions and deletions as necessary. The employee can make changes in spaces provided in the Employee's Outline.

STEP 1.   Explain the steps involved in checking on the table.

KEY CONCEPTS	TRAINER'S DIRECTIONS
6. Checking on the Table Within a few minutes of serving, check back with your guests to make sure everything is okay. Clear dishes and change ashtrays as needed. Refill water, bread, and condiments as needed. Ask to refill drinks before they are empty. Clear the table when guests are finished and remove crumbs from the table if needed.	• Explain the guidelines given for Checking on the Table.

STEP 2.   Demonstrate how to check on the table. Let the employee practice and coach.

Employee's Outline

■ **KEY POINTS TO REMEMBER**

6. Checking on the Table

- Within a few minutes of serving, check back with your guests to make sure everything is okay.
- Clear dishes and change ashtrays as needed.
- Refill water, bread, and condiments as needed.
- Ask to refill drinks before they are empty.
- Clear the table when guests are finished and remove crumbs from the table if needed.

Additional Instructions:

_____

_____

_____

_____

Trainer's Outline

■ **STEPS:**

1. Explain the steps involved in handling the check and processing payment.
2. Demonstrate how to handle the check and process payment.
   Let the employee practice and coach.

■ **TIME REQUIRED:**   10–15 minutes

■ **MATERIALS NEEDED:**   Employee's Outline

■ **AHEAD OF TIME:**   The guidelines presented under Key Concepts below are general in nature. Be sure to read them ahead of time to see how well they apply to your restaurant. Revise and make additions and deletions as necessary. The employee can make changes in spaces provided in the Employee's Outline.

STEP 1.   Explain the steps involved in handling the check and processing payment.

KEY CONCEPTS	TRAINER'S DIRECTIONS
7. Handling the Check and Processing Payment Prepare the check according to house procedures. Make sure it is legible and accurate. Once you are sure there is nothing else the guests want, present the check face down to the right of the host. If you are not sure who the host is, place it between the men at the table or in the center of the table. Thank the guests. Process check payment per house procedures.	• Explain the guidelines given for Handling the Check and Processing Payment.

STEP 2.   Demonstrate how to handle the check and process payment. Let the employee practice and coach.

Employee's Outline

■ **KEY POINTS TO REMEMBER**

7. Handling the Check

* Prepare the check according to house procedures. Make sure it is legible and accurate.
* Once you are sure there is nothing else the guests want, present the check face down to the right of the host. If you are not sure who the host is, place it between the men at the table or in the center of the table. Thank the guests.
* Process check payment per house procedures.

Additional Instructions:

_____

_____

_____

_____

Trainer's Outline

■ **STEPS:**

1. Explain the steps involved in saying thank you and goodbye.
2. Demonstrate how to say thank you and goodbye.
   Let the employee practice and coach.

■ **TIME REQUIRED:**   10–15 minutes

■ **MATERIALS NEEDED:**   Employee's Outline

■ **AHEAD OF TIME:**   The guidelines presented under Key Concepts below are general
in nature. Be sure to read them ahead of time to see how well
they apply to your restaurant. Revise and make additions and
deletions as necessary. The employee can make changes in
spaces provided in the Employee's Outline.

STEP 1.   *Explain the steps involved in saying thank you and goodbye.*

KEY CONCEPTS	TRAINER'S DIRECTIONS
8. Saying Thank You and Goodbye When you bring guests their change or credit card, thank them warmly for their visit and tell them you hope to see them again. Don't count your tip until after the guests leave.	• Explain the guidelines given for Saying Thank You and Goodbye.

STEP 2.   *Demonstrate how to say thank you and goodbye. Let the employee practice and coach.*

Employee's Outline

■ KEY POINTS TO REMEMBER

8. Saying Thank You and Goodbye

- When you bring guests their change or credit card, thank them warmly for their visit and tell them you hope to see them again.
- Don't count your tip until after the guests leave.

Additional Instructions:

_____

_____

_____

_____

Trainer's Outline

■ **STEPS:**

1. Describe ingredients, preparation methods and time, portion size, taste, and price of menu items in each section of your menu.
2. Give quiz.

■ **TIME REQUIRED:**	Will vary depending on length of menu
■ **MATERIALS NEEDED:**	Employee's Outline, Employee Quiz
■ **AHEAD OF TIME:**	Because it is easier for both the trainer and trainee, do this training in short segments, such as 15-minute blocks, until the entire menu has been reviewed.

STEP 1. *Describe ingredients, preparation methods and time, portion size, taste, and price of menu items in each section of your menu.*

KEY CONCEPTS	TRAINER'S DIRECTIONS
Menu Item and Price Key Ingredients Preparation Method Preparation Time Portion Size Taste	• Review your menu, item by item, covering the information under Key Concepts. As you review each item, ask the employee to write down the information in the Employee's Outline.
	• As much as is possible, let a cook help with this and also let the employee see and taste the actual menu items.
	• Another way to cover this information is to have your menu information typed and ready to review with employees. This could then be done with a tasting.

STEP 2. *Give quiz.*

KEY CONCEPTS	TRAINER'S DIRECTION
	• It is usually best to give the employee at least one week or more to become familiar with the menu. Therefore, give the quiz when you think the employee has had enough time to practice using the menu.

- Before giving the employee the quiz, write down five menu items (add more if you want) on the quiz for which the employee should give you the necessary information.

- Ask the employee to complete the quiz and review the correct answers.

Employee's Outline

■ **KEY POINTS TO REMEMBER**

Menu Section: _____

Menu Item: _____ Price: _____

Key Ingredients: _____

Preparation Method: _____

Preparation Time: _____ Portion Size: _____

Taste: _____

Menu Section: _____

Menu Item: _____ Price: _____

Key Ingredients: _____

Preparation Method: _____

Preparation Time: _____ Portion Size: _____

Taste: _____

Menu Section: _____

Menu Item: _____ Price: _____

Key Ingredients: _____

Preparation Method: _____

Preparation Time: _____ Portion Size: _____

Taste: _____

Menu Section: _____

Menu Item: _____ Price: _____

Key Ingredients: _____

Preparation Method: _____

Preparation Time: _____ Portion Size: _____

Taste: _____

EMPLOYEE'S OUTLINE *(continued)*

Menu Section: _____

Menu Item: _____ Price: _____

Key Ingredients: _____

Preparation Method: _____
Preparation Time: _____ Portion Size: _____
Taste: _____

Menu Section: _____

Menu Item: _____ Price: _____
Key Ingredients: _____
Preparation Method: _____
Preparation Time: _____ Portion Size: _____
Taste: _____

Menu Section: _____

Menu Item: _____ Price: _____
Key Ingredients: _____
Preparation Method: _____
Preparation Time: _____ Portion Size: _____
Taste: _____

Menu Section: _____

Menu Item: _____ Price: _____
Key Ingredients: _____
Preparation Method: _____
Preparation Time: _____ Portion Size: _____
Taste: _____

Menu Section: _____

Menu Item: _____ Price: _____
Key Ingredients: _____
Preparation Method: _____
Preparation Time: _____ Portion Size: _____
Taste: _____

Menu Section: _____

Menu Item: _____ Price: _____
Key Ingredients: _____

Preparation Method: _____
Preparation Time: _____ Portion Size: _____
Taste: _____

EMPLOYEE'S OUTLINE *(continued)*

Menu Section: _____

Menu Item: _____ Price: _____

Key Ingredients: _____

Preparation Method: _____

Preparation Time: _____ Portion Size: _____

Taste: _____

Menu Section: _____

Menu Item: _____ Price: _____

Key Ingredients: _____

Preparation Method: _____

Preparation Time: _____ Portion Size: _____

Taste: _____

Menu Section: _____

Menu Item: _____ Price: _____

Key Ingredients: _____

Preparation Method: _____

Preparation Time: _____ Portion Size: _____

Taste: _____

Menu Section: _____

Menu Item: _____ Price: _____

Key Ingredients: _____

Preparation Method: _____

Preparation Time: _____ Portion Size: _____

Taste: _____

Employee Quiz

Name: _____

Job Title: _____

Date: _____

Directions: *You will be given five menu items to describe as directed below.*

Menu Item #1: _____ Price: _____

Key Ingredients: _____

Preparation Method: _____

Preparation Time: _____ Portion Size: _____

Taste: _____

Menu Item #2: _____ Price: _____

Key Ingredients: _____

Preparation Method: _____

Preparation Time: _____ Portion Size: _____

Taste: _____

Menu Item #3: _____ Price: _____

Key Ingredients: _____

Preparation Method: _____

Preparation Time: _____ Portion Size: _____

Taste: _____

Menu Item #4: _____ Price: _____

Key Ingredients: _____

Preparation Method: _____

Preparation Time: _____ Portion Size: _____

Taste: _____

EMPLOYEE QUIZ *(continued)*

Menu Item #5: _____ Price: _____

Key Ingredients: _____

Preparation Method: _____

Preparation Time: _____ Portion Size: _____

Taste: _____

Trainer's Outline

■ **STEPS:**

1. Explain the major causes of foodborne illness.

2. Explain the Seven Steps for Serving Safe Food.

3. Give quiz.

■ **TIME REQUIRED:**   20–30 minutes

■ **MATERIALS NEEDED:**   Employee's Outline, Employee Quiz, Job Aid

STEP 1.   Explain the major causes of foodborne illness.

KEY CONCEPTS	TRAINER'S DIRECTIONS
	• Ask the employee what he/she thinks foodborne illness is (a disease carried to people by food that causes upset stomach, vomiting, etc. for one or more days). Explain that foodborne illness is preventable.
	• Asking the employee to follow along in the Employee's Outline, review the major causes of foodborne illness.
Major Causes of Foodborne Illness	
1. Food left in the Danger Zone (45–140 degrees F) for 4 or more hours, such as hot foods that are not chilled rapidly	• Explain that room temperature is normally 70 degrees F and refrigerators run below 45 degrees F, so room temperature is right in the Danger Zone.
2. An employee with sloppy personal hygiene habits	
3. Preparing food a day or more before serving	
4. Food that is served when it is not completely cooked	

STEP 2.   Explain the Seven Steps for Serving Safe Food.

KEY CONCEPTS	TRAINER'S DIRECTIONS
	• Asking the employee to follow along in the Employee's Outline, review the Seven Steps for Serving Safe Food.

Seven Steps for Serving Safe Food

1. Avoid contaminating the food-contact surfaces of tableware.

   Hold plate with thumb on top outside edge and other fingers under plate for support.

   Hold goblets and wine glasses by the stem.

   Hold tumblers by the base, keeping fingers away from top edge.

   Pick up coffee cup by the handle or base.

   Hold flatware by the handles only.

   - Ask employee what a food-contact surface is (the surface on which the food will be placed).
   - Demonstrate holding tableware.

2. Handle ice properly.

   Use clean scoops or tongs to pick up ice; don't use hands or a glass.

   Store scoops or tongs in a clean container, not in the ice.

   Don't store any food or beverage in the ice.

   - Ask: "Why?" Because hands carry bacteria and a glass might chip in the ice.
   - Ask: "Why?" To minimize contamination.
   - Ask: "Why?" To prevent contamination of the ice.

3. Keep hot food hot and cold foods cold.

   - Remind employees that foods needing refrigeration, such as milk, must be kept cold.

4. Keep your work area clean.

   Keep tables, serving trays, and counters clean with a cloth rinsed in a sanitizing solution.

   Keep chairs, floors, rugs, menus, etc. clean.

   Check tableware for cracks, chips, streaks, film, and dirt.

5. Prevent reusing of contaminated tableware.

   Bring a clean utensil to replace one that has fallen on the floor.

   Provide guests who are using self-service bars with a clean dish when they return for additional portions.

6. Dispose of waste properly.

   Throw out food that was served but not eaten (unless it is wrapped), falls on the floor, is outdated, does not meet quality standards, was exposed to hazardous chemicals, was in the Danger Zone over 3 hours, or was otherwise mishandled.

Store soiled linen in laundry bag or nonabsorbent container.

Cover garbage cans as much as possible.

- Ask: "Why?" To prevent contamination.

Remove garbage regularly.

- Ask: "Why?" To prevent odors and attracting bugs and animals.

7. Keep insects and animals out.

Keep work areas clean and uncluttered.

Keep garbage sealed and trash areas clean.

Don't provide a free meal.

Keep doors closed.

STEP 3. *Give quiz.*

KEY CONCEPTS	TRAINER'S DIRECTIONS
	- Ask the employee to complete the Employee Quiz and then review the answers (given at left).

Employee Quiz Answer Key

Directions: *Circle the correct answer.*

1. Wiping cloths should be stored in a water and soap solution.

   B. False

   Explain that wiping cloths should be stored in a water and sanitizing solution.

2. By keeping your work area clean and neat, it is less likely that bugs and animals will be found.

   A. True

3. Pick up coffee cups by the rim to prevent contamination.

   B. False

   Explain to hold coffee cups by the handle or base.

4. When guests return for a second helping from the salad bar, provide them with a new plate.

   A. True

5. Hold forks and knives by the handles to prevent contamination.

    A. True

6. Throw out foods that:

    A. Fall on the floor

    B. Were exposed to hazardous chemicals

    C. Are outdated

    D. All of the above

    The correct answer is D—all of the above.

7. The safest way to get ice out of an ice machine is to:

    B. Use tongs or a scoop

8. Check tableware for the following.

    A. Streaks

    B. Film

    C. Dirt

    D. Cracks

    E. All of the above

    The correct answer is E—all of the above.

9. If you notice a fork under a guest's table, you should:

    C. Remove it and give the guest a new fork

10. You have to store fresh milk for coffee at your server's station. It is best to:

    B. Place it in a bowl of ice

    • Explain that the ice will keep it colder than just using cold water.

Employee's Outline

■ KEY POINTS TO REMEMBER

Seven Steps for Serving Safe Food

1. Avoid contaminating the food-contact surfaces of tableware.

   Hold plate with thumb on top outside edge and other fingers under plate for support.

   Hold goblets and wine glasses by the stem.

   Hold tumblers by the base, keeping fingers away from top edge.

   Pick up coffee cup by the handle or base.

   Hold flatware by the handles only.

2. Handle ice properly.

   Use clean scoops or tongs to pick up ice; don't use your hands or a glass because your hands carry bacteria and a glass might chip in the ice.

   Store scoops or tongs in a clean container, not in the ice, so as to minimize contamination.

   Don't store any food or beverage in the ice to prevent contaminating the ice.

3. Keep hot foods hot and cold foods cold.

4. Keep your work area clean.

   Keep tables, serving trays, and counters clean with a cloth rinsed in a sanitizing solution.

   Keep chairs, floors, rugs, menus, and so forth clean.

   Check tableware for cracks, chips, streaks, film, and dirt.

5. Prevent reusing of contaminated tableware.

   Bring a clean utensil to replace one that has fallen on the floor.

   Provide guests using self-service bars with a clean dish when they return for additional portions.

6. Dispose of waste properly.

   Throw out food that was served but not eaten (unless it is wrapped), falls on the floor, is outdated, does not meet quality standards, was exposed to hazardous chemicals, or was otherwise mishandled.

   Store soiled linen in laundry bag or nonabsorbent container.

   Cover garbage cans as much as possible to prevent contamination.

   Remove garbage regularly to prevent odors and attracting bugs and animals.

7. Keep insects and animals out.

   Keep work areas clean and uncluttered.

   Keep garbage sealed and trash areas clean.

   Don't provide a free meal.

   Keep doors closed.

Employee Quiz

Name: _____

Job Title: _____

Date: _____

Directions: *Circle the correct answer.*

1. Wiping cloths should be stored in a water and soap solution.
   A. True
   B. False

   Correct Answer: _____

2. By keeping your work area clean and neat, it is less likely that bugs and animals will be found.
   A. True
   B. False

   Correct Answer: _____

3. Pick up coffee cups by the rim to prevent contamination.
   A. True
   B. False

   Correct Answer: _____

4. When guests return for a second helping from the salad bar, provide them with a new plate.
   A. True
   B. False

   Correct Answer: _____

5. Hold forks and knives by the handles to prevent contamination.
   A. True
   B. False

   Correct Answer: _____

6. Throw out foods that:
   A. Fall on the floor
   B. Were exposed to hazardous chemicals

    C. Are outdated

    D. All of the above

    Correct Answer: _____

7. The safest way to get ice out of an ice machine is to:

    A. Use your hands

    B. Use tongs or a scoop

    C. Use a glass

    Correct Answer:_____

8. Check tableware for the following.

    A. Streaks

    B. Film

    C. Dirt

    D. Cracks

    E. All of the above

    Correct Answer:_____

9. If you notice a fork under a guest's table, you should:

    A. Return it to the guest

    B. Ignore it until the guests leave

    C. Remove it and give the guest a new fork

    Correct Answer: _____

10. You have to store fresh milk for coffee at your server's station. It is best to:

    A. Just leave it on top of your station.

    B. Place it in a bowl of ice.

    C. Place it in a bowl of very cold water.

    Correct Answer: _____

1. Avoid contaminating the food-contact surfaces of tableware.

2. Handle ice with scoops or tongs.

3. Keep hot foods hot and cold foods cold.

4. Keep your work area clean.

5. Prevent reusing of contaminated tableware.

6. Dispose of waste properly.

7. Keep insects and animals out.

Trainer's Outline

■ **STEPS:**

1. Explain what suggestive selling is.
2. Discuss 10 suggestive selling techniques.
3. Give quiz.

■ **TIME REQUIRED:**   20–30 minutes

■ **MATERIALS NEEDED:**   Employee's Outline, Employee Quiz, Job Aid

---

STEP 1.   Explain what suggestive selling is.

KEY CONCEPTS	TRAINER'S DIRECTIONS
Suggestive selling is not pushy selling of your most expensive menu items to simply increase your tips. Suggestive selling is soft selling of the full range of menu items available at your restaurant in an attempt to better acquaint the guest with menu options and therefore better serve his/her needs.	• Asking the employee to follow along in the Employee's Outline, explain what suggestive selling is not. • Explain what suggestive selling is and how it benefits the restaurant (by increasing the check average) and the server (through higher tips).

STEP 2.   Discuss 10 suggestive selling techniques.

KEY CONCEPTS	TRAINER'S DIRECTIONS
	• Asking the employee to continue following along in the Employee's Outline, discuss 10 Suggestive Selling Techniques, giving an example for each one. Ask the employee for another example.

10 Suggestive Selling Techniques

1. Mention specific menu items from each area of your menu to interest guests. For instance, instead of saying: "Can I get you dessert?" say "May I recommend our homemade black forest cake or our brownie ice cream sundae?"

---

2. Suggest foods that complement each other. For instance, a side salad with an entree.

3. When describing menu items, use descriptive, accurate phrases and include a favorable evaluation. For instance, "Our deep dish vegetarian pizza is made with whole-wheat flour, three types of cheese, and five fresh vegetables. It is unique."

4. Know which foods are particularly popular so you can respond to guests' requests for good menu selections. For instance, "A very popular entree is our famous prime rib."

5. Find out what your guests want by listening. For instance, show you are interested in listening by maintaining good eye contact, leaning slightly toward the guest, and nodding your head affirmatively, while you remain relaxed and smile.

6. Find out what your guests want by observing and asking questions. For instance, if your guests arrive with children, be sure to tell them about the children's menu.

7. Keep an eye on refilling beverages throughout service, being sure to follow the rules for responsible alcohol service. For instance, "Our after-dinner drink list is quite extensive. May I suggest . . . ?"

8. Suggest a wine to go with the meal. For instance, "Have you decided on a wine for your meal?" Ask if the guest wants red or white wine, a dry or a fruity wine, or any specific variety, then make two suggestions.

9. Suggest name-brand liquors. For instance, when a guest asks for gin and tonic, ask: "Do you have a favorite gin?"

10. Have the right attitude for suggestive selling:

Take "no" for an answer.

Show genuine interest in enhancing the guests' dining experience.

Be tactful.

Don't be pushy, fast-talking, or dishonest.

Use suggestive selling with all your tables.

STEP 3.   *Give quiz.*

KEY CONCEPTS	TRAINER'S DIRECTIONS
	• Ask the employee to complete the Employee Quiz and then review the answers below.

Employee Quiz Answer Key

Directions: *Finish the sentence:*

1. Suggestive selling is not pushy selling of your most expensive menu items. Rather, suggestive selling is:

soft selling of the full range of menu items available at your restaurant in an attempt to better

acquaint the guest with menu options and therefore better serve his/her needs and wants.

2. One of today's specials is spaghetti with meatballs. How can you describe it to make it sound good?

Our spaghetti is prepared with a homemade tomato sauce and comes with several large juicy

meatballs.

3. How will you ask a couple if they want to buy wine?

Have you decided on a wine to go with dinner?

May I help you select a wine to go with your dinners?

4–6. Write down three pairs of menu items that complement each each other.

Sandwich with french fries, entree with salad, dessert with coffee (or whatever is appropriate

at your restaurant)

7. A couple comes in to celebrate an anniversary. What can you suggest to make their celebration special?

Wine, champagne, after-dinner drink, any special dinners for two (or whatever is appropriate

at your restaurant)

Employee's Outline

■ KEY POINTS TO REMEMBER

What is suggestive selling? Let's start by examining what it is *not*. Suggestive selling is not pushy selling of your most expensive menu items to simply increase your tips. Rather, suggestive selling is soft selling of the full range of menu items available at your restaurant in an attempt to better acquaint the guest with menu options and therefore better serve his/her needs and wants. It involves suggesting food and beverages that complement one another so as to heighten the dining experience of your guests.

Everyone wins when suggestive selling techniques are used. The guest enjoys special dishes and extras he or she may not otherwise enjoy, your restaurant increases the check average, and you therefore receive higher tips.

Suggestive selling is just one way to increase tips. You need first to provide high-quality service to your guests. Also, keep in mind that you are selling satisfaction, not just food.

Suggestive Selling Techniques

1. Mention specific menu items from each area of your menu to interest guests. For instance, instead of saying: "Can I get you dessert?" say "May I recommend our homemade black forest cake or our brownie ice cream sundae?"

2. Suggest foods that complement each other. For instance, a side salad with an entree.

3. When describing menu items, use descriptive, accurate phrases and include a favorable evaluation. For instance, "Our deep dish vegetarian pizza is made with whole-wheat flour, three types of cheese, and five fresh vegetables. It is unique."

4. Know which foods are particularly popular so you can respond to guests' requests for good menu selections. For instance, "A very popular entree is our famous prime rib."

5. Find out what your guests want by listening.

   Let the guest talk and don't interrupt!

   Show you are interested in listening by maintaining good eye contact, leaning slightly toward the guest, and nodding your head affirmatively, while you remain relaxed and smile.

   Concentrate on the guest's words and feelings.

   Ignore distractions and focus on the guest.

6. Find out what your guests want by observing and asking questions. For instance, if your guests arrive with children, be sure to tell them about the children's menu.

7. Keep an eye on refilling beverages throughout service, being sure to follow your rules for responsible alcohol service. For instance, "Our after-dinner drink list is quite extensive. May I suggest . . . ?"

8. Suggest a wine to go with the meal. For instance, "Have you decided on a wine for your meal?" Ask if the guest wants red or white wine, a dry or a fruity wine, or any specific variety, then make two suggestions.

9. Suggest name-brand liquors. For instance, when a guest asks for gin and tonic, ask: "Do you have a favorite gin?"

10. Have the right attitude for suggestive selling:

    Take "no" for an answer.

    Show genuine interest in enhancing the guests' dining experience.

    Be tactful.

    Don't be pushy, fast-talking, or dishonest.

    Use suggestive selling with all your tables.

Employee Quiz

Name: _____

Job Title: _____

Date: _____

Directions: *Finish the sentence:*

1. Suggestive selling is not pushy selling of your most expensive menu items. Rather, suggestive selling is:

_____

_____

_____

2. One of today's specials is spaghetti with meatballs. How can you describe it to make it sound good?

_____

_____

_____

3. How will you ask a couple if they want to buy wine?

_____

_____

_____

4–6. Write down three pairs of menu items that complement each other.

_____

_____

_____

7. A couple comes in to celebrate an anniversary. What can you suggest to make their celebration special?

_____

_____

1. Mention specific menu items from each area of your menu to interest guests.
2. Suggest foods that complement each other.
3. When describing menu items, use descriptive, accurate phrases and include a favorable evaluation.
4. Know which foods are particularly popular so you can respond to guests' requests for good menu selections.
5. Find out what your guests want by listening.
6. Find out what your guests want by observing and asking questions.
7. Keep an eye on refilling beverages throughout service, being sure to follow rules for responsible alcohol service.
8. Suggest a wine to go with the meal.
9. Suggest name-brand liquors.
10. Have the right attitude for suggestive selling:

    Take "no" for an answer.

    Show genuine interest in enhancing the guests' dining experience.

    Be tactful.

    Don't be pushy, fast-talking, or dishonest.

    Use suggestive selling with all your tables.

Trainer's Outline

■ **STEPS:**

1. Explain 10 listening tips.
2. Demonstrate how to listen to guests and let the employee practice.

■ **TIME REQUIRED:**   10–20 minutes

■ **MATERIALS NEEDED:**   Employee's Outline, Job Aid

STEP 1.   Explain 10 listening tips.

KEY CONCEPTS	TRAINER'S DIRECTIONS
	• Explain how important it is for employees to really listen to the guests.
	• Ask the employee for tips for better listening.
	• Asking the employee to follow along in the Employee's Outline, explain each of the 10 Listening Tips.

10 Listening Tips

1. Maintain good eye contact with the guest.
2. Do not interrupt.
3. Do not think about your next comment while listening to the guest.
4. Give your full attention to listening and not to doing something else.
5. Encourage the guest to continue talking by nodding your head or saying "yes."
6. Focus on what the guest is saying and concentrate on the main issues.
7. Ask questions at an appropriate time about any unclear points.
8. Repeat to the guest what he/she has said in your own words to confirm understanding.

9. Do not judge what the guest is saying, just accept his/her point of view. The guest may not always be right, but he/she is never wrong.

10. Control any emotional reactions you may have to what the guest is saying.

- Remind employees to not take personally anything a guest says to them. Explain that *to the guest, the server is the restaurant*—the chef, the manager, the host, and everybody else—so the server hears everything.

STEP 2. Demonstrate how to listen to guests and let the employee practice.

KEY CONCEPTS	TRAINER'S DIRECTIONS
	• While dealing with guests, let the employee observe how well you listen to several different guests.
	• Let the employee practice listening to guests and observe. Coach.

Employee's Outline

■ KEY POINTS TO REMEMBER

10 Listening Tips

Listening is a major factor in guest satisfaction. Following are ways to improve your listening skills.

1. Maintain good eye contact with the guest.
2. Do not interrupt.
3. Do not think about your next comment while listening to the guest.
4. Give your full attention to listening and not to doing something else.
5. Encourage the guest to continue talking by nodding your head or saying "yes."
6. Focus on what the guest is saying and concentrate on the main issues.
7. Ask questions at an appropriate time about any unclear points.
8. Repeat to the guest what he/she has said in your own words to confirm understanding.
9. Do not judge what the guest is saying, just accept his/her point of view. Be guided by this saying: *The guest may not always be right, but he/she is never wrong.*
10. Control any emotional reactions you may have to what the guest is saying. Don't take personally any comments a guest makes. *To the guest, the server is the restaurant*—the chef, the manager, the host, and everybody else—so the server hears everything.

1. Maintain good eye contact with the guest.

2. Do not interrupt.

3. Do not think about your next comment while listening to the guest.

4. Give your full attention to listening and not to doing something else.

5. Encourage the guest to continue talking by nodding your head or saying "yes."

6. Focus on what the guest is saying and concentrate on the main issues.

7. Ask questions at an appropriate time about any unclear points.

8. Repeat to the guest what he/she has said in your own words to confirm understanding.

9. Do not judge what the guest is saying, just accept his/her point of view. Be guided by this saying: *The guest may not always be right, but he/she is never wrong.*

10. Control any emotional reactions you may have to what the guest is saying. Don't take personally any comments a guest makes. *To the guest, the server is the restaurant*—the chef, the manager, the host, and everybody else—so the server hears everything.

Trainer's Outline

■ **STEPS:**

    1. Explain why we should be thankful for guest complaints.

    2. Discuss the steps for handling guest complaints.

    3. Discuss the do's and don'ts for resolving guest complaints.

    4. Demonstrate how to handle complaints and let the employee practice.

■ **TIME REQUIRED:**   15–25 minutes

■ **MATERIALS NEEDED:**   Employee's Outline, Job Aids

STEP 1.   Explain why we should be thankful for guest complaints.

KEY CONCEPTS	TRAINER'S DIRECTIONS
Be thankful for complaints because: **1.** The guest may be telling you about a problem that really needs correction and is probably being noticed by other guests as well. **2.** The guest cares enough to mention the problem to you and give you a second chance to provide good service. Most guests will simply not complain to you but will tell all their friends and never return.	• Ask the employee for reasons to be thankful for complaints. • Explain why as discussed under Key Concepts. • Also explain that if you can resolve a complaint to the guest's satisfaction, it is more likely that the guest will return.

STEP 2.   Discuss the steps for handling guest complaints.

KEY CONCEPTS	TRAINER'S DIRECTIONS
	• Asking the employee to follow along in the Employee's Outline, discuss the Steps for Handling Guest Complaints.
Steps for Handling Guest Complaints **1.** When a guest addresses a complaint to you, actively listen with sincere interest. **2.** Express a desire to help, and ask the guest for more information, if needed.	

3. State back to the guest what you think his/her complaint is to check on understanding.

4. Offer one or more solutions to the guest.

5. If the guest is happy with a solution, act on it quickly. If the guest is not happy with any of the solutions, or you do not have the authority to resolve the matter satisfactorily, get the manager.

- At this time you may want to review your policy on when a server needs to speak to the manager to resolve a problem.

6. Follow up with the guests to make sure they are satisfied.

STEP 3. Discuss the do's and don'ts for resolving guest complaints.

KEY CONCEPTS	TRAINER'S DIRECTIONS
	• Asking the employee to continue to follow along, discuss the Do's and Don'ts of Handling Complaints.

Do's and Don'ts of Handling Complaints

1. Do emphasize resolving the problem instead of finding someone to blame.

2. Do act positively and use positive language.

- For instance, use the word "concern" instead of "problem."

3. Do respond quickly.

4. Do respect the guest and treat him/her accordingly.

5. Do speak to your manager when in doubt about what to do.

6. Don't make excuses like "we're short."

- Explain that this does not help solve the problem, nor does it make the guest feel better.

7. Don't blame anyone.

- This also does not help solve the problem, and it reflects poorly on the restaurant.

8. Don't ask for sympathy or understanding.

- Remember, it's the guest who has the problem.

9. Don't argue.

- Nobody ever wins an argument with a guest. Keep in mind that the guest may not always be right, but he/she is never wrong.

10. Don't get defensive.

- Remember, if you don't take a guest's comments personally, you won't get defensive.

STEP 4. *Demonstrate how to handle complaints and let the employee practice.*

KEY CONCEPTS	TRAINER'S DIRECTIONS
	• While dealing with guests, let the employee observe how well you handle guest complaints.
	• Let the employee practice handling complaints and observe. Coach.

Employee's Outline

■ KEY POINTS TO REMEMBER

Why should you welcome employee complaints? Let's look at a few reasons.

1. The guest may be telling you about a problem that really needs correction and is probably being noticed by other guests as well.

2. The guest cares enough to mention the problem to you and give you a second chance to provide good service. Most guests will simply not complain to you but will tell all their friends and never return. If you can resolve a complaint to the guests' satisfaction, they are more likely to be repeat customers.

Steps for Handling Guest Complaints

Following is a six-step procedure for handling guest complaints.

1. When a guest addresses a complaint to you, actively listen with sincere interest.

2. Express a desire to help, and ask the guest for more information, if needed.

3. State back to the guest what you think his/her complaint is to check on understanding.

4. Offer one or more solutions to the guest.

5. If the guest is happy with a solution, act on it quickly. If the guest is not happy with any of the solutions, or you do not have the authority to resolve the matter satisfactorily, get the manager.

6. Follow up with the guests to make sure they are satisfied.

Do's and Don'ts of Handling Complaints

1. Do emphasize resolving the problem instead of finding someone to blame.

2. Do act positively and use positive language. For example, use the word "concern" instead of "problem."

3. Do respond quickly.

4. Do respect the guest and treat him/her accordingly.

5. Do speak to your manager when in doubt about what to do.

6. Don't make excuses like "we're short." This does not help solve the problem, nor does it make the guest feel better.

7. Don't blame anyone. This also does not help solve the problem, and it reflects poorly on the restaurant and you.

8. Don't ask for sympathy or understanding. Remember, it's the guest who has the problem.

9. Don't argue. Nobody ever wins an argument with a guest. Keep in mind that the guest may not always be right, but he/she is never wrong.

10. Don't get defensive. If you remember not to take a guest's comments personally, you won't get defensive.

1. When a guest addresses a complaint to you, actively listen with sincere interest.

2. Express a desire to help, and ask the guest for more information, if needed.

3. State back to the guest what you think his/her complaint is to check on understanding.

4. Offer one or more solutions to the guest.

5. If the guest is happy with a solution, act on it quickly. If the guest is not happy with any of the solutions, or you do not have the authority to resolve the matter satisfactorily, get the manager.

6. Follow up with the guests to make sure they are satisfied.

1. Do emphasize resolving the problem instead of finding someone to blame.
2. Do act positively and use positive language. For example, use the word "concern" instead of "problem."
3. Do respond quickly.
4. Do respect the guest and treat him/her accordingly.
5. Do speak to your manager when in doubt about what to do.
6. Don't make excuses like "we're short." This does not help solve the problem, nor does it make the guest feel better.
7. Don't blame anyone. This also does not help solve the problem, and it reflects poorly on the restaurant and you.
8. Don't ask for sympathy or understanding. Remember, it's the guest who has the problem.
9. Don't argue. Nobody ever wins an argument with a guest. Keep in mind that the guest may not always be right, but he/she is never wrong.
10. Don't get defensive. If you remember not to take a guest's comments personally, you won't get defensive.

Trainer's Outline

■ **STEPS:**

1. Explain the techniques for preventing a guest from becoming intoxicated.
2. Discuss the stages of intoxication and how to react to each of them.

■ **TIME REQUIRED:** 15–25 minutes

■ **MATERIALS NEEDED:** Employee's Outline, Job Aids

■ **AHEAD OF TIME:** The guidelines presented under Key Concepts below are general in nature. Be sure to read them ahead of time to check if they are applicable to your restaurant. Revise and make additions and deletions as necessary.

STEP 1. Explain the techniques for preventing a guest from becoming intoxicated.

KEY CONCEPTS	TRAINER'S DIRECTIONS
	• Explain that in many states, the restaurant and server can be held liable for damages caused by the intoxicated guest; therefore, it is important to prevent guests from becoming intoxicated.
	• Ask the employee for some ideas on how to prevent a guest from becoming intoxicated.
	• Review How to Prevent a Guest from Becoming Intoxicated.
How to Prevent a Guest from Becoming Intoxicated	
1. First, make sure the guest is old enough to drink. When to ask. Type of proof required. If proof appears forged or tampered, see manager.	• Review your policy on when to ask for proof of age, and what type of proof (such as a driver's license with photo) is required.
2. Measure drinks according to rules.	
3. Do not serve a guest more than one drink at a time.	

4. Do not serve several drinks to a guest within a short period of time.

5. Offer guests food when they are having a drink.

6. Have an idea of how many drinks guests are consuming.

7. Know the stages of intoxication, to be discussed next.

STEP 2. ***Discuss the stages of intoxication and how to react to each of them.***

KEY CONCEPTS	TRAINER'S DIRECTIONS
	• Asking the employee to follow along in the Employee's Outline, discuss the Yellow Zone and Red Zone, and what to do when guests get into these zones.

Yellow Zone Signs:

• Guest gets noticeably louder or more quiet.

• Guest becomes overly friendly with others.

• Guest complains about weak drinks and slow service.

What to Do:

• Keep an eye on guest.

• Keep count of the number of drinks served and the time span in which they are served.

• Recommend food.

• Serve drinks at a slower rate.

• Review your policy here and ask the employee to write it on the Employee's Outline.

Red Zone Signs:

• Guest has trouble walking and may fall or stumble.

• Guest asks for doubles.

• Guest has slurred speech and may be incoherent.

• Guest has hard time picking up change.

• Guest starts arguing with others.

What to Do:

- Tactfully, but firmly, inform guest that no more alcoholic drinks will be served.

- Offer nonalcoholic drinks and food.

- If guest is planning on driving home, offer a ride either in a taxi or company car or offer to call another party. Take guest's car keys if necessary (in a reasonable manner).

- If an intoxicated guest leaves in his or her car, get license plate number and notify police.

- Review your policy here and ask the employee to write it on the Employee Outline.

Employee's Outline

■ KEY POINTS TO REMEMBER

How to Prevent Guests from Getting Intoxicated

Your first defense in serving alcohol responsibly is to prevent guests from getting intoxicated. The following suggestions can help.

1. First, make sure the guest is old enough to drink.

   When to ask.

   Type of proof required.

   If proof appears forged or tampered, see manager.

2. Measure drinks according to rules.

3. Do not serve a guest more than one drink at a time.

4 Do not serve several drinks to a guest within a short period of time.

5. Offer guests food when they are having a drink.

6. Have an idea of how many drinks guests are consuming.

7. Know the stages of intoxication, to be discussed next.

Other Rules:

_____

_____

_____

_____

_____

The Stages of Intoxication

You can classify your guests who are drinking alcoholic beverages into any one of three categories, or zones, as follows.

- Green Zone: There are no noticeable behavior changes in the guest so drinks can continue to be served.

- Yellow Zone: There are some noticeable behavior changes so you need to monitor the guest.

- Red Zone: The guest is intoxicated and must be handled accordingly.

Following are specific signs you can recognize and actions you should take when guests are in the yellow or red zones.

EMPLOYEE'S OUTLINE *(continued)*

Yellow Zone

SIGNS	SERVER ACTIONS
• Guest gets noticeably louder or more quiet.	• Keep an eye on the guest.
• Guest becomes overly friendly with others.	• Keep count of the number of drinks served and the time span in which they they are served.
• Guest complains about weak drinks and slow service.	• Recommend food.
	• Serve drinks at a slower rate.

Other Rules:

_____

_____

_____

_____

Red Zone

SIGNS	SERVER ACTIONS
• Guest has trouble walking and may fall or stumble.	• Tactfully, but firmly, inform guest that no more alcoholic drinks will be served.
• Guest asks for doubles.	• Offer nonalcoholic drinks and food.
• Guest has slurred speech and may be incoherent.	• If guest is planning on driving home, offer a ride either in a taxi or company car or offer to call another party. Take guest's car keys if necessary (in a reasonable manner).
• Guest has hard time picking up change.	
• Guest starts arguing with others.	• If an intoxicated guest leaves in his or her car, get license plate number and notify police.

Other Rules:

_____

_____

_____

_____

1. First, make sure the guest is old enough to drink.

   When to ask.

   Type of proof required.

   If proof appears forged or tampered, see manager.

2. Measure drinks according to rules.

3. Do not serve a guest more than one drink at a time.

4. Do not serve several drinks to a guest within a short period of time.

5. Offer guests food when they are having a drink.

6. Have an idea of how many drinks guests are consuming.

7. Know the stages of intoxication.

SIGNS

- Guest gets noticeably louder or more quiet.
- Guest becomes overly friendly with others.
- Guest complains about weak drinks and slow service.

SERVER ACTIONS

- Keep an eye on the guest.
- Keep count of the number of drinks served and the time span in which they are served.
- Recommend food.
- Serve drinks at a slower rate.

SIGNS	SERVER ACTIONS
• Guest has trouble walking and may fall or stumble.	• Tactfully, but firmly, inform guest that no more alcoholic drinks will be served.
• Guest asks for doubles.	• Offer nonalcoholic drinks and food.
• Guest has slurred speech and may be incoherent.	• If guest is planning on driving home, offer a ride either in a taxi or company car or offer to call another party. Take guest's car keys if necessary (in a reasonable manner).
• Guest has hard time picking up change.	
• Guest starts arguing with others.	• If an intoxicated guest leaves in his or her car, get license plate number and notify police.

Trainer's Outline

■ **STEPS:**

1. Explain general safety guidelines.
2. Give quiz.

■ **TIME REQUIRED:**   15–25 minutes

■ **MATERIALS NEEDED:**   Employee's Outline, Employee Quiz, Job Aid

STEP 1.   Explain general safety guidelines.

KEY CONCEPTS	TRAINER'S DIRECTIONS
	• Asking the employee to follow along in the Employee's Outline, explain the General Safety Guidelines and ask "Why?" as directed.

General Safety Guidelines

1. Only use equipment you have been trained on.	
2. Pay attention!	
3. No plastic aprons by hot equipment.	• Ask: "Why?" They melt.
4. No bulky clothes or dangling jewelry near equipment.	• Ask: "Why?" They may get caught in the equipment.
5. Be sure safety devices are in place and use guards.	• Emphasize not to stick your hands inside equipment when it is on.
6. Turn machine off before making adjustments, or when walking away for a minute.	
7. Be sure electrical equipment is grounded, and cord and plug are in good condition.	
8. Be sure your hands are dry, and feet not in water, when using electrical equipment.	• Ask: "Why?" Otherwise you risk an electrical shock.
9. Use equipment only for its intended purpose.	• Stress not to use equipment for other purposes.
10. Report any problems to your supervisor.	• Problems include equipment not working or overheating, and frequent tripping of circuit breakers.

11. Do not use extension cords without asking your supervisor.

12. Turn machine off and unplug before cleaning.

13. Unplug by gently pulling the plug, not the cord.

- Ask: "Why?" You may damage the cord if you pull on it.

14. Be sure the pilot light is on before turning on gas equipment.

15. After cleaning, reassemble equipment and test it.

STEP 2. *Give quiz.*

KEY CONCEPTS	TRAINER'S DIRECTIONS
	• Ask the employee to complete the Employee Quiz and then review the answers (given at left).

Employee Quiz Answer Key

Directions: *Check off whether each of the following incidents are safe or unsafe.*

Safe	Unsafe	
	X	1. Unplugging a piece of electrical equipment by pulling the cord.
	X	2. Using a wet cloth on a piece of equipment that is plugged in.
X		3. Turning the steam table off and unplugging before cleaning.
	X	4. Adjusting the slicer while it is on.
X		5. Talking to your supervisor when the food chopper starts to make a strange noise.
	X	6. Using electrical equipment while standing on a floor that is wet.
	X	7. Using the slicer while wearing a bulky sweater.
	X	8. Using the deep-fat fryer without knowing anything about it.
X		9. Using the guard properly on the slicer.
	X	10. Not paying attention while using the mixer.

Employee's Outline

■ KEY POINTS TO REMEMBER

Following are general rules for working safely with equipment.

General Safety Guidelines

1. Only use equipment you have been trained on.
2. Pay attention when using any kitchen equipment.
3. No plastic aprons are permitted by hot equipment because they melt.
4. No bulky garments or dangling jewelry are permitted near equipment because they may get caught in equipment.
5. Be sure safety devices are in place, and use guards. Never put your hands inside equipment.
6. Turn machine off before making adjustments, or when walking away for a minute.
7. Be sure electrical equipment is grounded, and cord and plug are in good condition.
8. Be sure your hands are dry and your feet are not in water when using electrical equipment; otherwise you risk being shocked.
9. Use equipment only for its intended purpose.
10. Report any problems to your supervisor, such as equipment not working or overheating, or frequent tripping of circuit breakers.
11. Do not use extension cords without asking your supervisor.
12. Turn machine off and unplug before cleaning.
13. Unplug equipment by gently pulling the plug, not the cord.
14. Be sure the pilot light is on before turning on gas equipment.
15. After cleaning, reassemble and test equipment. Only reassemble dry parts.

Employee Quiz

Name: _____

Job Title: _____

Date: _____

Directions: *Check off whether the following incidents are safe or unsafe.*

Safe   **Unsafe**

_____   _____   **1.** Unplugging a piece of electrical equipment by pulling the cord.
Correct Answer: _____

_____   _____   **2.** Using a wet cloth on a piece of equipment that is plugged in.
Correct Answer: _____

_____   _____   **3.** Turning the steam table off and unplugging before cleaning.
Correct Answer: _____

_____   _____   **4.** Adjusting the slicer while it is on.
Correct Answer: _____

_____   _____   **5.** Talking to your supervisor when the food chopper starts to make a strange noise.
Correct Answer: _____

_____   _____   **6.** Using electrical equipment while standing on a floor that is wet.
Correct Answer: _____

_____   _____   **7.** Using the slicer while wearing a bulky sweater.
Correct Answer: _____

_____   _____   **8.** Using the deep-fat fryer without knowing anything about it.
Correct Answer: _____

_____   _____   **9.** Using the guard properly on the slicer.
Correct Answer: _____

_____   _____   **10.** Not paying attention while using the mixer.
Correct Answer: _____

1. Only use equipment you have been trained on.

2. Pay attention when using any kitchen equipment.

3. No plastic aprons are permitted by hot equipment because they melt.

4. No bulky garments or dangling jewelry are permitted near equipment because they may get caught in equipment.

5. Be sure safety devices are in place, and use guards. Never put your hands inside equipment.

6. Turn machine off before making adjustments or when walking away for a minute.

7. Be sure electrical equipment is grounded, and cord and plug are in good condition.

8. Be sure your hands are dry and your feet not in water when using electrical equipment; otherwise you risk being shocked.

9. Use equipment only for its intended purpose.

10. Report any problems to your supervisor, such as equipment not working or overheating, or frequent tripping of circuit breakers.

continued

11. Do not use extension cords without asking your supervisor.

12. Turn machine off and unplug before cleaning.

13. Unplug equipment by gently pulling the plug, not the cord.

14. Be sure the pilot light is on before turning on gas equipment.

15. After cleaning, reassemble and test equipment. Only reassemble dry parts.

Trainer's Outline

■ **STEPS:**

1. Tell the employee how to operate the range, including the safety tips.
2. Demonstrate how to operate the range, and let the employee practice.

■ **TIME REQUIRED:**   10–20 minutes

■ **MATERIALS NEEDED:**   Employee's Outline, Job Aid

STEP 1.   Tell the employee how to operate the range, including safety tips.

KEY CONCEPTS	TRAINER'S DIRECTIONS
	• Ask the employee if he/she has ever used the range before and what he/she might already know about it.
	• Asking the employee to follow along in the Employee's Outline, explain safety tips and the steps involved in operating the equipment.

How to Operate the Range

1. With flat top, preheat to desired temperature. Place pot or pan on hot top and cook food as directed on recipe. Do not keep these ranges on high heat except during cooking because top could be damaged.

2. With burners, place pot or pan on burner and turn burner to desired temperature. Cook food as directed on recipe.

Safety Tips: Avoid using plastic aprons or wet potholders. Don't let utensil handles hang over the range's edge.

Other Notes:

STEP 2.   Demonstrate how to operate the range, and let the employee practice.

Employee's Outline

■ **KEY POINTS TO REMEMBER**

How to Operate the Range

1. With flat top, preheat to desired temperature. Place pot or pan on hot top and cook food as directed on recipe. Do not keep these ranges on high heat except during cooking because top could be damaged.

2. With burners, place pot or pan on burner and turn burner to desired temperature. Cook food as directed on recipe.

Safety Tips: Avoid using plastic aprons or wet potholders. Don't let utensil handles hang over the range's edge.

Other Notes:

1. With flat top, preheat to desired temperature. Place pot or pan on hot top and cook food as directed on recipe. Do not keep these ranges on high heat except during cooking because top could be damaged.

2. With burners, place pot or pan on burner and turn burner to desired temperature. Cook food as directed on recipe.

Safety Tips: Avoid using plastic aprons or wet potholders. Don't let utensil handles hang over the range's edge.

Trainer's Outline

■ **STEPS:**

1. Tell the employee how to operate the conventional oven, including the safety tips.

2. Demonstrate how to operate the conventional oven, and let the employee practice.

■ **TIME REQUIRED:** 10–20 minutes

■ **MATERIALS NEEDED:** Employee's Outline, Job Aid

STEP 1. **Tell the employee how to operate the conventional oven, including safety tips.**

KEY CONCEPTS	TRAINER'S DIRECTIONS
	• Ask the employee if he/she has ever used a conventional oven before and what he/she might already know about it.
	• Asking the employee to follow along in the Employee's Outline, explain safety tips and the steps involved in operating the equipment.

How to Operate a Conventional Oven

1. Turn temperature control switch to medium or high.

2. Turn thermostat to desired temperature.

3. Place food in oven when proper temperature has been reached.

4. Place pans 2 inches away from each other and from sides of oven. Load oven as evenly as possible.

5. Cook as directed on recipe.

6. Avoid opening the oven too often during cooking.

7. Rotate the food during cooking.

Safety Tip: Do not rest heavy pans on the door.

Other Notes:

STEP 2. **Demonstrate how to operate the conventional oven and let the employee practice.**

Employee's Outline

■ **KEY POINTS TO REMEMBER**

How to Operate a Conventional Oven

1. Turn temperature control switch to medium or high.
2. Turn thermostat to desired temperature.
3. Place food in oven when proper temperature has been reached.
4. Place pans 2 inches away from each other and from sides of oven. Load oven as evenly as possible.
5. Cook as directed on recipe.
6. Avoid opening the oven too often during cooking.
7. Rotate the food during cooking.

Safety Tip: Do not rest heavy pans on the door.

Other Notes:

1. Turn temperature control switch to medium or high.

2. Turn thermostat to desired temperature.

3. Place food in oven when proper temperature has been reached.

4. Place pans 2 inches away from each other and from sides of oven. Load oven as evenly as possible.

5. Cook as directed on recipe.

6. Avoid opening the oven too often during cooking.

7. Rotate the food during cooking.

Safety Tip: Do not rest heavy pans on the door.

Trainer's Outline

■ **STEPS:**

  1. Tell the employee how to operate the convection oven, including the safety tips.

  2. Demonstrate how to operate the convection oven, and let the employee practice.

■ **TIME REQUIRED:**   10–20 minutes

■ **MATERIALS NEEDED:**   Employee's Outline, Job Aid

STEP 1.   Tell the employee how to operate the convection oven, including safety tips.

KEY CONCEPTS	TRAINER'S DIRECTIONS
	• Ask the employee if he/she has ever used the convection oven before and what he/she might already know about it.
	• Asking the employee to follow along in the Employee's Outline, explain safety tips and the steps involved in operating the equipment.

How to Operate a Convection Oven

  1. Turn thermostat to desired temperature. Use a lower temperature than for a conventional oven—about 25–50 degrees lower.

  2. Turn fan on, if necessary.

  3. Place food in oven when proper temperature has been reached.

  4. Place pans 2 inches away from each other and from sides of oven. Load oven as evenly as possible and don't overload.

  5. Cook as directed on recipe. Watch cooking time closely because convection oven cooks more quickly and tends to dry out foods.

  6. Avoid opening the oven too often during cooking.

7. Rotate the food during cooking.

Safety Tip: Face away from doors as you open them.

Other Notes:

STEP 2.   Demonstrate how to operate the convection oven and let the employee practice.

Employee's Outline

■ **KEY POINTS TO REMEMBER**

How to Operate a Convection Oven

1. Turn thermostat to desired temperature. Use a lower temperature than for a conventional oven—about 25–50 degrees lower.

2. Turn fan on, if necessary.

3. Place food in oven when proper temperature has been reached.

4. Place pans 2 inches away from each other and from sides of oven. Load oven as evenly as possible and don't overload.

5. Cook as directed on recipe. Watch cooking time closely because convection oven cooks more quickly and tends to dry out foods.

6. Avoid opening the oven too often during cooking.

7. Rotate the food during cooking.

Safety Tip: Face away from doors when you open them.

Other Notes:

1. Turn thermostat to desired temperature. Use a lower temperature than for a conventional oven—about 25–50 degrees lower.

2. Turn fan on, if necessary.

3. Place food in oven when proper temperature has been reached.

4. Place pans 2 inches away from each other and from sides of oven. Load oven as evenly as possible and don't overload.

5. Cook as directed on recipe. Watch cooking time closely because convection oven cooks more quickly and tends to dry out foods.

6. Avoid opening the oven too often during cooking.

7. Rotate the food during cooking.

Safety Tip: Face away from doors when you open them.

Trainer's Outline

■ **STEPS:**

1. Tell the employee how to operate the microwave oven, including the safety tips.

2. Demonstrate how to operate the microwave oven, and let the employee practice.

■ **TIME REQUIRED:** 10–20 minutes

■ **MATERIALS NEEDED:** Employee's Outline, Job Aid

STEP 1. Tell the employee how to operate the microwave oven, including the safety tips.

KEY CONCEPTS	TRAINER'S DIRECTIONS
	• Ask the employee if he/she has ever used the microwave oven before and what he/she might already know about it.
	• Asking the employee to follow along in the Employee's Outline, explain safety tips and the steps involved in operating the equipment.

How to Operate the Microwave

1. Place food no more than 3 inches deep on microwave-safe dish and place in oven.

2. Close door.

3. Set timer.

4. Cook according to directions. Be careful not to overcook as cooking is rapid and tends to dry out the food.

5. Stir or turn during the cooking for even cooking. (Microwaves tend to cook unevenly.)

Safety Tip: The microwave-safe dish may heat up during cooking so use a potholder.

Other Notes:

STEP 2. Demonstrate how to operate the microwave oven and let the employee practice.

Employee's Outline

■ **KEY POINTS TO REMEMBER**

How to Operate the Microwave

1. Place food no more than 3 inches deep on microwave-safe dish and place in oven.
2. Close door.
3. Set timer.
4. Cook according to directions. Be careful not to overcook because cooking is rapid and tends to dry out the food.
5. Stir or turn during the cooking for even cooking.

Safety Tip: The microwave-safe dish may heat up during cooking so use a potholder.

Other Notes:

1. Place food no more than 3 inches deep on microwave-safe dish and place in oven.

2. Close door.

3. Set timer.

4. Cook according to directions. Be careful not to overcook because cooking is rapid and tends to dry out the food.

5. Stir or turn during the cooking for even cooking.

Safety Tip: The microwave-safe dish may heat up during cooking so use a potholder.

Trainer's Outline

■ **STEPS:**

1. Tell the employee how to operate the broiler, including the safety tips.

2. Demonstrate how to operate the broiler, and let the employee practice.

■ **TIME REQUIRED:**   10–20 minutes

■ **MATERIALS NEEDED:**   Employee's Outline, Job Aid

STEP 1.   Tell the employee how to operate the broiler, including the safety tips.

KEY CONCEPTS	TRAINER'S DIRECTIONS
	• Ask the employee if he/she has ever used the broiler before and what he/she might already know about it.
	• Asking the employee to follow along in the Employee's Outline, explain the safety tips and steps involved in operating the equipment.

How to Operate the Broiler

1. Preheat 15 minutes to high temperature before using.

2. Adjust temperature per recipe.

3. Rub grid with oil if food is to be placed directly on grid. This prevents the food from sticking.

4. Place food on grid.

5. Locate grid at proper position for broiling according to the degree of doneness desired:

   Well-done—at least 4 inches from heat

   Medium—3–4 inches from heat

   Rare—1–2 inches from heat

6. Cook according to recipe and watch foods closely.

Safety Tip: Use elbow-length oven gloves.

Other Notes:

STEP 2.   Demonstrate how to operate the broiler and let the employee practice.

Employee's Outline

■ **KEY POINTS TO REMEMBER**

How to Operate the Broiler

1. Preheat 15 minutes to high temperature before using.
2. Adjust temperature per recipe.
3. Rub grid with oil if food is to be placed directly on grid. This prevents the food from sticking.
4. Place food on grid.
5. Locate grid at proper position for broiling according to the degree of doneness desired:
   Well-done—at least 4 inches from heat
   Medium—3–4 inches from heat
   Rare—1–2 inches from heat
6. Cook according to recipe and watch foods closely.

Safety Tip: Use elbow-length oven gloves.

Other Notes:

1. Preheat 15 minutes to high temperature before using.

2. Adjust temperature per recipe.

3. Rub grid with oil if food is to be placed directly on grid. This prevents the food from sticking.

4. Place food on grid.

5. Locate grid at proper position for broiling according to the degree of doneness desired:

   Well-done—at least 4 inches from heat

   Medium—3–4 inches from heat

   Rare—1–2 inches from heat

6. Cook according to recipe and watch foods closely.

Safety Tip: Use elbow-length oven gloves.

Trainer's Outline

■ **STEPS:**

1. Tell the employee how to operate the grill, including the safety tips.

2. Demonstrate how to operate the grill, and let the employee practice.

■ **TIME REQUIRED:**   10–20 minutes

■ **MATERIALS NEEDED:**   Employee's Outline, Job Aid

STEP 1.   Tell the employee how to operate the grill, including the safety tips.

KEY CONCEPTS	TRAINER'S DIRECTIONS
	• Ask the employee if he/she has ever used the grill before and what he/she might already know about it.
	• Asking the employee to follow along in the Employee's Outline, explain the safety tips and steps involved in operating the equipment.

How to Operate the Grill

1. Preheat grill to 400 degrees F.

2. Brush with thin layer of cooking oil to create a nonstick surface.

3. Allow oil to remain on grill for 2 minutes, then wipe excess.

4. Turn temperature dial to desired temperature.

5. Place food on grill and cook according to recipe.

Safety Tip: Wear a cloth, not plastic, apron.

Other Notes:

STEP 2.   Demonstrate how to operate the grill and let the employee practice.

Employee's Outline

■ **KEY POINTS TO REMEMBER**

How to Operate the Grill

1. Preheat grill to 400 degrees F.
2. Brush with thin layer of cooking oil to create a nonstick surface.
3. Allow oil to remain on grill for 2 minutes, then wipe excess.
4. Turn temperature dial to desired temperature.
5. Place food on grill and cook according to recipe.

Safety Tip: Wear a cloth, not a plastic, apron.

Other Notes:

1. Preheat grill to 400 degrees F.

2. Brush with thin layer of cooking oil to create a nonstick surface.

3. Allow oil to remain on grill for 2 minutes, then wipe excess.

4. Turn temperature dial to desired temperature.

5. Place food on grill and cook according to recipe.

Safety Tip: Wear a cloth, not a plastic, apron.

Trainer's Outline

■ **STEPS:**

1. Tell the employee how to operate the steamer, including the safety tips.

2. Demonstrate how to operate the steamer, and let the employee practice.

■ **TIME REQUIRED:**   10–20 minutes

■ **MATERIALS NEEDED:**   Employee's Outline, Job Aid

STEP 1.   Tell the employee how to operate the steamer, including the safety tips.

KEY CONCEPTS	TRAINER'S DIRECTIONS
	• Ask the employee if he/she has ever used the steamer before and what he/she might already know about it.
	• Asking the employee to follow along in the Employee's Outline, explain the safety tips and steps involved in operating the equipment.

How to Operate the Steamer

1. Place food in steamer.

2. Close and lock door securely.

3. Turn on steam. Set timer.

4. Reverse closing procedure when food is cooked.

Safety Tip: When opening, vent the steam away from you. Steam gives serious burns.

Other Notes:

STEP 2.   Demonstrate how to operate the steamer and let the employee practice.

Employee's Outline

■ **KEY POINTS TO REMEMBER**

How to Operate the Steamer

1. Place food in steamer.
2. Close and lock door securely.
3. Turn on steam. Set timer.
4. Reverse closing procedure when food is cooked.

Safety Tip: When opening, vent the steam away from you. Steam gives serious burns.

Other Notes:

1. Place food in steamer.

2. Close and lock door securely.

3. Turn on steam. Set timer.

4. Reverse closing procedure when food is cooked.

Safety Tip: When opening, vent the steam away from you. Steam gives serious burns.

Trainer's Outline

■ **STEPS:**

1. Tell the employee how to operate the steam-jacketed kettle, including the safety tips.

2. Demonstrate how to operate the steam-jacketed kettle, and let the employee practice.

■ **TIME REQUIRED:**   10–20 minutes

■ **MATERIALS NEEDED:**   Employee's Outline, Job Aid

STEP 1.   Tell the employee how to operate the steam-jacketed kettle, including the safety tips.

KEY CONCEPTS	TRAINER'S DIRECTIONS
	• Ask the employee if he/she has ever used the steam-jacketed kettle before and what he/she might already know about it.
	• Asking the employee to follow along in the Employee's Outline, explain the safety tips and steps involved in operating the equipment.

How to Operate the Steam-Jacketed Kettle

1. Adjust kettle to upright position.

2. Fill kettle with food or water to be heated. Don't fill more than three-quarters full.

3. Turn the steam control valve clockwise. Open completely for highest temperature; close partially for simmering.

4. Complete cooking according to recipe.

5. Close steam control valve by turning counterclockwise.

6. Remove food to prevent overcooking.

Safety Tips: Avoid touching the hot surfaces of the kettle. Watch that the kettle does not boil over.

Other Notes:

STEP 2.   Demonstrate how to operate the steam-jacketed kettle and let the employee practice.

Employee's Outline

■ KEY POINTS TO REMEMBER

How to Operate the Steam-Jacketed Kettle

1. Adjust kettle to upright position.
2. Fill kettle with food or water to be heated. Don't fill more than three-quarters full.
3. Turn the steam control valve clockwise. Open completely for highest temperature; close partially for simmering.
4. Complete cooking according to recipe.
5. Close steam control valve by turning counterclockwise.
6. Remove food to prevent overcooking.

Safety Tips: Avoid touching the hot surfaces of the kettle. Watch carefully that the kettle does not boil over.

Other Notes:

1. Adjust kettle to upright position.

2. Fill kettle with food or water to be heated. Don't fill more than three-quarters full.

3. Turn the steam control valve clockwise. Open completely for highest temperature; close partially for simmering.

4. Complete cooking according to recipe.

5. Close steam control valve by turning counterclockwise.

6. Remove food to prevent overcooking.

Safety Tips: Avoid touching the hot surfaces of the kettle. Watch carefully that the kettle does not boil over.

Trainer's Outline

■ **STEPS:**

1. Tell the employee how to operate the deep-fat fryer, including the safety tips.

2. Demonstrate how to operate the deep-fat fryer, and let the employee practice.

■ **TIME REQUIRED:** 10–20 minutes

■ **MATERIALS NEEDED:** Employee's Outline, Job Aid

STEP 1. Tell the employee how to operate the deep-fat fryer, including the safety tips.

KEY CONCEPTS	TRAINER'S DIRECTIONS
	• Ask the employee if he/she has ever used the deep-fat fryer before and what he/she might already know about it.
	• Asking the employee to follow along in the Employee's Outline, explain the safety tips and steps involved in operating the equipment.

How to Operate the Deep-Fat Fryer

1. Make sure fryer is filled just up to the fill line.

2. Set thermostat to desired temperature (fat should not be heated over 400 degrees F).

3. Fill baskets with food no more than two-thirds full.

4. Slowly lower the baskets into the fat to prevent the fat from splattering.

5. Shake the baskets if food starts to stick.

6. Hang baskets on hook to drain for 10–15 seconds when cooking is complete.

7. Pour food onto absorbent paper in pan.

8. Turn off heat when cooking is completed or lower thermostat to 200 degrees F during slow periods.

Safety Tip: Don't let oil build up on counters, etc. near the fryer because oil is a serious fire hazard.

Other Notes:

STEP 2. ***Demonstrate how to operate the deep-fat fryer and let the employee practice.***

Employee's Outline

■ **KEY POINTS TO REMEMBER**

How to Operate the Deep-Fat Fryer

1. Make sure fryer is filled just up to the fill line.
2. Set thermostat to desired temperature (fat should not be heated over 400 degrees F).
3. Fill baskets with food no more than two-thirds full.
4. Slowly lower the baskets into the fat to prevent the fat from splattering.
5. Shake the baskets if food starts to stick.
6. Hang baskets on hook to drain for 10–15 seconds when cooking is complete.
7. Pour food onto absorbent paper in pan.
8. Turn off heat when cooking is completed or lower thermostat to 200 degrees F during slow periods.

Safety Tip: Don't let oil build up on counters, etc. near the fryer because oil is a serious fire hazard.

Other Notes:

1. Make sure fryer is filled just up to the fill line.

2. Set thermostat to desired temperature (fat should not be heated over 400 degrees F).

3. Fill baskets with food no more than two-thirds full.

4. Slowly lower the baskets into the fat to prevent the fat from splattering.

5. Shake the baskets if food starts to stick.

6. Hang baskets on hook to drain for 10–15 seconds when cooking is complete.

7. Pour food onto absorbent paper in pan.

8. Turn off heat when cooking is completed or lower thermostat to 200 degrees F during slow periods.

Safety Tip: Don't let oil build up on counters, etc. near the fryer because oil is a serious fire hazard.

Trainer's Outline

■ **STEPS:**

   1. Tell the employee how to operate the tilt skillet, including the safety tips.

   2. Demonstrate how to operate the tilt skillet, and let the employee practice.

■ **TIME REQUIRED:**   10–20 minutes

■ **MATERIALS NEEDED:**   Employee's Outline, Job Aid

STEP 1.   *Tell the employee how to operate the tilt skillet, including the safety tips.*

KEY CONCEPTS	TRAINER'S DIRECTIONS
	• Ask the employee if he/she has ever used the tilt skillet before and what he/she might already know about it.
	• Asking the employee to follow along in the Employee's Outline, explain the safety tips and steps involved in operating the equipment.

How to Operate the Tilt Skillet

   1. Turn to upright position.

   2. Adjust thermometer to desired temperature.

   3. Place food into skillet.

   4. Follow recipe.

   5. Complete cooking process.

Safety Tip: Use long-handled utensils to avoid being burned.

Other Notes:

STEP 2.   *Demonstrate how to operate the tilt skillet and let the employee practice.*

Employee's Outline

■ **KEY POINTS TO REMEMBER**

How to Operate the Tilt Skillet

1. Turn to upright position.
2. Adjust thermometer to desired temperature.
3. Place food into skillet.
4. Follow recipe.
5. Complete cooking process.

Safety Tip: Use long-handled utensils to avoid being burned.

Other Notes:

1. Turn to upright position.

2. Adjust thermometer to desired temperature.

3. Place food into skillet.

4. Follow recipe.

5. Complete cooking process.

Safety Tip: Use long-handled utensils to avoid being burned.

Trainer's Outline

■ **STEPS:**

    1. Tell the employee how to operate the slicer, including the safety tips.

    2. Demonstrate how to operate the slicer, and let the employee practice.

■ **TIME REQUIRED:**   10–20 minutes

■ **MATERIALS NEEDED:**   Employee's Outline, Job Aid

STEP 1.   Tell the employee how to operate the slicer, including the safety tips.

KEY CONCEPTS	TRAINER'S DIRECTIONS
	• Ask the employee if he/she has ever used the slicer before and what he/she might already know about it.
	• Asking the employee to follow along in the Employee's Outline, explain the safety tips and steps involved in operating the equipment.

How to Operate the Slicer

    1. Be sure the slicer is properly assembled. Make sure the knife guard is in proper position and blade is set at zero.

    2. Place food on chute and cover with holder.

    3. Move arm to check free movement.

    4. Adjust indicator to desired number.

    5. Turn machine on.

    6. Slice 2–3 slices.

    7. Turn machine off.

    8. Examine food for proper size and accurate weight.

    9. Readjust indicator if necessary.

Safety Tips: Always keep hands and utensils away from moving blade. Never walk away from an automatic slicer. Clean

the blade from the center out. Turn the
indicator to zero when not in use.

Other Notes:

STEP 2. ***Demonstrate how to operate the slicer and let the employee practice.***

Employee's Outline

■ **KEY POINTS TO REMEMBER**

How to Operate the Slicer

1. Be sure the slicer is properly assembled. Make sure the knife guard is in proper position and blade is set at zero.

2. Place food on chute and cover with holder.

3. Move arm to check free movement.

4. Adjust indicator to desired number.

5. Turn machine on.

6. Slice 2–3 slices.

7. Turn machine off.

8. Examine food for proper size and accurate weight.

9. Readjust indicator if necessary.

Safety Tips: Always keep hands and utensils away from moving blade. Never walk away from an automatic slicer. Clean the blade from the center out. Turn the indicator to zero when not in use.

Other Notes:

1. Be sure the slicer is properly assembled. Make sure the knife guard is in proper position and blade is set at zero.

2. Place food on chute and cover with holder.

3. Move arm to check free movement.

4. Adjust indicator to desired number.

5. Turn machine on.

6. Slice 2–3 slices.

7. Turn machine off.

8. Examine food for proper size and accurate weight.

9. Readjust indicator if necessary.

Safety Tips: Always keep hands and utensils away from moving blade. Never walk away from an automatic slicer. Clean the blade from the center out. Turn the indicator to zero when not in use.

Trainer's Outline

■ **STEPS:**

   1. Tell the employee how to operate the mixer, including the safety tips.

   2. Demonstrate how to operate the mixer, and let the employee practice.

■ **TIME REQUIRED:** 10–20 minutes

■ **MATERIALS NEEDED:** Employee's Outline, Job Aid

STEP 1. Tell the employee how to operate the mixer, including the safety tips.

KEY CONCEPTS	TRAINER'S DIRECTIONS
	• Ask the employee if he/she has ever used the mixer before and what he/she might already know about it.
	• Asking the employee to follow along in the Employee's Outline, explain the safety tips and steps involved in operating the equipment.

How to Operate a Mixer

   1. Place bowl of desired size into position and put into the catch at back first, then onto the bowl pins on each side.

   2. Lower bowl to lowest level using the lever handle.

   3. Select the appropriate attachment and put on shaft.

   4. Clamp the attachment securely.

   5. Lift the bowl into position, making sure the attachment doesn't touch the bottom of the bowl.

   6. Lower bowl and place food to be mixed in bowl.

   7. Select speed.

   8. Raise bowl back to mixing position and push start button.

9. For scraping or filling, stop mixer and wait until the attachment has stopped.

10. Turn mixer off when done, and lower the bowl once the attachment has stopped.

11. Lower bowl and remove attachment before scraping out its contents.

Safety Tip: Never stick your hand or utensil into the bowl when operating.

Other Notes:

STEP 2.   Demonstrate how to operate the mixer and let the employee practice.

Employee's Outline

■ **KEY POINTS TO REMEMBER**

How to Operate a Mixer

1. Place bowl of desired size into position and put into the catch at back first, then onto the bowl pins at the side.
2. Lower bowl to lowest level with the lever handle.
3. Select the appropriate attachment and put on shaft.
4. Clamp the attachment securely.
5. Lift the bowl into position, making sure the attachment doesn't touch the bottom of the bowl.
6. Lower bowl and place food to be mixed in bowl.
7. Select speed.
8. Raise bowl back to mixing position and push start button.
9. For scraping or filling, stop mixer and wait until the attachment has stopped.
10. Turn mixer off when done, and lower the bowl once the attachment has stopped.
11. Remove attachment before scraping out its contents.

Safety Tip: Never stick your hand or utensil into the bowl when operating.

Other Notes:

1. Place bowl of desired size into position and put into the catch at back first, then onto the bowl pins at the side.
2. Lower bowl to lowest level with the lever handle.
3. Select the appropriate attachment and put on shaft.
4. Clamp the attachment securely.
5. Lift the bowl into position, making sure the attachment doesn't touch the bottom of the bowl.
6. Lower bowl and place food to be mixed in bowl.
7. Select speed.
8. Raise bowl back to mixing position and push start button.
9. For scraping or filling, stop mixer and wait until the attachment has stopped.
10. Turn mixer off when done, and lower the bowl once the attachment has stopped.
11. Remove attachment before scraping out its contents.

Safety Tip: Never stick your hand or utensil into the bowl when operating.

Trainer's Outline

■ **STEPS:**

1. Tell the employee how to operate the food chopper, including the safety tips.

2. Demonstrate how to operate the food chopper, and let the employee practice.

■ **TIME REQUIRED:** 10–20 minutes

■ **MATERIALS NEEDED:** Employee's Outline, Job Aid

STEP 1. Tell the employee how to operate the food chopper, including the safety tips.

KEY CONCEPTS	TRAINER'S DIRECTIONS
	• Ask the employee if he/she has ever used the food chopper before and what he/she might already know about it.
	• Asking the employee to follow along in the Employee's Outline, explain the safety tips and steps involved in operating the equipment.

How to Operate the Food Chopper

1. When unplugged, place bowl in position and rotate it counterclockwise to stop.

2. Place knife on knife shaft and screw hand knob into position to hold knives securely.

3. Place comb in position so the knives move through the teeth of the comb as they turn.

4. Place bowl cover in place, press down on the knob, and turn it clockwise to lock.

5. Plug in cord.

6. Fill bowl (no more than one-third full). More food may be added once the machine is running.

7. Turn on switch.

8. When completed, switch off, but do not lift cover until knives have stopped.

9. Open cover by turning the lock knob to a right angle with the machine and lift.

10. Unscrew hand knob and slide off knife.

11. Remove food from bowl.

Safety Tips: Never put your hand under the cover. If the blades are dull, tell your supervisor.

Other Notes:

STEP 2. Demonstrate how to operate the food chopper and let the employee practice.

Employee's Outline

■ **KEY POINTS TO REMEMBER**

How to Operate the Food Chopper

1. When unplugged, place bowl in position and rotate it counterclockwise to stop.
2. Place knife on knife shaft and screw hand knob into position to hold knives securely.
3. Place comb in position so the knives move through the teeth of the comb as they turn.
4. Place bowl cover in place, press down on the knob, and turn it clockwise to lock.
5. Plug in cord.
6. Fill bowl (no more than one-third full). More food may be added once the machine is running.
7. Turn on switch.
8. When completed, switch off, but do not lift cover until knives have stopped.
9. Open cover by turning the lock knob to a right angle with the machine and lift.
10. Unscrew hand knob and slide off knives.
11. Remove food from bowl.

Safety Tips: Never put your hand under the cover. If the blades are dull, tell your supervisor.

Other Notes:

1. When unplugged, place bowl in position and rotate it counterclockwise to stop.

2. Place knife on knife shaft and screw hand knob into position to hold knives securely.

3. Place comb in position so the knives move through the teeth of the comb as they turn.

4. Place bowl cover in place, press down on the knob, and turn it clockwise to lock.

5. Plug in cord.

6. Fill bowl (no more than one-third full). More food may be added once the machine is running.

7. Turn on switch.

8. When completed, switch off, but do not lift cover until knives have stopped.

9. Open cover by turning the lock knob to a right angle with the machine and lift.

10. Unscrew hand knob and slide off knives.

11. Remove food from bowl.

Safety Tips: Never put your hand under the cover. If the blades are dull, tell your supervisor.

Trainer's Outline

■ **STEPS:**

1. Explain and demonstrate how to measure by number, volume, and weight.
2. Review units of measure and recipe abbreviations.
3. Give quiz.

■ **TIME REQUIRED:**   20–30 minutes

■ **MATERIALS NEEDED:**   Employee's Outline, Employee Quiz, Job Aids; liquid measuring cups, a tablespoon, 1 pound of flour, portion scale

---

STEP 1.   Explain and demonstrate how to measure by number, volume, and weight.

KEY CONCEPTS	TRAINER'S DIRECTIONS
	• Asking the employee to follow along in the Employee's Outline, explain that we measure ingredients in one of three ways: number, volume, and weight.
Number • Examples: Count number of eggs for poached eggs or the number of apples for baked apples.	• Give examples of counting ingredients by number.
Volume • Measure amount of space	• Explain that when you measure ingredients by volume, you are actually measuring the amount of space the ingredient uses, such as 1 tablespoon. Ask employee for other examples, such as those at left.

• Examples: Measure 1 cup, 1 tablespoon, 1 fluid ounce, 1 quart, 1 gallon.
• How to measure volume:
  1. For dry ingredients, overfill the volume measure with the dry ingredient before leveling it off with a straight edge.
  2. For wet ingredients, put volume measure on a flat surface and fill to proper line. Check at eye level.
	• Demonstrate measuring a tablespoon of a dry ingredient, such as flour, and ½ cup of a liquid, such as water.

- Ask employee to measure a tablespoon of a dry ingredient and then a cup of a liquid ingredient. Coach.

- Explain that we measure ingredients by weight by using pounds and ounces, such as 1 pound of chopped celery.

- Demonstrate how to use a portion scale to weigh 1 pound of flour.

- Ask the employee to weigh ½ pound of flour. Coach.

Weight

- How to weigh:

  1. Place the empty container that will hold the ingredient on the scale and set the scale to zero.

  2. Place the ingredient on the scale until the scale reads the desired weight.

STEP 2.   Review units of measure and recipe abbreviations.

KEY CONCEPTS	TRAINER'S DIRECTIONS
	- Ask employee to complete the Units of Measure and Abbreviation Quiz in the Employee's Outline. Review the correct answers at left.

Units of Measure and Abbreviation Quiz Answer Key

1. 1 tablespoon = **3** teaspoons
2. 1 fluid ounce = **2** tablespoons
3. 1 cup = **16** tablespoons
4. 1 cup = **8** fluid ounces
5. 1 pint = **2** cups
6. 1 pint = **16** fluid ounces
7. 1 quart = **2** pints
8. 1 quart = **4** cups
9. 1 quart = **32** fluid ounces
10. 1 gallon = **4** quarts
11. 1 gallon = **8** pints
12. 1 pound = **16** ounces
13. # means **pound**
14. 1b. means **pound**
15. oz. means **ounce**
16. Tbsp., T., or Tb. means **Tablespoon**
17. tsp. or t. means **teaspoon**
18. C. or c. means **cup**
19. qt. means **quart**

20. gal. or G. means __gallon__
21. pt. means __pint__
22. fl. oz. means __fluid ounce__

STEP 3. *Give quiz.*

KEY CONCEPTS	TRAINER'S DIRECTIONS
	• Ask the employee to complete the Employee Quiz and then review the correct answers given at left.

Employee Quiz Answer Key

1. 1 tablespoon = __3__ teaspoons
2. 1 fluid ounce = __2__ tablespoons
3. 1 cup = __16__ tablespoons
4. 1 cup = __8__ fluid ounces
5. 1 pint = __2__ cups
6. 1 pint = __16__ fluid ounces
7. 1 quart = __2__ pints
8. 1 quart = __4__ cups
9. 1 quart = __32__ fluid ounces
10. 1 gallon = __4__ quarts
11. 1 gallon = __8__ pints
12. 1 gallon = __128__ ounces
13. tsp. means __teaspoon__
14. C. means __cup__
15. pt. means __pint__
16. tbsp. means __tablespoon__
17. oz. means __ounce__
18. G. means __gallon__
19. fl. oz. means __fluid ounce__
20. lb. means __pound__

Employee's Outline

■ **KEY POINTS TO REMEMBER**

We measure ingredients in one of three ways:

* Number
* Volume
* Weight

Number

You can count certain ingredients by number, such as the number of eggs for poached eggs or the number of apples for baked apples.

Volume

When you measure ingredients by volume, you are actually measuring the amount of space of the ingredients, such as in:

* 1 tablespoon
* 1 cup
* 1 fluid ounce
* 1 quart
* 1 gallon

To measure a dry ingredient, such as flour, overfill the volume measure with the dry ingredient before leveling it off with a straight edge.

To measure a wet ingredient, such as water, put the volume measure on a flat surface and fill to the proper line.

Weight

You can also measure many ingredients by weight, such as 1 pound or 6 ounces.

Here are the steps to use a portion scale.

1. Place the empty container that will hold the ingredient on the scale and set the scale to zero.
2. Place the ingredient on the scale until the scale reads the desired weight.

EMPLOYEE'S OUTLINE *(continued)*

Units of Measure and Abbreviation Quiz

		Your Answer	*Correct Answer*
1.	1 tablespoon =	_____ teaspoons	_____ teaspoons
2.	1 fluid ounce =	_____ tablespoons	_____ tablespoons
3.	1 cup =	_____ tablespoons	_____ tablespoons
4.	1 cup =	_____ fluid ounces	_____ fluid ounces
5.	1 pint =	_____ cups	_____ cups
6.	1 pint =	_____ fluid ounces	_____ fluid ounces
7.	1 quart =	_____ pints	_____ pints
8.	1 quart =	_____ cups	_____ cups
9.	1 quart =	_____ fluid ounces	_____ fluid ounces
10.	1 gallon =	_____ quarts	_____ quarts
11.	1 gallon =	_____ pints	_____ pints
12.	1 pound =	_____ ounces	_____ ounces
13.	# means	_____	_____
14.	lb. means	_____	_____
15.	oz. means	_____	_____
16.	Tbsp. or T. means	_____	_____
17.	tsp. or t. means	_____	_____
18.	C. or c. means	_____	_____
19.	qt. means	_____	_____
20.	gal. or G. means	_____	_____
21.	pt. means	_____	_____
22.	fl. oz. means	_____ _____	_____ _____

Employee Quiz

Name: _____

Job Title: _____

Date: _____

Directions: *Fill in the blank with the correct answer.*

		Your Answer	***Correct Answer***
1.	1 tablespoon =	_____ teaspoons	_____ teaspoons
2.	1 fluid ounce =	_____ tablespoons	_____ tablespoons
3.	1 cup =	_____ tablespoons	_____ tablespoons
4.	1 cup =	_____ fluid ounces	_____ fluid ounces
5.	1 pint =	_____ cups	_____ cups
6.	1 pint =	_____ fluid ounces	_____ fluid ounces
7.	1 quart =	_____ pints	_____ pints
8.	1 quart =	_____ cups	_____ cups
9.	1 quart =	_____ fluid ounces	_____ fluid ounces
10.	1 gallon =	_____ quarts	_____ quarts
11.	1 gallon =	_____ pints	_____ pints
12.	1 gallon =	_____ ounces	_____ ounces
13.	tsp. means	_____	_____
14.	C. means	_____	_____
15.	pt. means	_____	_____
16.	tbsp. means	_____	_____
17.	oz. means	_____	_____
18.	G. means	_____	_____
19.	fl. oz. means	_____ _____	_____ _____
20.	lb. means	_____	_____

1. Place the empty container that will hold the ingredient on the scale and set the scale to zero.

2. Place the ingredient on the scale until the scale reads the desired weight.

1. 1 tablespoon = 3 teaspoons
2. 1 fluid ounce = 2 tablespoons
3. 1 cup = 16 tablespoons
4. 1 cup = 8 fluid ounces
5. 1 pint = 2 cups
6. 1 pint = 16 fluid ounces
7. 1 quart = 2 pints
8. 1 quart = 4 cups
9. 1 quart = 32 fluid ounces
10. 1 gallon = 4 quarts
11. 1 gallon = 8 pints
12. 1 gallon = 128 ounces
13. tsp. means teaspoon

Trainer's Outline

■ **STEPS:**

1. Explain what portion control is and why it is important.
2. Identify various portion control tools.
3. Review portion sizes for menu items.
4. Give quiz. (Quiz is given at a later time.)

■ **TIME REQUIRED:**   20–30 minutes

■ **MATERIALS NEEDED:**   Employee's Outline, Employee Quiz, Job Aids, Portion control tools, a list of portion sizes for all menu items

STEP 1.   Explain what portion control is and why it is important.

KEY CONCEPTS	TRAINER'S DIRECTIONS
Portion control means that each serving of food must be measured to the appropriate size for that menu item as specified on the portion control list.	• Asking the employee to follow along in the Employee's Outline, explain what portion control is and give two or three examples of portion sizes for items on your menu.
Portion control is important: 　for the customer's satisfaction with the meals. 　to control and predict food costs. 　to avoid running out of food during service or having too many leftovers.	• Also explain why it is so important.

STEP 2.   Identify various portion control tools.

KEY CONCEPTS	TRAINER'S DIRECTIONS
Ladle and Spoodle Sizes 1 oz. = ⅛ cup 2 oz. = ¼ cup 3 oz. = ⅜ cup 4 oz. = ½ cup 6 oz. = ¾ cup 8 oz. = 1 cup	• Show the employee the various types of portion control tools that you use, such as those at left. Make sure Job Aids 44-1 and 44-2 that list ladle, spoodle, and scoop sizes are posted for easy reference by the employees. • Ask the employee to identify at least five different portion control tools. • Explain that ladles, spoodles, and scoops should be leveled off in order to serve the appropriate serving size.

Scoop Sizes

#6 = ⅔ cup

#8 = ½ cup

#10 = ⅜ cup

#12 = ⅓ cup

#16 = ¼ cup

#20 = 3 tablespoons

#24 = 2⅔ tablespoons

#30 = 2 tablespoons

Pans—can be divided, for example, into 4 × 8 to yield 32 portions.

Portion scale—measures by weight, such as 2 oz. meat or 1 oz. cheese.

Measuring cups, tablespoons, and teaspoons—measure by volume such as 1 cup milk or ½ cup juice or 1 tablespoon salad dressing or 1 teaspoon margarine.

Count—measures by number, such as number of slices in a cake or pie.

STEP 3.   Review portion sizes for menu items.

KEY CONCEPTS	TRAINER'S DIRECTIONS
Your portion sizes for each menu item	• Give the employee a listing of your portion sizes. If not available, give him/her a copy of your menu and review the portion sizes as the employee writes them on the menu.

STEP 4.   Give quiz.

KEY CONCEPTS	TRAINER'S DIRECTIONS
	• It is usually best to give the employee at least one week or more to become familiar with portion sizes. Therefore, give the quiz when you think the employee has had enough time to practice using the portion sizes.

- Before giving the employee the quiz, write down 10 menu items (add more if you want) on the quiz for the employee to give you the portion size.

- Ask the employee to complete the Employee Quiz and then review the correct answers.

Employee's Outline

■ KEY POINTS TO REMEMBER

Portion control means that each serving of food must be measured to the appropriate size for that menu item as specified on the portion control list.

Portion control is important:

- for the customer's satisfaction with the meals.
- to control and predict food costs.
- to avoid running out of food during service or having too many leftovers.

Ladle and Spoodle Sizes

1 oz. = ⅛ cup

2 oz. = ¼ cup

3 oz. = ⅜ cup

4 oz. = ½ cup

6 oz. = ¾ cup

8 oz. = 1 cup

Scoop Sizes

#6 = ⅔ cup

#8 = ½ cup

#10 = ⅜ cup

#12 = ⅓ cup

#16 = ¼ cup

#20 = 3 tablespoons

#24 = 2⅔ tablespoons

#30 = 2 tablespoons

Other Ways to Measure Portion Size

Pans—can be divided, for example, into 4 × 8 to yield 32 portions.

Portion scale—measures by weight, such as 2 oz. meat or 1 oz. cheese.

Measuring cups, tablespoons, and teaspoons—measure by volume such as 1 cup milk or ½ cup juice or 1 tablespoon salad dressing or 1 teaspoon margarine.

Count—measures by number, such as number of slices in a cake or pie.

Employee Quiz

Name: _____

Job Title: _____

Date: _____

Directions: *Fill in the appropriate portion sizes for the menu items listed below.*

1. Menu Item: _____
   Portion Size: _____

2. Menu Item: _____
   Portion Size: _____

3. Menu Item: _____
   Portion Size: _____

4. Menu Item: _____
   Portion Size: _____

5. Menu Item: _____
   Portion Size: _____

6. Menu Item: _____
   Portion Size: _____

7. Menu Item: _____
   Portion Size: _____

8. Menu Item: _____
   Portion Size: _____

9. Menu Item: _____
   Portion Size: _____

10. Menu Item: _____
    Portion Size: _____

LADLE AND SPOODLE SIZES

1 oz. = ⅛ cup

2 oz. = ¼ cup

3 oz. = ⅜ cup

4 oz. = ½ cup

6 oz. = ¾ cup

8 oz. = 1 cup

SCOOP SIZES

#6 = ⅔ cup

#8 = ½ cup

#10 = ⅜ cup

#12 = ⅓ cup

#16 = ¼ cup

#20 = 3 tablespoons

#24 = 2⅔ tablespoons

#30 = 2 tablespoons

Trainer's Outline

■ **STEPS:**

1. Explain how to correctly convert recipes to higher or lower yields and demonstrate.

2. Let the employee practice.

3. Give quiz.

■ **TIME REQUIRED:** 15–25 minutes

■ **MATERIALS NEEDED:** Employee's Outline, Employee Quiz, Job Aid

■ **AHEAD OF TIME:** Pick a recipe that the employee can convert for the Employee Quiz.

STEP 1. Explain how to correctly convert recipes to higher or lower yields and demonstrate.

KEY CONCEPTS	TRAINER'S DIRECTIONS
	• Asking the employee to follow along in the Employee's Outline, explain How to Convert a Recipe.

How to Convert a Recipe

1. Divide the desired yield by the current recipe yield to determine the multiplier.

For example: $\dfrac{\text{Desired yield}}{\text{Current yield}} = \dfrac{200}{100} = 2 \text{ (multiplier)}$

2. Multiply the quantity of each ingredient in the recipe by the multiplier.

• Go through the following example of converting a recipe from 100 to 200 servings. The multiplier is 2.

Ingredients	*100 servings*	×	2	=	*200 servings*
Flour	12 lb.	×	2	=	24 lb.
Water	8 lb.	×	2	=	16 lb.
Yeast	6 oz.	×	2	=	12 oz.

STEP 2.   Let the employee practice.

KEY CONCEPTS	TRAINER'S DIRECTIONS
	• Ask the employee to complete the Recipe Conversion Exercise.
	• Review the correct answers.

Recipe Conversion Exercise

1. Your recipe is for 50 portions. You need to adjust it to 125 portions. What is the multiplier?

$$\frac{125}{50} = 2.5$$

2. Your recipe is for 100 portions. You only need to feed 60. What is the multiplier?

$$\frac{60}{100} = .6 \text{ or } \frac{6}{10}$$

3. Convert the following recipe to yield 150 portions.

Soft Roll Dough

100 portions   *150 portions*

12 lb. flour	$\times$	1.5	=	16 lb.
8 lb. water	$\times$	1.5	=	12 lb.
6 oz. yeast	$\times$	1.5	=	9 oz.
1½ lb. dry milk	$\times$	1.5	=	2 lb. 4 oz.
12 oz. sugar	$\times$	1.5	=	1 lb. 2 oz.

• Explain that it is sometimes easier to convert pounds to ounces and volume measurements to fluid ounces before multiplying. This is the case with the dry milk, which can be converted to 24 oz. $\times$ 1.5 = 36 oz. or 2 lb. 4 oz.

• If employees use calculators, explain that fractions of pounds, such as 0.75, can be converted to ounces by multiplying by 16.

STEP 3.   Give quiz.

KEY CONCEPTS	TRAINER'S DIRECTIONS
	• Ask the employee to complete the Employee Quiz and then review the answers.

Employee's Outline

■ KEY POINTS TO REMEMBER

Converting recipes to new yields involves two steps.

1. Divide the desired yield by the current recipe yield to determine the multiplier.
2. Multiply the quantity of each ingredient in the recipe by the multiplier.
   For example, let's convert the following recipe from 100 to 200 servings.

$$\frac{\text{Desired yield}}{\text{Current yield}} = \frac{200}{100} = 2 \text{ (the multiplier)}$$

Now let's multiply each ingredient in the recipe by the multiplier, 2.

Ingredients	100 servings	×	2	=	200 servings
Flour	12 lb.	×	2	=	24 lb.
Water	8 lb.	×	2	=	16 lb.
Yeast	6 oz.	×	2	=	12 oz.

■ RECIPE CONVERSION EXERCISE

1. Your recipe is for 50 portions. You need to adjust it to 125 portions. What is the multiplier?
2. Your recipe is for 100 portions. You only need to feed 60. What is the multiplier?
3. Convert the following recipe to yield 150 portions.

Soft Roll Dough

100 portions	150 portions
12 lb. flour	
8 lb. water	
6 oz. yeast	
1½ lb. dry milk	
12 oz. sugar	

Employee Quiz

Name: _____

Job Title: _____

Date: _____

Directions: *Your trainer will give you a recipe to convert.*

1. Divide the desired yield by the current recipe yield to determine the multiplier.

    For example: $\dfrac{\text{Desired yield}}{\text{Current yield}} = \dfrac{200}{100} = 2$

2. Multiply the quantity of each ingredient in the recipe by the multiplier.

Trainer's Outline

■ **STEPS:**

1. Explain knife safety tips.
2. Give quiz.

■ **TIME REQUIRED:**   15–25 minutes

■ **MATERIALS NEEDED:**   Employee's Outline, Employee Quiz, Job Aids

STEP 1.   Explain knife safety tips.

KEY CONCEPTS	TRAINER'S DIRECTIONS
	• Ask the employee for ways that he/she handles knives safely.
	• Asking the employee to follow along in the Employee's Outline, review Knife Safety Tips.

Knife Safety Tips

Using Knives Safely

1. Cut away from the body.
2. Cut away from anyone near you.
3. Use a cutting board and put a damp cloth under it.

   • Explain that the damp cloth keeps the board from slipping.

4. Use the right knife for the job. Don't use a lightweight knife for a heavy-duty job.
5. Keep knives sharp. Since a dull knife requires more pressure to cut, it is more dangerous than a sharp knife.
6. Always pick up a knife by its handle.
7. Don't use knives to open cases, cans, or bottles.
8. Use metal mesh gloves if using knives constantly as the gloves prevent cuts.

Carrying Knives Safely

1. Carry the knife beside you, point down, and cutting edge back and away from you.

2. For carrying knives, it is preferable to use a sheath or covering.

3. If a knife falls, do not try to catch it. Get out of the way.

- Ask: "Why?" If you catch it by the blade, you will cut yourself.

Cleaning Knives

1. Do not put a knife in a sink full of water; instead put it on the drain board.

- Ask: "Why?" So another employee does not get cut when he/she puts hands into the sink.

2. Wipe from dull to sharp edge.

Storing Knives

1. Never put a knife loosely in a drawer. Instead use a rack or a case so the blade is protected.

2. Don't leave knives near the edge of a table.

- Ask: "Why?" So the knives are not knocked off the table.

STEP 2.   Give quiz.

KEY CONCEPTS	TRAINER'S DIRECTIONS
	• Ask the employee to complete the Employee Quiz and then review the answers (given at left).

Employee Quiz Answer Key

Directions: Circle "True" or "False."

1. If a knife falls, try to catch it.
   B. False
   Explain to just let the knife fall; otherwise you could get cut.

2. A dull knife is more dangerous than a sharp knife.
   A. True

3. It is safe to store your knife loose in a drawer.
   B. False

Explain that the knife should be in a rack or case to protect the blade and protect you from getting cut.

4. When nothing else is handy, use your knife to open up a case.

   B. False

   Explain that you can ruin your knife and hurt yourself by using your knife on cardboard.

5. When carrying a knife, carry it beside you with the point down and cutting edge back and away from you.

   A. True

6. Always put your dirty knife on the drain board by the sink, not in the sink.

   A. True

Employee's Outline

■ **KEY POINTS TO REMEMBER**

Using Knives Safely

The following tips are important to avoid being injured by knives.

1. Cut away from the body.
2. Cut away from anyone near you.
3. Use a cutting board and put a damp cloth under it to keep the board from slipping.
4. Use the right knife for the job. Don't use a lightweight knife for a heavy-duty job.
5. Keep knives sharp. Since a dull knife requires more pressure to cut, it is more dangerous than a sharp knife.
6. Always pick up a knife by its handle.
7. Don't use knives to open cases, cans, or bottles.
8. Use metal mesh gloves if using knives constantly as the gloves prevent cuts.

Carrying Knives Safely

Do the following to carry knives in a safe manner.

1. Carry the knife beside you, point down, and cutting edge back and away from you.
2. For carrying knives, it is preferable to use a sheath or covering.
3. If a knife falls, do not try to catch it. Get out of the way.

Cleaning Knives

Do the following to clean knives in a safe manner.

1. Do not put a knife in a sink full of water; instead put it on the drain board.
2. Wipe from dull to sharp edge.

Storing Knives

1. Never put a knife loosely in a drawer. Instead use a rack or a case so the blade is protected.
2. Don't leave knives near the edge of a table because they can be easily knocked off.

Employee Quiz

Name: _____

Job Title: _____

Date: _____

Directions: *Circle "True" or "False."*

1. If a knife falls, try to catch it.

   A. True

   B. False

   Correct Answer: _____

2. A dull knife is more dangerous than a sharp knife.

   A. True

   B. False

   Correct Answer: _____

3. It is safe to store your knife loose in a drawer.

   A. True

   B. False

   Correct Answer: _____

4. When nothing else is handy, use your knife to open up a case.

   A. True

   B. False

   Correct Answer: _____

5. When carrying a knife, carry it beside you with the point down and cutting edge back and away from you.

   A. True

   B. False

   Correct Answer: _____

6. Always put your dirty knife on the drain board by the sink, not in the sink.

   A. True

   B. False

   Correct Answer: _____

USING KNIVES SAFELY

1. Cut away from the body.

2. Cut away from anyone near you.

3. Use a cutting board and put a damp cloth under it to keep the board from slipping.

4. Use the right knife for the job. Don't use a lightweight knife for a heavy-duty job.

5. Keep knives sharp. Since a dull knife requires more pressure to cut, it is more dangerous than a sharp knife.

6. Always pick up a knife by its handle.

7. Don't use knives to open cases, cans, or bottles.

8. Use metal mesh gloves if using knives constantly as the gloves prevent cuts.

CARRYING KNIVES SAFELY

1. Carry the knife beside you, point down, and cutting edge back and away from you.

2. For carrying knives, it is preferable to use a sheath or covering.

3. If a knife falls, do not try to catch it. Get out of the way.

CLEANING KNIVES

1. Do not put a knife in a sink full of water; instead put it on the drain board.

2. Wipe from dull to sharp edge.

STORING KNIVES

1. Never put a knife loosely in a drawer. Instead use a rack or a case so the blade is protected.

2. Don't leave knives near the edge of a table because they can be easily knocked off.

Trainer's Outline

■ **STEPS:**

1. Show the different types of knives and explain their uses.
2. Give quiz.

■ **TIME REQUIRED:**   15–25 minutes

■ **MATERIALS NEEDED:**   Employee's Outline; Employee Quiz; chef's, paring, slicing, utility, and boning knives

STEP 1.   Show the different types of knives and explain their uses.

KEY CONCEPTS	TRAINER'S DIRECTIONS
	• Have a table set up with each of the types of knives listed at left.
	• Ask the employee to identify each type of knife.
	• Make sure each knife is correctly identified and the uses explained.

Types of Knives

1. Chef's knife or French knife: all-purpose knife used most frequently in kitchen
2. Paring knife: used to trim and peel fruits and vegetables
3. Utility knife: used mostly in cold food preparation for jobs such as cutting lettuce, fruits, and other vegetables
4. Slicer: used to carve and slice cooked meats
5. Boning knife: used to bone raw meats, poultry, and fish

STEP 2.   Give quiz.

KEY CONCEPTS	TRAINER'S DIRECTIONS
	• Ask the employee to complete the Employee Quiz and then review the answers as follow.

Employee Quiz Answer Key

Directions: *Match the term in column 1 with the correct use in column 2. Put the letter in the blank space.*

	Type of Knife	*Use*
__E__	**1.** Boning knife	**A.** A knife used to carve and slice cooked meats
__C__	**2.** Paring knife	**B.** An all-purpose knife
__D__	**3.** Utility knife	**C.** A knife used to trim and peel fruits and vegetables
__A__	**4.** Slicer	**D.** A knife used mostly in cold food preparation
__B__	**5.** Chef's knife	**E.** A knife used to bone raw meats, poultry, and fish

Employee's Outline

■ **KEY POINTS TO REMEMBER**

Types of Knives

1. A chef's knife or French knife is an all-purpose knife used most frequently in kitchens. The blade is wide at the heel and tapers to the point.

2. A paring knife is used to trim and peel fruits and vegetables. It has a short, pointed blade and is often 2 to 2½ inches in length.

3. A utility knife is used mostly in cold food preparation for jobs such as cutting lettuce, fruits, and other vegetables. It has a tapered blade usually 6 to 8 inches in length.

4. A slicer is used to carve and slice cooked meats. It has a long, narrow blade that is flexible and may be up to 14 inches in length. When a slicer's blade is serrated, the slicer is used to cut breads, cakes, and other soft foods that might otherwise be crushed.

5. A boning knife is used to bone raw meats, poultry, and fish. It has a narrow, tapered blade that is usually 6 inches in length.

Employee Quiz

Name: _____

Job Title: _____

Date: _____

Directions: *Match the term in column 1 with the correct use in Column 2. Put the letter in the blank space.*

		Type of Knife	*Use*
Your Answer	*Correct Answer*		
_____	_____	**1.** Boning knife	**A.** A knife used to carve and slice cooked meats
_____	_____	**2.** Paring knife	**B.** An all-purpose knife
_____	_____	**3.** Utility knife	**C.** A knife used to trim and peel fruits and vegetables
_____	_____	**4.** Slicer	**D.** A knife used mostly in cold food preparation
_____	_____	**5.** Chef's knife	**E.** A knife used to bone raw meats, poultry, and fish

Trainer's Outline

■ **STEPS:**

1. Have employee complete exercise and review correct answers.

■ **TIME REQUIRED:**   10–15 minutes

■ **MATERIALS NEEDED:**   Employee's Outline, Employee Quiz; chef's knife, cutting board, vegetables

STEP 1.   Have employee complete exercise and review correct answers.

KEY CONCEPTS	TRAINER'S DIRECTIONS
	• Ask employee to complete Cutting Terms Exercise and review correct answers at left.
	• When discussing dice, explain that small dice is ¼-inch cube, medium dice is ½-inch cube, and large dice is ¾-inch cube.
	• You may want to cut a carrot or other vegetable to show how each cut looks.

Cutting Terms Exercise

Directions: *Put the letter of the appropriate definition in front of each term listed below.*

	Cutting Terms		Definitions
B	1. Slice	**A.**	To cut into thin strips
D	2. Dice	**B.**	To cut into uniform slices or cross cuts
E	3. Chop	**C.**	To cut into small, thin strips about ⅛ inch by ⅛ inch by 2½ inches long
F	4. Mince	**D.**	To cut into uniform cubes
A	5. Shred	**E.**	To cut into irregularly shaped pieces
C	6. Julienne	**F.**	To chop very fine

Employee's Outline

■ CUTTING TERMS EXERCISE

Directions: *Put the letter of the appropriate definition in front of each term listed below.*

		Cutting Terms	Definitions
Your Answer	*Correct Answer*		
_____	_____	**1.** Slice	**A.** To cut into thin strips
_____	_____	**2.** Dice	**B.** To cut into uniform slices or cross cuts
_____	_____	**3.** Chop	**C.** To cut into small, thin strips about ⅛ inch by ⅛ inch by 2½ inches long
_____	_____	**4.** Mince	
_____	_____	**5.** Shred	**D.** To cut into uniform cubes
_____	_____	**6.** Julienne	**E.** To cut into irregularly shaped pieces
			F. To chop very fine

■ KEY POINTS TO REMEMBER

Following are cutting terms with which you need to be familiar before using knives.

1. Slice: to cut into uniform slices or cross cuts
2. Dice: to cut into uniform cubes
   small dice: ¼-inch cube
   medium dice: ½-inch cube
   large dice: ¾-inch cube
3. Chop: to cut into irregularly shaped pieces
4. Mince: to chop very fine
5. Shred: to cut into thin strips
6. Julienne: to cut into small, thin strips, about ⅛ inch by ⅛ inch by 2½ inches long

Trainer's Outline

■ **STEPS:**

1. Demonstrate how to handle a chef's knife and let the employee practice.

2. Demonstrate how to slice and let the employee practice.

3. Demonstrate how to dice and let the employee practice.

4. Demonstrate how to chop and mince and let the employee practice.

■ **TIME REQUIRED:**   20–30 minutes

■ **MATERIALS NEEDED:**   Employee's Outline, Job Aids; chef's knives, cutting boards, items for cutting

■ **AHEAD OF TIME:**   You may want to post the Job Aids in your work area.

STEP 1.   Demonstrate how to handle a chef's knife and let the employee practice.

KEY CONCEPTS	TRAINER'S DIRECTIONS
	• Give the employee a knife and ask him/her to hold it properly.
	• Make any corrections and demonstrate each of the points below.

How to Handle a Chef's Knife

1. To hold the knife, grasp the heel of the blade with part of the thumb on one side and part of the forefinger on the other. The remaining fingers fit under the handle. The grip should be secure but relaxed.

    • Explain that this grip gives you the most control and force.

2. The other hand holds the item being cut with the fingertips curled under and your knuckles guiding the blade. Fingertips are always curled under to protect them from cuts.

3. Use the tip of the blade for cutting small items, the center of the blade for most work, and the heel of the blade for heavy or coarse work.

STEP 2. Demonstrate how to slice and let the employee practice.

KEY CONCEPTS	TRAINER'S DIRECTIONS
	• Ask the employee what he/she knows about slicing.
	• Asking the employee to follow along on posted Job Aid 49-2, review how to slice.
	• Demonstrate how to slice, then let the employee practice. Coach.

How to Slice

1. The knife is placed at a 45-degree angle to the cutting board.

2. Move the knife forward and down, slicing the item to the desired width. Let the knife do the work.

3. When the slice is completed, the heel of the knife is on the cutting board. For the next slice, raise the heel and pull it back.

4. When cutting thin foods, keep the tip of the knife on the cutting board.

STEP 3. Demonstrate how to dice and let the employee practice.

KEY CONCEPTS	TRAINER'S DIRECTIONS
	• Ask the employee what he/she knows about dicing.
	• Asking the employee to follow along on posted Job Aid 49-2, review how to dice.
	• Demonstrate how to dice, then let the employee practice. Coach.

How to Dice

1. First, cut the item into lengthwise slices of the appropriate thickness (¼ inch, ½ inch, or ¾ inch).

2. Stack the slices and cut into lengthwise strips, again to the desired thickness.

3. Placing the strips in a pile, cut them crosswise into the dice of desired size.

STEP 4. *Demonstrate how to chop and mince and let the employee practice.*

KEY CONCEPTS	TRAINER'S DIRECTIONS
	• Ask the employee what he/she knows about chopping and mincing.
	• Asking the employee to follow along on posted Job Aid 49-4, review how to chop and mince.
	• Demonstrate how to chop and mince, then let the employee practice. Coach.

How to Chop

1. While holding the tip of the knife against the cutting board with three or four fingers of one hand, rock the knife up and down at a quick pace.

2. At the same time, swivel the knife gradually around the board to evenly distribute the chopping action across all of the items being cut.

3. After making several passes with your knife, redistribute the pile.

4. Wipe the blade with a clean and dry cloth when it has excessive food clinging to it.

How to Mince

1. Use the same procedure as chopping and chop into very fine pieces.

Employee's Outline

■ **KEY POINTS TO REMEMBER**

Following are instructions on how to handle a chef's knife, as well as how to slice, dice, chop, and mince.

How to Handle a Chef's Knife

1. To hold the knife, grasp the heel of the blade with part of the thumb on one side and part of the forefinger on the other. The remaining fingers fit under the handle. The grip should be secure but relaxed. This grip gives you the most control and force.

2. The other hand holds the item being cut with the fingertips curled under and your knuckles guiding the blade. Fingertips are always curled under to protect them from cuts.

3. Use the tip of the blade for cutting small items, the center of the blade for most work, and the heel of the blade for heavy or coarse work.

How to Slice

1. The knife is placed at a 45-degree angle to the cutting board.

2. Move the knife forward and down, slicing the items to the desired width. Let the knife do the work.

3. When the slice is completed, the heel of the knife is on the cutting board. For the next slice, raise the heel and pull it back.

4. When cutting thin foods, keep the tip of the knife on the cutting board.

How to Dice

1. First, cut the item into lengthwise slices of the appropriate thickness (¼ inch, ½ inch, or ¾ inch).

2. Stack the slices and cut into lengthwise strips, again to the desired thickness.

3. Placing the strips in a pile, cut them crosswise into the dice of desired size.

How to Chop

1. While holding the tip of the knife against the cutting board with three or four fingers of one hand, rock the knife up and down at a quick pace.

2. At the same time, swivel the knife gradually around the board to evenly distribute the chopping action across all of the items being cut.

3. After making several passes with your knife, redistribute the pile.

4. Wipe the blade with a clean and dry cloth when it has excessive food clinging to it.

How to Mince

1. Use the same procedure as chopping and chop into fine pieces.

1. To hold the knife, grasp the heel of the blade with part of the thumb on one side and part of the forefinger on the other. The remaining fingers fit under the handle. The grip should be secure but relaxed. This grip gives you the most control and force.

2. The other hand holds the item being cut with the fingertips curled under and your knuckles guiding the blade. Fingertips are always curled under to protect them from cuts.

3. Use the tip of the blade for cutting small items, the center of the blade for most work, and the heel of the blade for heavy or coarse work.

HOW TO SLICE

1. The knife is placed at a 45-degree angle to the cutting board.

2. Move the knife forward and down, slicing the items to the desired width. Let the knife do the work.

3. When the slice is completed, the heel of the knife is on the cutting board. For the next slice, raise the heel and pull it back.

4. When cutting thin foods, keep the tip of the knife on the cutting board.

HOW TO DICE

1. First, cut the item into lengthwise slices of the appropriate thickness (¼ inch, ½ inch, or ¾ inch).

2. Stack the slices and cut into lengthwise strips, again to the desired thickness.

3. Placing the strips in a pile, cut them crosswise into dice of desired size.

CHOPPING

1. While holding the tip of the knife against the cutting board with three or four fingers of one hand, rock the knife up and down at a quick pace.

2. At the same time, swivel the knife gradually around the board to evenly distribute the chopping action across all of the items being cut.

3. After making several passes with your knife, redistribute the pile.

4. Wipe the blade with a clean and dry cloth when it has excessive food clinging to it.

MINCING

1. Use the same procedure as chopping and chop into fine pieces.

Trainer's Outline

■ **STEPS:**

1. Demonstrate how to sharpen a knife blade and let the employee practice.

2. Demonstrate how to true a knife blade and let the employee practice.

■ **TIME REQUIRED:**   10–20 minutes

■ **MATERIALS NEEDED:**   Employee's Outline, Job Aids; chef's knives, sharpening stone, steel

■ **AHEAD OF TIME:**   You may want to post the Job Aids in your work area.

STEP 1. *Demonstrate how to sharpen a knife blade and let the employee practice.*

KEY CONCEPTS	TRAINER'S DIRECTIONS
	• Ask the employee what he/she knows about sharpening a knife.
	• Asking the employee to follow along on posted Job Aid 50-1, review how to sharpen.
	• Demonstrate how to sharpen a knife, then let the employee practice. Coach.

How to Sharpen a Knife Blade Using a Sharpening Stone

1. You may want to lubricate the stone by thoroughly rubbing in a tablespoon of oil.

2. Hold the knife firmly with one hand on the top and the other hand gripping the handle.

3. Holding the knife blade at a 20-degree angle to the stone, place the tip at one end of the stone and slowly draw the knife across the stone while pressing gently on the blade.

4. Draw the knife smoothly across the stone to the heel of the blade.

5. Make the same number (five is common) of strokes on each side of

the blade. Only a few strokes should
be necessary unless the knife has been
mishandled. Make sure strokes are
even and in one direction only.

STEP 2. *Demonstrate how to true a knife blade and let the employee practice.*

KEY CONCEPTS	TRAINER'S DIRECTIONS
	• Ask the employee what he/she knows about using a steel to true a blade.
	• Asking the employee to follow along on posted Job Aid 50-2, review how to true a blade.
	• Demonstrate how to true a blade, then let the employee practice. Coach.

How to True a Knife Blade Using a Steel

1. Hold the steel in one hand, away from your body, at a 45-degree angle.

2. Hold the knife vertically in your other hand, with the blade at a 20-degree angle to the steel. Touch the steel with the heel of the blade.

3. Draw the knife lightly along the steel, using an even and regular stroke.

4. Repeat this motion on the other side of the steel for the other side of the knife. Five or six strokes for each side is sufficient. Too much steeling can make the blade dull.

Employee's Outline

■ KEY POINTS TO REMEMBER

Another important aspect of using knives is keeping them sharp. A sharpening stone can do the sharpening, while a steel can true a blade so as to perfect the edge and maintain a sharp edge.

How to Sharpen a Knife Blade Using a Sharpening Stone

1. You may want to lubricate the stone by thoroughly rubbing in a tablespoon of oil.
2. Hold the knife firmly with one hand on the top and the other hand gripping the handle.
3. Holding the knife blade at a 20-degree angle to the stone, place the tip at one end of the stone and slowly draw the knife across the stone while pressing gently on the blade.
4. Draw the knife smoothly across the stone to the heel of the blade.
5. Make the same number (five is common) of strokes on each side of the blade. Only a few strokes should be necessary unless the knife has been mishandled. Make sure strokes are even and in one direction only.

How to True a Knife Blade Using a Steel

1. Hold the steel in one hand, away from your body, at a 45-degree angle.
2. Hold the knife vertically in your other hand, with the blade at a 20-degree angle to the steel. Touch the steel with the heel of the blade.
3. Draw the knife lightly along the steel, using an even and regular stroke.
4. Repeat this motion on the other side of the steel for the other side of the knife. Five or six strokes for each side is sufficient. Too much steeling can make the blade dull.

1. You may want to lubricate the stone by thoroughly rubbing in a tablespoon of oil.

2. Hold the knife firmly with one hand on the top and the other hand gripping the handle.

3. Holding the knife blade at a 20-degree angle to the stone, place the tip at one end of the stone and slowly draw the knife across the stone while pressing gently on the blade.

4. Draw the knife smoothly across the stone to the heel of the blade.

5. Make the same number (five is common) of strokes on each side of the blade. Only a few strokes should be necessary unless the knife has been mishandled. Make sure strokes are even and in one direction only.

HOW TO TRUE A KNIFE BLADE USING A STEEL

1. Hold the steel in one hand, away from your body, at a 45-degree angle.

2. Hold the knife vertically in your other hand, with the blade at a 20-degree angle to the steel. Touch the steel with the heel of the blade.

3. Draw the knife lightly along the steel, using an even and regular stroke.

4. Repeat this motion on the other side of the steel for the other side of the knife. Five or six strokes for each side are sufficient. Too much steeling can make the blade dull.

CHAPTER 4

Group Training Outlines

How to Use Group Training Outlines

This chapter contains eight ready-to-use *Group Training Outlines* on the following topics.

Sanitation and Safety

Group Training Outline 1:	**HAND WASHING**
Group Training Outline 2:	**SAFE FOOD HANDLING TECHNIQUES**
Group Training Outline 3:	**KITCHEN SAFETY RULES**
Group Training Outline 4:	**BACK SAFETY**

Service Skills

Group Training Outline 5:	**QUALITY SERVICE**
Group Training Outline 6:	**SUGGESTIVE SELLING**
Group Training Outline 7:	**HANDLING COMPLAINTS**
Group Training Outline 8:	**RESPONSIBLE ALCOHOL SERVICE**

These topics were chosen as they seem the most likely to be taught in group training. The topics are either very important or seem quite likely to be used for training or retraining groups of current employees. Figure 4-1 shows which outlines are best suited to specific positions in your restaurant.

The Group Training Outlines are designed to be used with your hourly foodservice employees in group classroom training. There are also ready-to-photocopy employee materials, called *Employee Guides*, that contain exercises, key points, and quizzes. In addition to the Group Training Outlines and Employee Guides, there are *Teaching Aid Masters*.

FIGURE 4-1 *Training Guide: Group Training Outlines*

	1: Hand Washing	2: Safe Food Handling Techniques	3: Kitchen Safety Rules	4: Back Safety	5: Quality Service	6: Suggestive Selling	7: Handling Complaints	8: Responsible Alcohol Service
Cooks	✓	✓	✓	✓				
Bakers	✓	✓	✓	✓				
Salads/Cold Food Preparation	✓	✓	✓	✓				
Storeroom	✓	✓	✓	✓				
Dishroom	✓	✓	✓	✓				
Pot and Pan Washer	✓	✓	✓	✓				
Porter-Utility-Cleaning Personnel	✓	✓	✓	✓				
Host/Hostess	✓			✓	✓	✓	✓	✓
Server	✓			✓	✓	✓	✓	✓
Busperson	✓			✓	✓		✓	
Bartender	✓			✓	✓	✓	✓	✓
Beverage Server	✓			✓	✓	✓	✓	✓

Each Group Training Outline explains *what* employees need to know, as well as *how* the trainer can get the content across to the employees. Standard industry practices and procedures are given, and trainers are instructed at many points to customize the procedures to their own operations. Various training methods (see Table 2-1) are used and most actively involve the employee in his or her learning. Each Group Training Outline can be used in tandem with videotape training programs. A list of sources for videotape training programs appears in Appendix A.

Each Group Training Outline starts with these three headings.

1. Learning Goals: The Learning Goals answer the question "What do I want my employees to get out of this?" Because only one Learning Goal is taught at a time, it is possible to teach only those goals that are relevant.

2. Time Required: This is an estimate of how much time the training will require. It is only a rough estimate because the actual time needed will depend on the size of the group, the amount of interaction that occurs, how knowledgeable the group is, and how many questions are raised.

3. Materials Needed: This list tells you what is needed to do the training and what to bring to the training session.

The remainder of the Training Outline is broken down into three sections: Introduction, Learning Goals, and Summary. Because this is the actual outline you use during the class, it has two columns. The left column, Key Concepts, contains the content of the class—in other words, "what to teach." The right column, Trainer's Directions, gives instructions on how to teach the material.

1. Introduction

The purpose of this section is to interest the employees in the topic and also to explain the learning goals for the training session so the employees see what's in it for them. A common introductory technique is to have the employees do a brief exercise that they grade themselves while the answers are briefly reviewed in class (the answers are discussed more later in the training session).

You will notice that the names of the training methods (such as Exercise) to be used are listed after the Introduction heading. Different training methods are discussed in detail in Table 2-1.

2. Learning Goals

The training outline is now broken down by learning goals. The names of the teaching methods you are to use again appear after the Learning Goal heading. When there are Teaching Aids available to help teach different sections, they are noted in the Trainer's Directions column. There are also notes in this column that direct you to discuss your own policies and procedures on such topics as responsible alcohol service.

3. *Summary*

Each training session ends with a summary section. A common summary technique is to redo the Warmup Questions by reading the questions out loud and asking the employees for the correct responses. In this manner, many important points are summarized and the employees feel that they have mastered some key points.

The final page(s) of the Employee Guide is a quiz that you are instructed to let the employee complete at the end of class and hand in for correction. You may want to review the answers so that the employees get immediate feedback. The quizzes have different types of questions such as true/false, multiple choice, and fill-in-the-blank.

It is crucial to read over the Group Training Outline and Employee Guide some time before conducting the training. You may decide to do demonstrations or other techniques that require preparation. Always make sure you have all your materials together before class starts, including pencils for the employees to use as well as a writing surface such as a blackboard or easel pad.

How to Use the Employee Guides

At the beginning of each training session, as employees walk in, hand out the Employee Guide, which you can easily photocopy for each of your employees and staple together. Each Employee Guide is organized as follows:

- Introduction: This section briefly introduces the topic and spells out the Learning Goals.
- Exercises: Most classes have one or more Exercises and they are located at the front of the Employee Guide. Each Exercise has its own set of instructions and space for completion.
- Key Points to Remember: In this section, all Key Concepts from the Training Outline are covered. In this manner the employee has all the class material at his/her fingertips.
- Quiz: The final page(s) of the Employee Guide is a quiz that you are instructed to let the employee complete at the end of class and hand in for correction.

How to Use the Teaching Aids

You can do either of the following with the Teaching Aids:

1. Make the Teaching Aids into transparencies by putting transparency film made for copiers into your copier's paper tray and photocopying the Teaching Aids onto the transparencies.
2. Enlarge the Teaching Aids onto larger and possibly heavier paper for use as posters in your training. These posters can also be hung in your restaurant to reinforce your training messages.

■ **TIME REQUIRED:**   20–30 minutes

■ **MATERIALS NEEDED:**

Employee Guides

Teaching Aids

Board or easel pad

Handwashing sink with soap and paper towels

Tongs, scoop

Plastic gloves

Plates, bowls, glasses, cups, and utensils

■ **LEARNING GOALS:**

The employee will be able to:

1. explain why clean hands are so vital in a foodservice.

2. recognize situations when hand washing is necessary.

3. demonstrate how to wash his/her hands.

4. handle food and tableware without contaminating it with his/her hands.

KEY CONCEPTS	TRAINER'S DIRECTIONS
INTRODUCTION	

Method: Exercise

Warmup Exercise

How many seconds does it take to wash your hands—meaning the time you need to rub your hands together with soap and wash between your fingers, under your rings and nails, and up your forearms?

Answer: 20 seconds

- Hand out Employee Guides and ask employees to complete the Warmup Exercise in a few minutes. Ask the employees for the correct answer, which is 20 seconds. Explain that many people spend much less time actually washing their hands than this, but that 20 seconds is a guideline to do the job well.

- Explain learning goals.

LEARNING GOAL 1

The employee will be able to explain why clean hands are so vital in a foodservice.

Hand Washing: Why?

- Hand washing removes dirt and grime from your hands that you do not want in the food or on the dishes.

- Hand washing reduces the number of bacteria on your hands so you are less likely to contaminate foods or dishes.

Method: Guided discussion

- Ask employees why they think they should wash their hands. List their responses on a board or easel pad. Be sure all Key Concepts are covered.

LEARNING GOAL 2

The employee will be able to recognize situations when hand washing is necessary.

Method: Buzz Groups

- Ask employees to work in groups of two or three people and complete the Handwashing Exercise in 5 minutes. Ask each group to tell you their responses and write them on a board or easel pad. Be sure all Key Concepts are covered, and ask "Why?" as directed.

I wash my hands after I:

1. Smoke

   - Ask: "Why?" When smoking, your fingers come in contact with saliva in your mouth.

2. Eat
   - Ask: "Why?" Same as #1.

3. Use the rest room
   - Ask: "Why?" Your body, feces, and urine are full of bacteria.

4. Touch money
   - Ask: "Why?" Money is very dirty.

5. Touch raw foods
   - Ask: "Why?" They may contain harmful bacteria.

6. Touch my face, hair, or skin
   - Ask: "Why?" Bacteria are all over your body.

7. Cough, sneeze, or blow my nose
   - Ask: "Why?" These actions spread bacteria.

8. Comb my hair
   - Ask: "Why?" Your hair is full of bacteria.

9. Handle anything dirty (including your apron)

10. You take a break (and also before)

- Ask: "Why?" Dirt and grime get on your hands.

LEARNING GOAL 3

The employee will be able to demonstrate how to wash his/her hands.

Hand Washing: How?

1. First, pick a handwashing sink.

2. If wearing a watch, remove it.

3. Turn water to as hot as you can stand.

4. Moisten hands and exposed forearms. Soap thoroughly and lather.

5. Wash for 20 seconds by rubbing hands and wash between fingers, under rings and nails, and up forearms. Use brush for nails if provided.

6. Rinse hands and forearms well with hot water.

7. Dry hands and forearms thoroughly.

8. Turn water off, preferably with a paper towel.

9. Tell your supervisor if there is no soap or paper towels.

Method: Tell/show/do/review

- Using Teaching Aid 1-1, explain how to wash your hands.

- Demonstrate how to wash hands.

- Ask employees to practice washing their hands and coach.

- Review steps.

LEARNING GOAL 4

The employee will be able to handle food and tableware without contaminating it with his or her hands

Handy Tips

1. Use scoops, tongs, spatulas, etc. to handle food and ice.

2. Use plastic gloves as directed. Change often.

Method: Demonstration

- Using Teaching Aid 1-2, explain how to decrease the chance of contaminating food with your hands. Demonstrate each tip.

3. Avoid touching food-contact surfaces of dishes, utensils, etc. The food-contact surface is the surface that will be touched by food or drink.

- Demonstrate handling plates by the bottom or edge, keeping hands off the eating surface. Show how to handle glasses, bowls, and cups by the bottom to avoid touching the rims. Lastly, show how to pick up knives, forks, and spoons by handles.

- Have employees work in pairs and demonstrate to each other proper handling of tableware.

SUMMARY

Method:

- Using Teaching Aid 1-3, review when to wash hands.

- Ask employees to complete Handwashing Quiz and review answers at left.

Handwashing Quiz Answer Key

I should wash my hands after I:

__X__	**1.**	Smoke
__X__	**2.**	Eat
__X__	**3.**	Use the rest room
__X__	**4.**	Touch money
__X__	**5.**	Touch raw foods
_____	**6.**	Talk to a friend
__X__	**7.**	Touch a dirty uniform or apron
__X__	**8.**	Blow my nose
__X__	**9.**	Comb my hair
_____	**10.**	Check my schedule

■ INTRODUCTION

Today's class covers why, when, and how to wash your hands. By the end of today's session, you should be able to:

1. explain why clean hands are so vital in a foodservice.
2. recognize situations when hand washing is necessary.
3. demonstrate how to wash your hands.
4. handle food and tableware without contaminating it with your hands.

■ WARMUP EXERCISE

Directions: *Put your answer to the following question in the space below.*

Question:

How many seconds does it take to wash your hands—meaning the time you need to rub your hands together with soap and wash between your fingers, under your rings and nails, and up your forearms?

Your Answer: _____ seconds

■ HANDWASHING EXERCISE

Directions: *Finish the following sentence. Write down as many situations as possible in the spaces provided.*

I wash my hands after I:

1. _____

2. _____

3. _____

4. _____

5. _____

6.
_____

7.
_____

8.
_____

9.
_____

10.
_____

11.
_____

12.
_____

13.
_____

14.
_____

15.
_____

■ KEY POINTS TO REMEMBER

Let's take a look at why we wash our hands, when we need to do it, and how.

Why?   Hand washing removes dirt and grime from your hands that you do not want in food or on dishes. Hand washing also reduces the number of bacteria on your hands so you are less likely to contaminate foods or dishes.

When?   You should wash your hands after you:

- Smoke (when smoking, your fingers come in contact with the saliva in your mouth).
- Eat (when eating, your fingers come in contact with the saliva in your mouth).
- Use the rest room (your body, feces, and urine contain bacteria).
- Touch money (money is very dirty—it never gets washed!).

EMPLOYEE GUIDE *(continued)*

- Touch raw foods (they may contain harmful bacteria).
- Touch your face, hair, or skin (bacteria are all over your body).
- Cough, sneeze, or blow your nose (these actions spread bacteria).
- Comb your hair (your hair is full of bacteria!).
- Handle anything dirty (including your apron).
- Take a break (wash both before and after).

How? Following are the steps for washing your hands correctly.

1. First, pick a handwashing sink.
2. If wearing a watch, remove it.
3. Turn water to as hot as you can stand.
4. Moisten hands and exposed forearms. Soap thoroughly and lather.
5. Wash for 20 seconds by rubbing hands and wash between fingers, under rings and nails, and up forearms. Use a brush for your nails if provided.
6. Rinse hands and forearms well with hot water.
7. Dry hands and forearms thoroughly.
8. Turn water off, preferably with a paper towel.
9. Tell your supervisor if there is no soap or paper towels.

Other handy tips include the following.

1. Use scoops, tongs, spatulas, etc. to handle food and ice. Don't use your hands!
2. Use plastic gloves as directed. Change often.
3. Avoid touching food-contact surfaces of dishes, utensils, and equipment. The food-contact surface is the surface that will be touched by food or drink.
   Handle plates by the bottom or edge, keeping fingers off the eating surface.
   Handle glasses, bowls, and cups by the bottom or handle to avoid touching the rims.
   Pick up utensils by their handles.

HANDWASHING QUIZ

Name: _____

Date: _____

Trainer: _____

Directions: *Check off in the space provided when appropriate.*

I should wash my hands after I:

Correct Answer	*Your Answer*	
_____	_____	**1.** Smoke
_____	_____	**2.** Eat
_____	_____	**3.** Use the rest room
_____	_____	**4.** Touch money
_____	_____	**5.** Touch raw foods
_____	_____	**6.** Talk to a friend
_____	_____	**7.** Touch a dirty uniform or apron
_____	_____	**8.** Blow my nose
_____	_____	**9.** Comb my hair
_____	_____	**10.** Check my schedule

1. First, pick a handwashing sink.

2. If wearing a watch, remove it.

3. Turn water to as hot as you can stand.

4. Moisten hands and exposed forearms. Soap thoroughly and lather.

5. Wash for 20 seconds by rubbing hands and wash between fingers, under rings and nails, and up forearms. Use a brush for your nails if provided.

6. Rinse hands and forearms well with hot water.

7. Dry hands and forearms thoroughly.

8. Turn water off, preferably with a paper towel.

9. Tell your supervisor if there is no soap or paper towels.

1. Use scoops, tongs, spatulas, and so forth to handle food and ice. Don't use your hands!

2. Use plastic gloves as directed. Change often.

3. Avoid touching food-contact surfaces of dishes, utensils, and equipment. The food-contact surface is the surface that will be touched by food or drink.

   Handle plates by the bottom or edge, keeping fingers off the eating surface.

   Handle glasses, bowls, and cups by the bottom or handle to avoid touching the rims.

   Pick up utensils by their handles.

WASH HANDS AFTER YOU:

- Smoke.
- Eat.
- Use the rest room.
- Touch money.
- Touch raw foods.
- Touch your face, hair, or skin.
- Cough, sneeze, or blow your nose.
- Comb your hair.
- Handle anything dirty.
- Take a break.

■ **TIME REQUIRED:**   30–40 minutes

■ **MATERIALS NEEDED:**

Employee Guides

Teaching Aid

Ice Bath

Thermometer

Sanitizing Solution

■ **LEARNING GOALS:**

The employee will be able to:

1. recognize major factors leading to foodborne illness.

2. recognize safe and unsafe handling practices.

KEY CONCEPTS	TRAINER'S DIRECTIONS

INTRODUCTION

Method: Exercise

Warmup Exercise Answer Key

• Pass out Employee Guide and ask employees to complete Warmup Exercise in 5 minutes. Ask for correct answers (at left) and review.

1. An outbreak of food poisoning can cause which of the following problems?

   E. all of the above

2. An average cost to a foodservice for an outbreak of food poisoning (to cover medical and legal fees, etc.) is:

   C. $75,000

3. The amount of time it takes 8 gallons of soup to cool down to 60 degrees F from 140 degrees F in a stockpot is:

   D. 4 hours

4. Leftover foods should be:

   D. all of the above

5. The number one factor that contributes to foodborne illness is:

A. inadequate cooling

• Review learning goals.

LEARNING GOAL 1

The employee will be able to recognize major factors leading to foodborne illness.

Foodborne Illness Exercise Answer Key

1. Inadequate cooling

2. A day or more between cooking and serving

3. Infected employee

4. Inadequate cooking

5. Inadequate hot storage

Method: Exercise

• Ask employees to complete Foodborne Illness Exercise. The correct ranking of factors leading to foodborne illness is at left.

LEARNING GOAL 2

The employee will be able to apply safe food handling techniques.

10 Essentials of Safe Food Handling

Method: Buzz Groups

• Using Teaching Aid 2-1, list the 10 Essentials of Safe Food Handling.

• Ask employees for examples of each Essential and write on board or easel pad. Before going to the next Essential, check under Key Concepts for additional applications or examples that were not discussed. Check below for additional notes and techniques you may want to demonstrate.

1. Keep foods out of the danger zone (45–140 degrees F).

Keep hot foods hot and cold foods cold.

Handle foods quickly during delivery and put refrigerated and frozen foods away as soon as possible.

Thaw foods in refrigerator, microwave, or under cold running water for not more than 2 hours (followed immediately by cooking).

Handle foods quickly during preparation. Only handle enough food that can be either cooked or refrigerated in 1 hour or less.

Don't use hot food holding equipment such as a steam table to heat or reheat food.

Cook and serve foods at a temperature of at least 140 degrees F. Heat leftovers to at least 165 degrees F. and pork to at least 150 degrees F.

To cool down hot foods, use shallow pans and/or ice bath. Stir hot foods to remove heat. Cut large pieces of meat, etc. into smaller pieces to allow heat loss. Cool foods to 45 degrees F or less in less than 4 hours.

Use thermometers to check food temperature during storing, cooking, serving, cooling, and reheating.

- Emphasize never to thaw foods at room temperature.

- Show the class examples of shallow pans (2½ inches deep). You may want to demonstrate an ice bath: Pans of food are placed in ice water.

- You may want to demonstrate how to use a thermometer by putting it into the center, or thickest, part of the food. Show that the thermometer must be immersed up to the dimple on the stem in order to get an accurate reading.

2. Inspect foods thoroughly for freshness and wholesomeness upon receipt and before cooking and serving.

Check incoming canned goods for rust, dents, and bulges.

Be sure to first use foods in storage that have been there the longest.

Check that foods are not outdated.

Check for off-colors and odors.

Do not use eggs that are cracked.

- Ask: "Why?" They may indicate the presence of a bacteria in the can that causes a deadly disease known as botulism.

- Ask: "Why?" They may contain significant amounts of a bacteria that can cause foodborne illness.

Wash thoroughly raw foods such as fruits and vegetables before use.

When in doubt, throw it out.

3. Store foods and equipment properly.

   Cover, label, and date foods in storage.

   Do not store food in open cans.

   Store new foods behind old ones.

   Store food off the floor and away from the wall.

   Check temperatures of refrigerators and freezers daily.

   Defrost freezers as necessary. Frost buildup causes freezers to warm up.

   Dry goods storage areas should be cool and dry for good food quality.

   Do not store food or equipment under exposed sewer or water lines.

   Keep storage areas clean.

   Store all equipment so dust can't settle on it.

   Store chemicals and pesticides separately from food.

4. Only use sanitized equipment and table surfaces.

   Clean and sanitize all equipment, tools, tables, dishes, etc. after each use.

   Store wiping cloths in sanitizing solution.

   Store equipment, tools, etc. so they do not collect dust.

5. Avoid letting the microorganisms from one food contaminate another food.

   Keep separate cutting boards for raw and cooked foods.

   Never mix leftovers with fresh food.

   Store fresh raw meats, poultry, and fish on lowest racks.

   Sanitize thermometers after each use.

- Explain your policy.

- Ask: "Why?" It helps prevent pests and animals from getting a free meal.

- Ask: "Why?" To prevent contamination of the food.

- Demonstrate this by using an alcohol swab or a sanitizing solution.

When thawing raw foods in the refrigerator, place them on the lowest shelf.

- Ask: "Why?" To avoid cross-contamination of foods.

6. Observe good grooming and hygiene practices including frequent hand washing.

- This is covered in detail in Training Outline 2.

7. Avoid preparing food further in advance than absolutely necessary.

8. Dispose of waste properly.

Cover garbage cans as much as possible.

- Ask: "Why?" To prevent contamination.

Remove garbage regularly.

- Ask: "Why?" To prevent odors and to prevent attracting bugs and animals.

Clean and sanitize garbage cans regularly.

- Review your policy. Mention the importance of washing cans in areas away from food, equipment, or tableware.

Keep outside garbage containers closed with tight-fitting lids.

Throw out food that was served but not eaten (unless it is wrapped), falls on the floor, is outdated, does not meet quality standards, was exposed to hazardous chemicals, was in the Danger Zone over 3 hours, or was otherwise mishandled.

Store soiled linen in laundry bag or nonabsorbent container.

9. Keep insects and animals out.

Keep doors closed.

Take garbage out frequently.

Keep garbage areas clean and garbage sealed.

Report any holes where an animal could enter.

Don't provide a free meal.

Keep work areas clean and uncluttered.

10. Handle ice properly.

Use clean scoops or tongs to pick up ice; don't use hands or a glass.

- Ask: "Why?" Because hands carry bacteria and a glass might chip in the ice.

Store scoops or tongs in a clean container, not in the ice.

- Ask: "Why?" To minimize contamination.

Don't store any food or beverage in the ice.

- Ask: "Why?" To prevent contamination of the ice.

SUMMARY

Method: Guided Discussion

- Ask the employees to identify a menu item that contains a potentially hazardous food. Write down the name on the top of a board or easel pad.

- Ask the employees to list all the steps involved in the receiving, storing, cooking, holding, and serving of this item. Write these steps down.

- Next, ask the employees to identify hazards at each step when the product might be mishandled. For each hazard identified, ask for a safe food handling technique that would apply.

- You may want to do this exercise with other menu items.

- Ask employees to complete Safe Food Handling Techniques Quiz and review answers at left.

Safe Food Handling Techniques Quiz Answer Key

1. Meats should be thawed at room temperature because it is the fastest method.

   A. True

   B. False

   ___B___ Correct Answer

   Explain that this method is neither safe nor fast.

2. Soups, stews, and sauces should be cooled in shallow pans and stirred to help release the heat.

   A. True

   B. False

   ___A___ Correct Answer

3. To cook frozen vegetables, put them in the steam table a few hours before needed to warm up.

   A. True

   B. False

   ___**B**___ Correct Answer

   Explain that the steam table can only keep hot foods hot, not warm them up.

4. Cooked leftovers should be chilled to a temperature under 45 degrees F in less than 4 hours.

   A. True

   B. False

   ___**A**___ Correct Answer

5. Wiping cloths should be stored in a water and soap solution.

   A. True

   B. False

   ___**B**___ Correct Answer

   Explain that wiping cloths should be stored in a water and sanitizing solution.

6. When you are stocking foods, put the new stock in front of the old stock.

   A. True

   B. False

   ___**B**___ Correct Answer

   Explain that new stock goes behind old stock so the old stock gets used up first.

7. When putting meats in the refrigerator that need to thaw, put them on any shelf where there is space.

   A. True

   B. False

   ___**B**___ Correct Answer

   Explain that the meats should go on the lowest shelf so they do not drip into other foods, particularly cooked foods.

8. When storing foods, be sure to label them with name and date.

   A. True

   B. False

   ___A___ Correct Answer

9. When in doubt, throw it out.

   A. True

   B. False

   ___A___ Correct Answer

   Explain also to ask your supervisor.

10. You can check the temperature of foods by feel.

    A. True

    B. False

    ___B___ Correct Answer

    Explain that a thermometer is the only reliable method.

11. When thawing meats under cold running water, do so for not more than:

    A. 4 hours

    B. 3 hours

    C. 2 hours

    D. 1 hour

    ___C___ Correct Answer

12. Leftovers should be heated to:

    A. 140 degrees F

    B. 150 degrees F

    C. 165 degrees F

    D. 180 degrees F

    ___C___ Correct Answer

13. Throw out food that:

    A. Falls on the floor

    B. Was exposed to hazardous chemicals

    C. Was in the Danger Zone over 3 hours

    D. All of the above

    ___D___ Correct Answer

14. The safest way to get ice out of an ice machine is to:

    A. Use your hands

    B. Use tongs or a scoop

    C. Use a glass

    ___**B**___ Correct Answer

15. Clean and sanitize equipment:

    A. At the end of the day

    B. After each use

    C. When you get to it

    ___**B**___ Correct Answer

■ INTRODUCTION

In today's class, we will discuss how to handle food safely so our guests do not become victims of foodborne illness. By the end of today's session, you should be able to:

1. recognize major factors leading to foodborne illness.
2. recognize safe and unsafe handling practices.

■ WARMUP EXERCISE

Directions: *Circle the correct answer.*

1. An outbreak of food poisoning can cause which of the following problems?
   A. Loss of customers and sales
   B. Loss of reputation
   C. Low employee morale
   D. Need to retrain employees
   E. All of the above

2. An average cost to a foodservice for an outbreak of food poisoning (to cover medical and legal fees, etc.) is:
   A. $10,000
   B. $50,000
   C. $75,000

3. The amount of time it takes 8 gallons of soup to cool down to 60 degrees F from 140 degrees F in a stockpot is:
   A. 1 hour
   B. 2 hours
   C. 3 hours
   D. 4 hours

4. Leftover foods should be:
   A. Covered
   B. Labeled with name
   C. Labeled with date
   D. All of the above

5. The number one factor that contributes to foodborne illness is:
   A. Inadequate cooling
   B. Inadequate cooking

Copyright © 1992 by John Wiley & Sons, Inc.

EMPLOYEE GUIDE *(continued)*

      C. Infected employee

      D. A day or more between cooking and serving

■ FOODBORNE ILLNESS EXERCISE

Directions: *Following are the five major factors, or reasons, for the occurrence of foodborne illness. Rank them in order of importance from 1 to 5.*

Factor	*Ranking*
Infected employee	_____
Inadequate hot storage	_____
Inadequate cooling	_____
A day or more between cooking and serving	_____
Inadequate cooking	_____

■ KEY POINTS TO REMEMBER

Major Factors Leading to Foodborne Illness

There are a number of factors such as inadequate cooking that can cause foodborne illness. The common causes are listed below, starting with the most common.

1. Inadequate cooling
2. A day or more between cooking and serving
3. Infected employee
4. Inadequate cooking
5. Inadequate hot storage

10 Essentials of Safe Food Handling

1. Keep foods out of the Danger Zone (45–140 degrees F).
   - Keep hot foods hot and cold foods cold.
   - Handle foods quickly during delivery and get refrigerated and frozen foods away as soon as possible.
   - Thaw foods in refrigerator, microwave, or under cold running water for not more than 2 hours (followed immediately by cooking). Never thaw at room temperature.
   - Handle foods quickly during preparation. Only handle enough food that can be either cooked or refrigerated in 1 hour or less.
   - Don't use hot food holding equipment such as a steam table to heat or reheat food.

EMPLOYEE GUIDE *(continued)*

- Cook and serve foods at a temperature of at least 140 degrees F. Heat leftovers to at least 165 degrees F. and pork to at least 150 degrees F.

- To cool down hot foods, use shallow pans and/or ice bath. To make an ice bath, place the container holding the hot food into a larger container filled with ice and cold water. Stir hot foods to remove heat. Cut large pieces of meat, etc. into smaller pieces to allow heat loss. Cool foods to 45 degrees F or less in less than 4 hours.

- Use thermometers to check food temperature during storing, cooking, serving, cooling, and reheating. Place the thermometer into the center, or thickest, part of the food and make sure it is immersed up to the dimple on the stem in order to get an accurate reading.

2. Inspect foods thoroughly for freshness and wholesomeness upon receipt and before cooking and serving.

- Check incoming canned goods for rust, dents, and bulges. They may indicate the growth of a bacteria in the can that causes a deadly disease known as botulism. Also check for leaking.

- Be sure to first use foods in storage that have been there the longest.

- Check that foods are not outdated.

- Check for off-colors and odors.

- Do not use eggs that are cracked because they may contain significant amounts of a bacteria that can cause foodborne illness.

- Wash thoroughly raw foods such as fruits and vegetables before use.

- When in doubt, throw it out.

3. Store foods and equipment properly.

- Cover, label, and date foods in storage.

- Do not store food in open cans.

- Store new foods behind old ones.

- Store food off the floor and away from the wall to help prevent pests and animals from getting a free meal.

- Check temperatures of refrigerators and freezers daily.

- Defrost freezers as necessary. Frost buildup causes freezers to warm up.

- Dry goods storage areas should be cool and dry for good food quality.

- Do not store food or equipment under exposed sewer or water lines.

- Keep storage areas clean.

- Store all equipment so dust can't settle on it.

- Store chemicals and pesticides separately from food to avoid contamination.

4. Only use sanitized equipment and table surfaces.

- Clean and sanitize all equipment, tools, tables, dishes, etc. after each use.

- Store wiping cloths in sanitizing solution.
- Store equipment, tools, etc. so they do not collect dust.

5. Avoid letting the microorganisms from one food contaminate another food.
   - Keep separate cutting boards for raw and cooked foods.
   - Never mix leftovers with fresh food.
   - Store fresh raw meats, poultry, and fish on lowest racks so they don't drip into cooked foods.
   - Sanitize thermometers after each use.
   - When thawing raw foods in the refrigerator, place them on the lowest shelf so they don't drip into cooked foods.

6. Observe good grooming and hygiene practices including frequent hand washing.
   - Wear a clean and pressed uniform and apron because soiled clothing harbors bacteria that may be transferred to food.
   - Do not use your apron as a hand towel because the apron will become contaminated and possibly transfer bacteria to food.
   - Wear a hair restraint or covering because you lose about 50 strands of hair daily.
   - Avoid excessive makeup, cologne, and jewelry as they may get into the food. Also, jewelry is a bacterial breeding ground and is hard to keep clean.
   - Cover all coughs and sneezes as they transmit bacteria far and wide. Wash your hands after coughing and sneezing.
   - Don't touch your face or other parts of your body while handling food because bacteria on your skin can then be introduced into food.
   - Taste food properly. Don't use your fingers or a spoon that is reused. Use a plastic spoon or the two-spoon method—use one spoon to dip into the food and the other to eat from.
   - If feeling sick, even with a minor cold, speak to your supervisor immediately so you do not contaminate food. You may be temporarily assigned to a job that doesn't handle food.
   - Cover all cuts, burns, and boils with a bandage and plastic glove, and report to your supervisor immediately.
   - Wear plastic gloves as directed.
   - Use utensils such as tongs and spoons to handle food so bacteria from your hands will not contaminate the food.
   - Smoke and eat only in designated areas. When you smoke or eat, your hands come in contact with your mouth.
   - No gum chewing because you can contaminate food when blowing bubbles.

7. Avoid preparing food further in advance than absolutely necessary.

8. Dispose of waste properly.
   - Cover garbage cans as much as possible to avoid contamination.
   - Remove garbage promptly to prevent odors and to prevent attracting bugs and animals.

EMPLOYEE GUIDE *(continued)*

- Clean and sanitize garbage cans regularly. Wash cans in areas away from any food, equipment, or tableware.
- Keep outside garbage containers closed with tight-fitting lids.
- Throw out food that was served but not eaten (unless it is wrapped), falls on the floor, is outdated, does not meet quality standards, was exposed to hazardous chemicals, was in the Danger Zone over 3 hours, or was otherwise mishandled.
- Store soiled linen in a laundry bag or nonabsorbent container.

9. Keep insects and animals out.
   - Keep doors closed.
   - Take garbage out frequently.
   - Keep garbage areas clean and garbage sealed.
   - Report any holes where an animal could enter.
   - Don't provide a free meal.
   - Keep work areas clean and uncluttered.

10. Handle ice properly.
    - Use clean scoops or tongs to pick up ice; don't use hands (they're contaminated) or a glass (it could chip and leave glass fragments in the ice).
    - Store scoops or tongs in a clean container, not in the ice.
    - Don't store any food or beverage in the ice because it could contaminate the ice.

SAFE FOOD HANDLING TECHNIQUES QUIZ

Name: _____

Date: _____

Trainer: _____

Directions: *Circle the correct answer.*

1. Meats should be thawed at room temperature because it is the fastest method.
   A. True
   B. False
   _____ Correct Answer

2. Soups, stews, and sauces should be cooled in shallow pans and stirred to help release the heat.
   A. True
   B. False
   _____ Correct Answer

3. To cook frozen vegetables, put them in the steam table a few hours before needed to warm up.
   A. True
   B. False
   _____ Correct Answer

4. Cooked leftovers should be chilled to a temperature under 45 degrees F in less than 4 hours.
   A. True
   B. False
   _____ Correct Answer

5. Wiping cloths should be stored in a water and soap solution.
   A. True
   B. False
   _____ Correct Answer

6. When you are stocking foods, put the new stock in front of the old stock.
   A. True
   B. False
   _____ Correct Answer

7. When putting meats that need to thaw in the refrigerator, put them on any shelf where there is space.

SAFE FOOD HANDLING TECHNIQUES QUIZ (continued)

    A. True

    B. False

    _____ Correct Answer

8. When storing foods, be sure to label them with name and date.

    A. True

    B. False

    _____ Correct Answer

9. When in doubt, throw it out.

    A. True

    B. False

    _____ Correct Answer

10. You can check the temperature of foods by feel.

    A. True

    B. False

    _____ Correct Answer

11. When thawing meats under cold running water, do so for not more than:

    A. 4 hours

    B. 3 hours

    C. 2 hours

    D. 1 hour

    _____ Correct Answer

12. Leftovers should be heated to:

    A. 140 degrees F

    B. 150 degrees F

    C. 165 degrees F

    D. 180 degrees F

    _____ Correct Answer

13. Throw out food that:

    A. Falls on the floor

    B. Was exposed to hazardous chemicals

    C. Was in the Danger Zone over 3 hours

    D. All of the above

    _____ Correct Answer

14. The safest way to get ice out of an ice machine is to:

    A. Use your hands

    B. Use tongs or a scoop

    C. Use a glass

    _____ Correct Answer

15. Clean and sanitize equipment:

    A. At the end of the day

    B. After each use

    C. When you get to it

    _____ Correct Answer

1. Keep foods out of the danger zone (45–140 degrees F).

2. Inspect foods thoroughly for freshness and wholesomeness upon receipt and before cooking and serving.

3. Store foods and equipment properly.

4. Only use sanitized equipment and table surfaces.

5. Avoid letting the microorganisms from one food contaminate another food.

6. Observe good grooming and hygiene practices including frequent hand washing.

7. Avoid preparing food further in advance than absolutely necessary.

8. Dispose of waste properly.

9. Keep insects and animals out.

10. Handle ice properly.

■ **TIME REQUIRED:**   30–45 minutes

■ **MATERIALS NEEDED:**

Employee Guides

Teaching Aids

Board or easel pad

Pot and lid

First aid kit

■ **LEARNING GOALS:**

The employee will be able to:

1. recognize causes and consequences of accidents.

2. recognize how to prevent each of the following: cuts, burns, fires, falls, and electric shock.

3. describe what steps to take when an accident occurs.

KEY CONCEPTS	TRAINER'S DIRECTIONS
INTRODUCTION	

	Method: Exercise
Typical Foodservice Accidents	• Ask employees to describe to you and the class a situation when they got hurt working in a kitchen, and why the accident happened. List some typical foodservice accidents on a board or easel pad.
Cuts	
Burns	
Fires	
Falls	• Explain learning goals.
Electric shock	

LEARNING GOAL 1	

The employee will be able to recognize causes and consequences of accidents.

Method: Guided Discussion

Why Accidents Occur

Fooling around

Rushing

Being careless

Working under the influence of drugs or alcohol

Not paying attention

Overdoing it

Ignorance

Feeling they are bound to happen

- Ask employees why accidents occur here. Write them on a board or easel pad. Be sure to include all reasons to the left.

- Ask employee what all these reasons have in common—a human being.

Consequences of Accidents

Painful

Costly

Lowered morale

Lost work time

Damaged reputations

- Ask employees for some suggestions as to the consequences of accidents. Be sure to include all Key Concepts.

LEARNING GOAL 2

The employee will be able to recognize how to prevent each of the following: cuts, burns, fires, falls, and electric shock.

Method: Guided Discussion

Guide to Foodservice Safety

Preventing Cuts

1. Know how to operate equipment.

2. Pay attention when using sharp equipment.

3. Use guards when provided on equipment.

- Using Teaching Aids 3-1 to 3-5, review the Guide to Foodservice Safety asking questions as directed below.

- Ask employees to name sharp equipment they work with.

- Ask employees which equipment has guards.

4. Use tampers to push food into equipment, not your hands!

5. Turn equipment off before adjusting.

- Why? You could be hurt by moving gears and/or blades.

6. No loose sleeves, ties, or dangling jewelry is permitted by equipment.

- Why? They can get caught in equipment and also pull in your arm, for example.

7. Use knives carefully.

- This is covered more in Training Outline 24.

8. Carry dishes and glassware carefully.

- Why? They break easily and shatter.

9. Sweep up broken glass.

- Emphasize not to use your hands to pick up broken glass.

10. Use a special container to dispose of broken glass, dishes, and other sharp objects.

- Why? Sharp items can cut through bags and cut the person removing the trash.

11. Remove nails and staples in shipping cartons and crates, and wear gloves.

12. Remove can lids entirely from cans and put them back into empty cans for disposal.

Preventing Burns

1. Pay attention when working around hot equipment.

- Ask employees which equipment they need to be cautious about in their work areas.

2. Use dry potholders.

- Emphasize first the need to use potholders. Next explain that wet potholders conduct heat to your hands.

3. Keep pot handles turned in from the edge of the range and away from open flames.

- Why? Otherwise they may be hit by someone causing hot foods to spill.

4. Avoid overfilling containers with hot foods.

- Why? They may spill and cause burns.

5. Get help lifting heavy pots of food.

- Why? To avoid spills and burns.

6. Open lids of pots and doors of steamers away from you, and do so slowly.

- Why? To avoid steam burns, which are worse than burns from boiling water. Demonstrate with a pot and lid.

7. Stir foods with long-handled spoons.

8. Warn others of hot surfaces.

- Ask the employees what phrases they use to warn each other of hot surfaces, such as "Coming through!"

9. Let equipment cool before cleaning. Don't use wet rags to clean hot equipment.

10. Don't put icy frozen foods into the fryer. Put foods slowly into the fryer and stand back.
   - Why? Grease may splatter.

11. Strike match before turning on gas equipment.
   - Why? Otherwise you risk a flare-up or large flame.

12. Wear closed-toe and closed-heel shoes that don't absorb liquids.
   - Why? They protect your feet in case of a spill.

13. Warn guests of hot dishes.

Preventing Fires

1. Smoke only where allowed.
   - Mention also the importance of using and having available ashtrays in smoking areas.

2. Don't turn your back on hot fat.
   - Why? It may burst into flames.

3. Keep equipment and hoods free from grease buildup.
   - Emphasize again that grease causes many fires. Ask employees where they need to pay attention to grease buildup in your kitchen.

4. Don't set the fryer at too high a temperature.
   - Why? Overheated grease can burst into flames.

5. Store matches in a covered container away from heat.

6. Keep garbage in covered containers.

7. Store chemicals away from heat.
   - Why? Many chemicals are flammable.

Preventing Falls

1. Wipe up spills immediately.

2. Use "Wet Floor" signs.

3. Wear shoes with nonskid soles and heels.

4. Keep aisles and stairs clear.

5. Walk, don't run.

6. Follow established traffic patterns.

7. Turn lights on to see.

8. Don't carry anything that blocks your vision.

9. Keep drawers closed.

10. Use ladders properly. Never stand on a chair, table, or box.

11. Use handrails.

12. Make sure there are no dangling electric cords.

- Mention not to stand on the top rung of a ladder and do not overreach.

Preventing Electric Shock

1. Never touch electrical equipment or outlets with wet hands or while standing in water.

2. Unplug equipment before cleaning or disassembling.

- Why? A damp cloth on a piece of equipment that is plugged in can cause shocks.

3. Do not yank plugs out by the cord.

- Why? It may cause damage to the cords, which may then cause shocks.

4. Report damaged and worn plugs and cords to your supervisor.

5. Make sure all electrical equipment is grounded.

- Why? It prevents many shocks. Normally it is accomplished by a third prong.

LEARNING GOAL 3

The employee will be able to describe what steps to take when an accident occurs.

Method: Guided Discussion/Demonstration

- Using Teaching Aid 3–6, explain the steps to take when an accident occurs, including basic first aid for the injuries listed.

When an Accident Occurs

1. Apply emergency first aid if needed.

Cuts: Apply pressure with clean cloth to stop bleeding.

Burns: Apply cool water or ice.

Sprains and strains: Apply ice and elevate the injury.

Broken bones: Do not move the person; cover with blanket.

Electrical shock: Remove source of electricity.

2. Call for medical help if needed.

3. Tell your supervisor.

- Show the employees where the first aid kit is, as well as the list of emergency telephone numbers. Review the contents of your first aid kit so employees know what is available.

SUMMARY

Method: Exercise

- Ask employees to complete Personal Safety Goals.

- Ask employees to complete Kitchen Safety Quiz and review answers at left.

Kitchen Safety Quiz Answer Key

Directions: *Check off whether each of the following actions is safe or unsafe.*

Safe	Unsafe	
X		**1.** Removing can lids and putting them back into empty container for disposal
	X	**2.** Using a damp potholder
	X	**3.** Striking a match after turning on gas equipment
X		**4.** Opening lids of pots away from you
	X	**5.** Leaving to go to the bathroom while deep-fat frying chicken
	X	**6.** Standing on a chair to reach supplies
	X	**7.** Yanking a plug out by the cord
X		**8.** Unplugging equipment before cleaning
X		**9.** Wiping up spills immediately
X		**10.** Knowing how to operate equipment before doing so

■ INTRODUCTION

In today's class, we will discuss kitchen safety rules. By the end of today's session, you should be able to:

1. recognize causes and consequences of accidents.
2. recognize how to prevent each of the following: cuts, burns, fires, falls, and electric shock.
3. describe what steps to take when an accident occurs.

■ PERSONAL SAFETY GOALS

Write below one or two unsafe on-the-job habits that you would like to improve. Next, write down a goal you will use as a guide to work more safely. These are for your use only! Sign your name below, signifying that you are going to work toward these goals.

1. Unsafe habit to improve:

    Goal:

2. Unsafe habit to improve:

    Goal:

_____   _____
           Employee Signature   Date

■ KEY POINTS TO REMEMBER

Accidents all have one thing in common: a human being. We cause accidents by fooling or clowning around, rushing, being careless, not paying attention, overdoing it, or simply not knowing what we are doing. Accidents also occur when we accept wrongly that they are a part of life, or when we are working under the influence of drugs or alcohol. Unfortunately accidents cause many kinds of problems. To begin with, accidents usually cause pain and discomfort to those who get hurt. Besides being painful, work time may be lost, and medical bills are costly. Accidents can also lower morale and damage reputations.

What are the major types of accidents that occur in foodservice? Common accidents include cuts, burns, fires, falls, and electrical shock. When an accident occurs, always tell a supervisor and ask others for help if needed. Be sure to know where a first aid kit is located, how to use it, and how to telephone for medical help.

Guide to Foodservice Safety

Preventing Cuts

1. Know how to operate equipment.
2. Pay attention when using sharp equipment. Never touch edge of sharp blades, and wipe away from sharp edges when cleaning.
3. Use guards when provided on equipment.
4. Use tampers to push food into equipment.
5. Turn equipment off before adjusting to avoid being cut by moving gears and/or blades.
6. No loose sleeves, ties, or dangling jewelry are permitted by equipment because they may get caught and pull in your arm, for example.
7. Use knives carefully.
8. Carry dishes and glassware carefully.
9. Sweep up broken glass; don't use your hands.
10. Use a special container to dispose of broken glass, dishes, and other sharp objects because they tend to cut through bags and cut the person removing the trash.
11. Remove nails and staples in shipping cartons and crates, and wear gloves.
12. Remove can lids entirely from cans and put them back into empty cans for disposal.

Preventing Burns

1. Pay attention when working around hot equipment.
2. Use dry potholders. Wet potholders conduct heat to your hands.
3. Keep pot handles turned in from the edge of the range so they are not accidentally knocked and spilled. Keep pot handles away from open flames because the flame will heat them up.
4. Avoid overfilling containers with hot foods.
5. Get help lifting heavy pots of food.
6. Open lids of pots and doors of steamers away from you, and do so slowly to avoid a steam burn. Steam burns are worse than burns from boiling water.
7. Stir foods with long-handled spoons.
8. Warn others of hot surfaces.
9. Let equipment cool before cleaning. Don't use wet rags to clean hot equipment.
10. Don't put icy frozen foods into the fryer. Put foods slowly into the fryer and stand back to avoid being splattered with grease.
11. Strike match before turning on gas equipment to avoid a flare-up or large flame.
12. Wear closed-toe and closed-heel shoes that don't absorb liquids.
13. Warn guests of hot dishes.

EMPLOYEE GUIDE *(continued)*

Preventing Fires

1. Smoke only where allowed.
2. Don't turn your back on hot fat as it may burst into flames.
3. Keep equipment and hoods free from grease buildup because grease causes many foodservice fires.
4. Don't set the fryer at too high a temperature.
5. Store matches in a covered container away from heat.
6. Keep garbage in covered containers.
7. Store chemicals away from heat because many chemicals are flammable.

Preventing Falls

1. Wipe up spills immediately.
2. Use "Wet Floor" signs.
3. Wear shoes with nonskid soles and heels.
4. Keep aisles and stairs clear.
5. Walk, don't run.
6. Follow established traffic patterns.
7. Turn lights on to see.
8. Don't carry anything that blocks your vision.
9. Keep drawers closed.
10. Use ladders properly. Never stand on a chair, table, or box. Don't stand on the top rung of a ladder and do not overreach.
11. Use handrails.
12. Make sure there are no dangling electric cords.

Preventing Electric Shock

1. Never touch electrical equipment or outlets with wet hands or while standing in water.
2. Unplug equipment before cleaning or disassembling to avoid shocks.
3. Do not yank plugs out by the cord because it can cause damage to the cords, which may then cause shocks.
4. Report damaged and worn plugs and cords to your supervisor.
5. Make sure all electrical equipment is grounded. Normally this is accomplished by a third prong.

KITCHEN SAFETY QUIZ

Name: _____

Date: _____

Trainer: _____

Directions: *Check off whether each of the following actions is safe or unsafe.*

Safe	*Unsafe*	
_____	_____	**1.** Removing can lids and put them back into the empty container for disposal _____ Correct Answer
_____	_____	**2.** Using a damp potholder _____ Correct Answer
_____	_____	**3.** Striking a match after turning on gas equipment _____ Correct Answer
_____	_____	**4.** Opening lids of pots away from you _____ Correct Answer
_____	_____	**5.** Leaving to go to the bathroom while deep-fat frying chicken _____ Correct Answer
_____	_____	**6.** Standing on a chair to reach supplies _____ Correct Answer
_____	_____	**7.** Yanking a plug out by the cord _____ Correct Answer
_____	_____	**8.** Unplugging equipment before cleaning _____ Correct Answer
_____	_____	**9.** Wiping up spills immediately _____ Correct Answer
_____	_____	**10.** Knowing how to operate equipment before doing so _____ Correct Answer

PREVENTING CUTS

1. Know how to operate equipment.

2. Pay attention when using sharp equipment. Never touch the edge of sharp blades, and wipe away from sharp edges when cleaning.

3. Use guards when provided on equipment.

4. Use tampers to push food into equipment.

5. Turn equipment off before adjusting to avoid being cut by moving gears and/or blades.

6. No loose sleeves, ties, or dangling jewelry should be near equipment because they may get caught and drag in your arm, for example.

7. Use knives carefully.

8. Carry dishes and glassware carefully.

9. Sweep up broken glass; don't use your hands.

10. Use a special container to dispose of broken glass, dishes, and other sharp objects because they tend to cut through bags and may cut the person removing the trash.

11. Remove nails and staples in shipping cartons and crates, and wear gloves.

12. Remove can lids entirely from cans and put them back into empty cans for disposal.

PREVENTING BURNS

1. Pay attention when working around hot equipment.

2. Use dry potholders. Wet potholders conduct heat to your hands.

3. Keep pot handles turned in from the edge of the range so they are not accidentally knocked and spilled. Keep pot handles away from open flames because the flame will heat them up.

4. Avoid overfilling containers with hot foods.

5. Get help lifting heavy pots of food.

6. Open lids of pots and doors of steamers away from you, and do so slowly to avoid a steam burn. Steam burns are worse than burns from boiling water.

7. Stir foods with long-handled spoons.

8. Warn others of hot surfaces.

9. Let equipment cool before cleaning. Don't use wet rags to clean hot equipment.

10. Don't put icy frozen foods into the fryer. Put foods slowly into the fryer and stand back to avoid being splattered with grease.

continued

11. Strike match before turning on gas equipment to avoid a flare-up or large flame.

12. Wear closed-toe and closed-heel shoes that don't absorb liquids.

PREVENTING FIRES

1. Smoke only where allowed.

2. Don't turn your back on hot fat as it may burst into flames.

3. Keep equipment and hoods free from grease buildup because grease causes many foodservice fires.

4. Don't set the fryer at too high a temperature.

5. Store matches in a covered container away from heat.

6. Keep garbage in covered containers.

7. Store chemicals away from heat because many chemicals are flammable.

PREVENTING FALLS

1. Wipe up spills immediately.

2. Use "Wet Floor" signs.

3. Wear shoes with nonskid soles and heels.

4. Keep aisles and stairs clear.

5. Walk, don't run.

6. Follow established traffic patterns.

7. Turn lights on to see.

8. Don't carry anything that blocks your vision.

9. Keep drawers closed.

10. Use ladders properly. Never stand on a chair, table, or box. Don't stand on the top rung of a ladder and do not overreach.

11. Use handrails.

12. Do not allow dangling electric cords.

PREVENTING ELECTRIC SHOCK

1. Never touch electrical equipment or outlets with wet hands or while standing in water.

2. Unplug equipment before cleaning or disassembling to avoid shocks.

3. Do not yank plugs out by the cord because it can cause damage to the cords, which may then cause shocks.

4. Report damaged and worn plugs and cords to your supervisor.

5. Make sure all electrical equipment is grounded. Normally this is accomplished by a third prong.

WHEN AN ACCIDENT OCCURS

1. Apply emergency first aid if needed.

   Cuts: Apply pressure with clean cloth to stop bleeding.

   Burns: Apply cool water or ice.

   Sprains and strains: Apply ice and elevate the injury.

   Broken bones: Do not move the person; cover him/her with a blanket.

   Electrical shock: Remove source of electricity.

2. Call for medical help if needed.

3. Tell your supervisor.

■ **TIME REQUIRED:**   30–45 minutes

■ **MATERIALS NEEDED:**   Employee Guides, Teaching Aids, boxes for lifting, a cart or truck

■ **LEARNING GOALS:**

The employee will be able to:

1. demonstrate how to lift properly.

2. demonstrate how to properly move a cart or a truck.

KEY CONCEPTS	TRAINER'S DIRECTIONS

INTRODUCTION

Warmup Exercise

1. What is the most common on-the-job accident?

   B. Back injury

2. What is the most costly on-the-job accident?

   B. Back injury

3. Back injuries are preventable.

   A. True

4. When lifting, use your legs, not your back.

   A. True

5. It is better and easier to pull, rather than push, a cart.

   B. False

Method: Exercise

• Hand out Employee Guide and ask employees to complete Warmup Exercise in 5 minutes. Ask for correct answers and review.

• Explain learning goals.

LEARNING GOAL 1

How to Lift

1. Plan it!

   Do you need help?

   Could you use a cart?

Method: Tell/Show/Do/Review

• Using Teaching Aids 4-1 and 4-2, explain how to lift properly, including the additional notes below.

Where is it going?

Which route is best?

2. Get ready!

Spread your feet shoulder width apart.

Put one foot slightly in front of the other for a good support base.

Squat down with back straight and head up. Don't bend over from the waist!

Grip the object firmly with both hands. Keep elbows and arms close to body. Tuck in chin. If lifting a tray, squat down alongside the tray stand and slide the tray onto your shoulder and hand.

3. Lift it!

Straighten your knees slowly and smoothly to a stand. Avoid doing this in a quick or jerky manner.

Don't lift and twist at the same time.

4. Move it!

Keep object close to you.

To change position, move your feet and entire body. Don't twist from the waist!

Look where you are going.

Call out "Coming through" as needed.

5. Set it down!

Bend your knees slowly and smoothly.

Slide load into place—watch your fingers and toes!

- Emphasize using your leg muscles to lift, not your back muscles, because back muscles become injured much more easily.

- This is the cause of most back injuries and it puts undue stress on your lower back. Instead of twisting, stand up straight and move your feet to change position.
- This gives you more control and lessens the pressure.

- Demonstrate how to lift properly.
- Let employees practice and coach.
- Review steps.

LEARNING GOAL 2

The employee will be able to demonstrate how to properly move a cart or a truck.

How to Move a Cart or Truck

1. Push rather than pull.

2. Spread your feet wide, one in front of the other, with your front knee bent.

3. Keep back straight.

4. Slowly push into the cart with your body weight, using your leg muscles to do much of the pushing.

5. Push slowly and smoothly. Avoid sudden motions or twisting your back.

Method: Tell/Show/Do/Review

- Using Teaching Aid 4-2, explain how to properly move a cart or truck.

- Demonstrate how to push a cart or truck.

- Let employees practice and coach.

- Review.

SUMMARY

Method: Exercise

- Redo Warmup Questions. You may want to read each question out loud and ask for the correct answer.

- Ask employees to complete Back Safety Quiz and review answers given at left.

Back Safety Quiz Answer Key

Directions: *Circle the appropriate answer.*

1. When lifting, you should use your:
   A. Arm muscles
   B. Leg muscles
   C. Back muscles
   Correct Answer: B.

2. Instead of twisting your back when lifting, you should wait until you are standing up and then move your feet into the desired position.
   A. True
   B. False
   Correct Answer: A. Otherwise you will hurt your back.

3. Push, don't pull, trucks.

A. True

B. False

Correct Answer: A. Pulling hurts your back.

4. When lifting, do it quickly.

A. True

B. False

Correct Answer: B. Take your time.

5. Keep your back straight when moving a cart.

A. True

B. False

Correct Answer: A.

6. Squat down and get your shoulder under a tray before lifting it.

A. True

B. False

Correct Answer: A.

■ INTRODUCTION

In today's class, we will discuss back safety. By the end of today's session, you should be able to:

1. demonstrate how to lift properly.
2. demonstrate how to properly move a cart or a truck.

■ WARMUP EXERCISE

Directions: *Circle the correct answer.*

1. What is the most common on-the-job accident?
   A. Burns
   B. Back injury
   C. Cuts
2. What is the most costly on-the-job accident?
   A. Burns
   B. Back injury
   C. Cuts
3. Back injuries are rarely preventable.
   A. True
   B. False
4. When lifting, use your legs, not your back.
   A. True
   B. False
5. It is better and easier to pull, rather than push, a cart.
   A. True
   B. False

■ KEY POINTS TO REMEMBER

Back safety is a topic of crucial importance to foodservice employees because almost everybody does some lifting in their jobs, and when done improperly, lifting can cause serious back problems. The bad news is that the most common, as well as the most costly, type of accident involves an employee's back. The good news is that hurting your back is preventable if you follow these steps when lifting or moving a cart or truck.

EMPLOYEE GUIDE *(continued)*

How to Lift

1. Plan it!

   Do you need help?

   Could you use a cart?

   Where is it going?

   Which route is best?

2. Get ready!

   Spread your feet shoulder width apart.

   Put one foot slightly in front of the other for a good support base.

   Squat down with back straight and head up. Don't bend over from the waist!

   Grip the object firmly with both hands. Keep elbows and arms close to body. Tuck in chin. If lifting a tray, squat down alongside the tray stand and slide the tray onto your shoulder and hand.

3. Lift it!

   Straighten your knees slowly and smoothly to a stand. Avoid doing this in a quick or jerky manner.

   Don't lift and twist at the same time.

4. Move it!

   Keep object close to you.

   To change position, move your feet and entire body. Don't twist from the waist!

   Look where you are going.

   Call out "Coming through" as needed.

5. Set it down!

   Bend your knees slowly and smoothly.

   Slide load into place—watch your fingers and toes!

How to Move a Cart or Truck

1. Push rather than pull.
2. Spread your feet wide, one in front of the other, with your front knee bent.
3. Keep back straight.
4. Slowly push into the cart with your body weight, using your leg muscles to do much of the pushing.
5. Push slowly and smoothly. Avoid sudden motions or twisting your back.

BACK SAFETY QUIZ

Name: _____

Date: _____

Trainer: _____

Directions: *Circle the appropriate answer.*

1. When lifting, you should use your:
   A. Arm muscles
   B. Leg muscles
   C. Back muscles
   _____ Correct Answer

2. Instead of twisting your back when lifting, you should wait until you are standing up and then move your feet into the desired position.
   A. True
   B. False
   _____ Correct Answer

3. Push, don't pull, trucks.
   A. True
   B. False
   _____ Correct Answer

4. When lifting, do it quickly.
   A. True
   B. False
   _____ Correct Answer

5. Keep your back straight when moving a cart.
   A. True
   B. False
   _____ Correct Answer

6. Squat down and get your shoulder under a tray before lifting it.
   A. True
   B. False
   _____ Correct Answer

1. **Plan it!**

   Do you need help?

   Could you use a cart?

   Where is it going?

   Which route is best?

2. **Get ready!**

   Spread your feet shoulder width apart.

   Put one foot slightly in front of the other for a good support base.

   Squat down with back straight and head up. Don't bend over from the waist!

   Grip the object firmly with both hands. Keep elbows and arms close to body. Tuck in chin. If lifting a tray, squat down alongside the tray stand and slide the tray onto your shoulder and hand.

3. **Lift it!**

   Straighten your knees slowly and smoothly to a stand. Avoid doing this in a quick or jerky manner.

   Don't lift and twist at the same time.

continued

4. Move it!

Keep object close to you.

To change position, move your feet and entire body. Don't twist from the waist!

Look where you are going.

Call out "Coming through" as needed.

5. Set it down!

Bend your knees slowly and smoothly.

Slide load into place—watch your fingers and toes!

1. Push rather than pull.

2. Spread your feet wide, one in front of the other, with your front knee bent.

3. Keep back straight.

4. Slowly push into the cart with your body weight, using your leg muscles to do much of the pushing.

5. Push slowly and smoothly. Avoid sudden motions or twisting your back.

■ **TIME REQUIRED:**   30–45 minutes

■ **MATERIALS NEEDED:**   Employee Guides
Board or easel pad

■ **LEARNING GOALS:**

The employee will be able to:

1. recognize facets of quality service.

2. set personal goals to provide quality service.

KEY CONCEPTS	TRAINER'S DIRECTIONS

INTRODUCTION

Warmup Exercise

1. Your job is not to serve food, but to serve guests.

   A. True

2. Even when you may be having personal problems, it is important to take an interest in and work with, not against, your co-workers.

   A. True

3. By coming to work properly groomed and dressed, you are taking pride in yourself and your job.

   A. True

4. Working together as a team can make your job much more pleasant.

   A. True

5. Learning to anticipate a guest's needs is a worthwhile skill.

   A. True

Method: Exercise

• Hand out Employee Guide and ask employees to complete Warmup Exercise in 5 minutes. Ask for correct answers and review.

• Explain learning goals.

LEARNING GOAL 1

The employee will be able to recognize facets of quality service.

Quality service is when the server:

1. Reports to his/her station on time, with proper uniform, and is well-groomed.

2. Is friendly, courteous, tactful, and cooperative with guests and co-workers.

3. Treats guests and co-workers with respect.

4. Genuinely smiles.

5. Actively listens to guests and co-workers and makes eye contact.

6. Calls guests and co-workers by name.

7. Doesn't let the hustle-bustle or the occasional complaining guest disturb his/her positive attitude.

8. Knows the menu and daily specials.

9. Assists guests in making selections.

10. Knows all aspects of his/her job and works in an organized manner.

11. Provides service in a timely manner consistent with guest needs.

12. Actively anticipates and plans for meeting guest needs.

13. Responds quickly and courteously to guest requests and complaints without judging their validity.

14. Explains delays in advance to guests.

15. Says "please," "thank you," and "come back again" often.

16. Tries to meet the needs of special guests (handicapped, special diet, celebrations).

17. Helps co-workers out when they need help.

Method: Guided Discussion

- Ask employees to finish the sentence "Quality service is when the server _____."

- Write their responses on a board or easel pad.

- Be sure to include all Key Concepts.

354

18. Talks quietly and briefly with co-workers when necessary.

19. Leaves any problems at home.

LEARNING GOAL 2

The employee will be able to set personal goals to provide quality service.

Method: Exercise

• Ask employees to complete the Personal Quality Service Goals Exercise in the next 10 minutes.

• When all the employees have completed the exercise, ask each one to arrange for a short meeting with his/her supervisor to discuss these goals and to let the supervisor give ideas and support.

• Mention also that the supervisor will be following up at a later date to discuss how successfully the goals have been met.

SUMMARY

Method: Exercise

• Redo Warmup Questions. You may want to read each question out loud and ask for the correct answer.

• Ask employees to complete Quality Service Quiz and hand it in. The answers are any of the Quality Service Skills discussed.

■ INTRODUCTION

Today's training covers how to provide quality service. By the end of today's training, you should be able to:

1. recognize facets of quality service.
2. set personal goals to provide quality service.

■ WARMUP EXERCISE

Directions: *Circle the appropriate answer.*

1. Your job is not to serve food, but to serve guests.
   A. True
   B. False

2. Even when you may be having personal problems, it is important to take an interest in and work with, not against, your co-workers.
   A. True
   B. False

3. By coming to work properly groomed and dressed, you are taking pride in yourself and your job.
   A. True
   B. False

4. Working together as a team can make your job much more pleasant.
   A. True
   B. False

5. Learning to anticipate a guest's needs is a worthwhile skill.
   A. True
   B. False

■ PERSONAL QUALITY SERVICE GOALS EXERCISE

Directions: *In the blank before each quality service skill listed as follows, write down the number of the statement below that is most appropriate. This exercise will help you identify skills you can work on.*

1. I perform this skill well now.
2. I perform this skill fairly well, but I could work harder on it.
3. I could really work on this skill and improve the quality of guest services I provide.

EMPLOYEE GUIDE (continued)

Quality Service Skills

_____ 1. Reports to his/her station on time, with proper uniform, and well-groomed

_____ 2. Is friendly, courteous, tactful, and cooperative with guests and co-workers

_____ 3. Treats guests and co-workers with respect

_____ 4. Genuinely smiles

_____ 5. Actively listens to guests and co-workers and makes eye contact

_____ 6. Calls guests and co-workers by name

_____ 7. Doesn't let the hustle-bustle or the occasional complaining guest disturb his/her positive attitude

_____ 8. Knows the menu and daily specials

_____ 9. Assists guests in making selections

_____ 10. Knows all aspects of his/her job and works in an organized manner

_____ 11. Provides service in a timely manner consistent with guest needs

_____ 12. Actively anticipates and plans for meeting guest needs

_____ 13. Responds quickly and courteously to guest requests and complaints without judging their validity

_____ 14. Explains delays in advance to guests

_____ 15. Says "please," "thank you," and "come back again" often

_____ 16. Tries to meet the needs of special guests (handicapped, special diet, celebrations)

_____ 17. Helps co-workers out when they need help

_____ 18. Talks quietly and briefly with co-workers when necessary

_____ 19. Leaves any problems at home

QUALITY SERVICE QUIZ

Name: _____

Date: _____

Trainer: _____

1. Describe five quality service skills you use when you perform your job.

_____

_____

_____

_____

_____

_____

_____

_____

_____

_____

_____

- **TIME REQUIRED:**   30–45 minutes

- **MATERIALS NEEDED:**   Employee Guides
                                           Teaching Aids

- **LEARNING GOALS:**

The employee will be able to:

1. explain what suggestive selling is.

2. apply suggestive selling techniques.

KEY CONCEPTS	TIME REQUIRED

Warmup Exercise

Method: Exercise
- Hand out Employee Guide and ask employees to complete Warmup Exercise. Ask for correct answers and review.

1. Which of the following statements made by servers are poor examples of suggestive selling?
   1. Everything on the menu is good here.
   3. Any dessert?
   5. Anything else?

2. Which of the following statements made by servers are good examples of suggestive selling?
   2. May I recommend an appetizer? Our jumbo grilled shrimp are a specialty of the house.
   4. We have a wonderful split pea soup to go with your sandwich, if you like.

- Explain learning goals.

LEARNING GOAL 1

The employee will be able to explain what suggestive selling is.

Suggestive selling is not pushy selling of your most expensive menu items to simply increase your tips.

Method: Guided Discussion
- Explain what suggestive selling is and is not.

Suggestive selling is soft selling of the full range of menu items available at your restaurant in an attempt to better acquaint the guest with menu options and therefore better serve his/her needs and wants.

Three Ways to Increase Tips

1. Give good service.

2. Makes sales; don't just take orders.

3. Sell satisfaction, not food.

LEARNING GOAL 2

The employee will be able to apply suggestive selling techniques.

Suggestive Selling Techniques

1. Mention specific menu items from each area of your menu to interest guests. For instance, instead of saying: "Can I get you dessert?" say "May I recommend our homemade black forest cake or our brownie ice cream sundae?"

2. Suggest foods that complement each other. For instance, a side salad with an entree.

3. When describing menu items, use descriptive, accurate phrases and include a favorable evaluation. For instance, "Our deep dish vegetarian pizza is made with whole-wheat flour, three types of cheese, and five fresh vegetables. It is unique."

4. Know which foods are particularly popular so you can respond to guests' requests for good menu selections. For instance, "A very popular entree is our famous prime rib."

5. Find out what your guests want by listening.

- Explain that suggestive selling also benefits the restaurant (by increasing the check average) and the server (through higher tips).

- Using Teaching Aid 6-1, explain the three ways to increase tips. Explain that suggestive selling is just one way. A server needs first to provide high-quality service through anticipating guests' needs, etc.

Method: Guided Discussion/Exercise

- Using Teaching Aid 6-2, explain the Suggestive Selling Techniques, give an example of each.

Let the guest talk and don't interrupt!

Show you are interested in listening by maintaining good eye contact, leaning slightly toward the guest, and nodding your head affirmatively, while you remain relaxed and smile.

Concentrate on the guest's words and feelings.

Ignore distractions and focus on the guest.

6. Find out what your guests want by observing and asking questions. For instance, if your guests arrive with children, be sure to tell them about the children's menu.

7. Keep an eye on refilling beverages throughout service, being sure to follow your rules for responsible alcohol service. For instance, "Our after-dinner drink list is quite extensive. May I suggest . . . ?"

8. Suggest a wine to go with the meal. For instance, "Have you decided on a wine for your meal?" Ask if the guest wants red or white wine, a dry or a fruity wine, or any specific variety, then make two suggestions.

9. Suggest name-brand liquors. For instance, when a guest asks for gin and tonic, ask: "Do you have a favorite gin?"

10. Have the right attitude for suggestive selling:

Take "no" for an answer.

Show genuine interest in enhancing the guests' dining experience.

Be tactful.

Don't be pushy, fast-talking, or dishonest.

Use suggestive selling with all your tables.

- Ask the employees to work in groups of two and complete the Suggestive Selling Techniques Exercise.

- Coach each group as they work on applying each technique in the exercise.

SUMMARY

Method: Employee Practice

- Ask each group of two employees to read to the larger group the applications they came up with to suggestively sell in their exercise.

- Ask employees to complete the Suggestive Selling Quiz and review the answers given at left.

Suggestive Selling Quiz Answer Key

Directions: *Finish the sentence:*

1. Suggestive selling is not pushy selling of your most expensive menu items. Rather, suggestive selling is:

soft selling of the full range of menu items available at your restaurant in an attempt to better acquaint the guest with menu options and therefore better serve his/her needs and wants.

2. One of today's specials is spaghetti with meatballs. How can you describe it to make it sound good?

Our spaghetti is prepared with a homemade tomato sauce and comes with several large juicy meatballs.

3. How will you ask a couple if they want to buy wine?

Have you decided on a wine to go with dinner?

May I help you select a wine to go with your dinners?

4–6. Write down three pairs of menu items that complement each other.

Sandwich with french fries, entree with salad, dessert with coffee (or whatever is appropriate at your restaurant)

7. A couple comes in to celebrate an anniversary. What can you suggest to make their celebration special?

Wine, champagne, after-dinner drink, any special dinners-for-two (or whatever is appropriate at your restaurant)

■ INTRODUCTION

The topic of today's training is suggestive selling, a technique that you can use to both increase your tips and better meet your guests' needs and wants. By the end of today's training, you should be able to:

1. explain what suggestive selling is.
2. apply suggestive selling techniques.

■ WARMUP EXERCISE

1. Which of the following statements made by servers are poor examples of suggestive selling? Place the numbers of the statements here. _____

2. Which of the following statements made by servers are good examples of suggestive selling? Place the numbers of the statements here. _____

Server Statements

1. "Everything on the menu is good here."
2. "May I recommend an appetizer? Our jumbo grilled shrimp are a specialty of the house."
3. "Any dessert?"
4. "We have a wonderful split pea soup to go with your sandwich, if you like."
5. "Anything else?"

■ SUGGESTIVE SELLING TECHNIQUES EXERCISE

Directions: *Following are the suggestive selling techniques just discussed. After reading each one, write two examples of how you can apply this technique in your restaurant.*

1. Mention specific menu items from each area of your menu to interest guests. For instance, instead of saying: "Can I get you dessert?" say "May I recommend our homemade black forest cake or our brownie ice cream sundae?" Another way to recommend specific menu items is to use the following:

   Our chef's own favorite is

   We are famous for our

   An unusual item we make is

Copyright © 1992 by John Wiley & Sons, Inc.

EMPLOYEE GUIDE *(continued)*

Applications:

_____

_____

_____

_____

_____

2. Suggest foods that complement each other. For instance, a side salad with an entree. Other examples of foods that complement each other are:

   juice with breakfast

   french fries with sandwich

   soup with sandwich

   appetizer with cocktails

   wine with meals

Applications:

_____

_____

_____

_____

_____

3. When describing menu items, use descriptive, accurate phrases and include a favorable evaluation. For instance, "Our deep dish vegetarian pizza is made with whole-wheat flour, three types of cheese, and five fresh vegetables. It is unique." Following are descriptive phrases and adjectives.

baked	light
broiled	moist
crisp	refreshing
creamy	rich
delicious	roasted
delicate	scrumptious
fluffy	simmered
homemade	spicy
juicy	tasty
luscious	tender

EMPLOYEE GUIDE *(continued)*

Applications:

_____

_____

_____

_____

_____

4. Know which foods are particularly popular so you can respond to guests' requests for good menu selections. For instance, "A very popular entree is our famous prime rib."

Applications:

_____

_____

_____

_____

_____

5. Find out what your guests want by observing and asking questions. For instance, if your guests arrive with children, be sure to tell them about the children's menu. What kinds of questions can you ask to get more of an idea of what your guests want?

Applications:

_____

_____

_____

_____

_____

6. Keep an eye on refilling beverages throughout service, being sure to follow your rules for responsible alcohol service. For instance, "Our after-dinner drink list is quite extensive. May I suggest . . . ?"

Applications:

_____

_____

_____

_____

_____

EMPLOYEE GUIDE (continued)

7. Suggest a wine to go with the meal. For instance, "Have you decided on a wine for your meal?" Ask if the guest wants red or white wine, a dry or a fruity wine, or any specific variety, then make two suggestions.

Applications:

_____

_____

_____

_____

_____

8. Suggest name-brand liquors. For instance, when a guest asks for gin and tonic, ask: "Do you have a favorite gin?"

Applications:

_____

_____

_____

_____

_____

■ KEY POINTS TO REMEMBER

What is suggestive selling? Let's start by examining what it is *not*. Suggestive selling is not pushy selling of your most expensive menu items to simply increase your tips. Rather, suggestive selling is soft selling of the full range of menu items available at your restaurant in an attempt to better acquaint the guest with menu options and therefore better serve his/her needs and wants. It involves suggesting food and beverages that complement one another so as to heighten the dining experience of your guests.

Everyone wins when suggestive selling techniques are used. The guest enjoys special dishes and extras he or she may not otherwise enjoy, your restaurant increases the check average, and you therefore receive higher tips.

Suggestive selling is just one way to increase tips. You need first to provide high-quality service to your guests. Also, keep in mind that you are selling satisfaction, not just food.

Suggestive Selling Techniques

1. Mention specific menu items from each area of your menu to interest guests. For instance, instead of saying: "Can I get you dessert?" say "May I recommend our homemade black forest cake or our brownie ice cream sundae?"
2. Suggest foods that complement each other. For instance, a side salad with an entree.

EMPLOYEE GUIDE (continued)

3. When describing menu items, use descriptive, accurate phrases and include a favorable evaluation. For instance, "Our deep dish vegetarian pizza is made with whole-wheat flour, three types of cheese, and five fresh vegetables. It is unique."

4. Know which foods are particularly popular so you can respond to guests' requests for good menu selections. For instance, "A very popular entree is our famous prime rib."

5. Find out what your guests want by listening.

   Let the guest talk and don't interrupt!

   Show you are interested in listening by maintaining good eye contact, leaning slightly toward the guest, and nodding your head affirmatively while you remain relaxed and smile.

   Concentrate on the guest's words and feelings.

   Ignore distractions and focus on the guest.

6. Find out what your guests want by observing and asking questions. For instance, if your guests arrive with children, be sure to tell them about the children's menu.

7. Keep an eye on refilling beverages throughout service, being sure to follow your rules for responsible alcohol service. For instance, "Our after-dinner drink list is quite extensive. May I suggest . . . ?"

8. Suggest a wine to go with the meal. For instance, "Have you decided on a wine for your meal?" Ask if the guest wants red or white wine, a dry or a fruity wine, or any specific variety, then make two suggestions.

9. Suggest name-brand liquors. For instance, when a guest asks for gin and tonic, ask: "Do you have a favorite gin?"

10. Have the right attitude for suggestive selling:

    Take "no" for an answer.

    Show genuine interest in enhancing the guests' dining experience.

    Be tactful.

    Don't be pushy, fast-talking, or dishonest.

    Use suggestive selling with all your tables.

SUGGESTIVE SELLING QUIZ

Name: _____

Date: _____

Trainer: _____

Directions: *Finish the sentence:*

1. Suggestive selling is not pushy selling of your most expensive menu items. Rather, suggestive selling is:

   _____

   _____

   _____

2. One of today's specials is spaghetti with meatballs. How can you describe it to make it sound good?

   _____

   _____

   _____

3. How will you ask a couple if they want to buy wine?

   _____

   _____

   _____

4–6. Write down three pairs of menu items that complement each other.

   _____

   _____

   _____

7. A couple comes in to celebrate an anniversary. What can you suggest to make their celebration special?

   _____

   _____

1. Give good service.

2. Make sales; don't just take orders.

3. Sell satisfaction, not food.

1. Mention specific menu items from each area of your menu to interest guests.

2. Suggest foods that complement each other.

3. When describing menu items, use descriptive, accurate phrases and include a favorable evaluation.

4. Know which foods are particularly popular so you can respond to guests' requests for good menu selections.

5. Find out what your guests want by listening.

6. Find out what your guests want by observing and asking questions.

7. Keep an eye on refilling beverages throughout service, being sure to follow your rules for responsible alcohol service.

8. Suggest a wine to go with the meal.

9. Suggest name-brand liquors.

10. Have the right attitude for suggestive selling:
    Take "no" for an answer.
    Show genuine interest in enhancing the guests' dining experience.
    Be tactful.
    Don't be pushy, fast-talking, or dishonest.
    Use suggestive selling with all your tables.

■ **TIME REQUIRED:**   50–70 minutes

■ **MATERIALS NEEDED:** Employee Guides
                         Teaching Aids
                         Board or easel pad

■ **LEARNING GOALS:**   The employee will be able to:

       1. give two reasons to be thankful for complaints.

       2. state three ways to improve listening skills.

       3. demonstrate how to handle complaints in an appropriate manner.

KEY CONCEPTS	TRAINER'S DIRECTIONS

INTRODUCTION

Warmup Exercise

  1. If the level of service is excellent, there should be no complaints.

    B. False

  2. We should be grateful for guest complaints.

    A. True

  3. Active listening is a skill most people are born with.

    B. False

  4. When a listener's emotional level is high, he/she will not be as good a listener.

    A. True

  5. The customer may not always be right, but he is never wrong.

    A. True

Method: Exercise

• Hand out Employee Guide and ask employees to complete Warmup Exercise. Ask for correct answers and review.

• Explain the learning goals.

LEARNING GOAL 1

The employee will be able to give two reasons to be thankful for complaints.

Be thankful for complaints because:

1. The guest may be telling you about a problem that really needs correction and is probably being noticed by other guests as well.

2. The guest cares enough to mention the problem to you and give you a second chance to provide good service. Most guests will simply not complain to you but will tell all their friends and never return.

3. The way you help solve guest concerns ultimately impacts on the success of the restaurant.

Method: Guided Discussion

• Ask the employees for reasons why they should be thankful for complaints. Write their responses on a board or easel pad. Be sure to cover all Key Concepts.

• Explain that if you can resolve a complaint to the guest's satisfaction, you are more likely to see that guest return.

LEARNING GOAL 2

The employee will be able to state three ways to improve listening skills.

Listening Tips

1. Maintain good eye contact with the guest.

2. Do not interrupt.

3. Do not think about your next comment while listening to the guest.

4. Give your full attention to listening and not to doing something else.

5. Encourage the guest to continue talking by nodding your head or saying "yes."

6. Focus on what the guest is saying and concentrate on the main issues.

7. Ask questions at an appropriate time about any unclear points.

8. Repeat to the guest what he/she has said in your own words to confirm understanding.

Method: Guided Discussion

• Using Teaching Aid 7-1, review Listening Tips. Tell employees that listening is crucial to satisfactorily resolving guest complaints and that it is a skill that can be learned.

9. Do not judge what the guest is saying; just accept his/her point of view. The guest may not always be right, but he/she is never wrong.

10. Control any emotional reactions you may have to what the guest is saying.

- Remind employees to not take personally anything a guest says to them. Explain that to the guest, the server is the restaurant—the chef, the manager, the host, and everybody else—so the server hears everything.

LEARNING GOAL 3

The employee will be able to demonstrate how to handle complaints in an appropriate manner.

Method: Tell/Show/Do/Review

Steps for Handling Guest Complaints

1. When a guest addresses a complaint to you, actively listen with sincere interest.

2. Express a desire to help, and ask the guest for more information, if needed.

3. State back to the guest what you think his/her complaint is to check on understanding.

4. Offer one or more solutions to the guest.

5. If the guest is happy with a solution, act on it quickly. If the guest is not happy with any of the solutions, or you do not have the authority to resolve the matter satisfactorily, get the manager.

6. Follow up with the guests to make sure they are satisfied.

- Using Teaching Aid 7-2, explain Steps for Handling Guest Complaints.

- At this time you may want to review your policy on when a server needs to speak to the manager to resolve a problem.

Do's and Don'ts of Handling Complaints

1. Do emphasize resolving the problem instead of finding someone to blame.

- Using Teaching Aid 7-3, review the Do's and Don'ts of Handling Complaints.

2. Do act positively and use positive language.

3. Do respond quickly.

4. Do respect the guest and treat him/her accordingly.

5. Do speak to your manager when in doubt about what to do.

- For instance, use the word *concern* instead of *problem*.

6. Don't make excuses like "we're short."

7. Don't blame anyone.

- This does not help solve the problem or make the guest feel better.

- This also does not help solve the problem, and it reflects poorly on the restaurant.

8. Don't ask for sympathy or understanding.

9. Don't argue.

- Remember, it's the guest who has the problem.

- Nobody ever wins an argument with a guest. Keep in mind that the guest may not always be right, but he/she is never wrong.

10. Don't get defensive.

- Remember, if you don't take a guest's comments personally, you won't get defensive.

- Ask an employee to role-play with you a scene in which a guest makes a complaint. Let the employee choose the complaint and act as the guest. You act as the server who handles and resolves the complaint.

- Now ask employees to break into groups of two and do the same using any of the following complaints (or any of their own), which you can write on a board or easel pad: cold food, waiting for a table, don't like location of table, slow service, food is not as expected, noisy.

- Coach employees and make sure each employee has a turn.

- Review the steps and do's and don'ts.

SUMMARY

Method: Exercise

- Redo Warmup Exercise by reading the questions out loud and asking your employees to tell you the correct answers.

- Ask employees to complete the Handling Complaints Quiz and review answers at left.

Handling Complaints Quiz Answer Key

1–2. Write below the reasons why you should be grateful when a guest complains.
   1. The guest may be telling you about a problem that really needs correction and is probably being noticed by other guests as well.
   2. The guest cares enough to mention the problem to you and give you a second chance to provide good service. Most guests will simply not complain to you but will tell all their friends and never return. If you can resolve a complaint to the guests' satisfaction, they are more likely to be repeat customers.
   3. The way you help solve guest concerns ultimately impacts on the success of the restaurant.

3. What does this expression mean to you? "The guest may not always be right, but he/she is never wrong."

   Although guests' requests may sometimes seem unreasonable, you must always try to meet their needs to the best of your abilities.

4. A guest complains to you that the service is slow and he must leave shortly, but his entree has yet to arrive. Describe the steps you would take to resolve his complaint.
   1. Actively listen with sincere interest.

2. Express a desire to help.

3. State back to the guest what you think his/her complaint is to check on understanding.

4. Offer one or more solutions to the guest.

5. If the guest is happy with a solution, act on it quickly. If the guest is not happy with any of the solutions, or you do not have the authority to resolve the matter satisfactorily, get the manager.

6. Follow up with the guests to make sure they are satisfied.

■ INTRODUCTION

In the restaurant business, as in any business, there are complaints. How we handle complaints will impact on how well the restaurant does, so it is especially important to learn how to handle complaints from your guests. By the end of today's training, you should be able to:

1. give two reasons to be thankful for complaints.
2. state three ways to improve listening skills.
3. demonstrate how to handle complaints in an appropriate manner.

■ WARMUP EXERCISE

1. If the level of service is excellent, there should be no complaints.

   A. True

   B. False

2. We should be grateful for guest complaints.

   A. True

   B. False

3. Active listening is a skill most people are born with.

   A. True

   B. False

4. When a listener's emotional level is high, he/she will not be as good a listener.

   A. True

   B. False

5. The customer may not always be right, but he/she is never wrong.

   A. True

   B. False

■ KEY POINTS TO REMEMBER

Why should you welcome employee complaints? Let's look at a few reasons.

1. The guest may be telling you about a problem that really needs correction and is probably being noticed by other guests as well.
2. The guest cares enough to mention the problem to you and give you a second chance to provide good service. Most guests will simply not complain to you but will tell all their friends and never return. If you can resolve a complaint to the guests' satisfaction, they are more likely to be repeat customers.
3. The way you help solve guest concerns ultimately impacts on the success of the restaurant.

EMPLOYEE GUIDE *(continued)*

Listening

Before discussing exactly how to respond to guest complaints, it is a good idea to review some listening tips. Listening is a major factor in satisfactorily resolving guest complaints and it is a skill that can be learned.

Listening Tips

1. Maintain good eye contact with the guest.
2. Do not interrupt.
3. Do not think about your next comment while listening to the guest.
4. Give your full attention to listening and not to doing something else.
5. Encourage the guest to continue talking by nodding your head or saying "yes."
6. Focus on what the guest is saying and concentrate on the main issues.
7. Ask questions at an appropriate time about any unclear points.
8. Repeat to the guest what he/she has said in your own words to confirm understanding.
9. Do not judge what the guests are saying; just accept their point of view. Be guided by this saying: The guest may not always be right, but he/she is never wrong.
10. Control any emotional reactions you may have to what the guest is saying. Don't take personally any comments a guest makes. To the guest, the server is the restaurant—the chef, the manager, the host, and everybody else—so the server hears everything.

Steps for Handling Guest Complaints

Following is a six-step procedure for handling guest complaints.

1. When a guest addresses a complaint to you, actively listen with sincere interest.
2. Express a desire to help, and ask the guest for more information, if needed.
3. State back to the guest what you think his/her complaint is to check on understanding.
4. Offer one or more solutions to the guest.
5. If the guest is happy with a solution, act on it quickly. If the guest is not happy with any of the solutions, or you do not have the authority to resolve the matter satisfactorily, get the manager.
6. Follow up with the guests to make sure they are satisfied.

Do's and Don'ts of Handling Complaints

1. Do emphasize resolving the problem instead of finding someone to blame.
2. Do act positively and use positive language. For example, use the word *concern* instead of *problem*.
3. Do respond quickly.

4. Do respect the guest and treat him/her accordingly.

5. Do speak to your manager when in doubt about what to do.

6. Don't make excuses like "we're short." This does not help solve the problem or make the guest feel better.

7. Don't blame anyone. This also does not help solve the problem, and it reflects poorly on the restaurant and you.

8. Don't ask for sympathy or understanding. Remember, it's the guest who has the problem.

9. Don't argue. Nobody ever wins an argument with a guest. Keep in mind that the guest may not always be right, but he/she is never wrong.

10. Don't get defensive. If you remember not to take a guest's comments personally, you won't get defensive.

HANDLING COMPLAINTS QUIZ

Name: _____

Date: _____

Trainer: _____

1–2. Write below two reasons why you should be grateful when a guest complains.

_____

_____

_____

_____

3. What does this expression mean to you? "The guest may not always be right, but he/she is never wrong."

_____

_____

_____

_____

4. A guest complains to you that the service is slow and he must leave shortly, but his entree has yet to arrive. Describe the steps you would take to resolve his complaint.

_____

_____

_____

_____

_____

_____

1. Maintain good eye contact with the guest.

2. Do not interrupt.

3. Do not think about your next comment while listening to the guest.

4. Give your full attention to listening and not to doing something else.

5. Encourage the guest to continue talking by nodding your head or saying "yes."

6. Focus on what the guest is saying and concentrate on the main issues.

7. Ask questions at an appropriate time about any unclear points.

8. Repeat to the guest what he/she has said in your own words to confirm understanding.

9. Do not judge what the guests are saying; just accept their point of view. Be guided by this saying: The guest may not always be right, but he/she is never wrong.

10. Control any emotional reactions you may have to what the guest is saying. Don't take personally any comments a guest makes. To the guest, the server is the restaurant—the chef, the manager, the host, and everybody else—so the server hears everything.

1. When a guest addresses a complaint to you, actively listen with sincere interest.

2. Express a desire to help, and ask the guest for more information, if needed.

3. State back to the guest what you think his/her complaint is to check on understanding.

4. Offer one or more solutions to the guest.

5. If the guest is happy with a solution, act on it quickly. If the guest is not happy with any of the solutions, or you do not have the authority to resolve the matter satisfactorily, get the manager.

6. Follow up with the guests to make sure they are satisfied.

1. Do emphasize resolving the problem instead of finding someone to blame.

2. Do act positively and use positive language. For example, use the word *concern* instead of *problem*.

3. Do respond quickly.

4. Do respect the guest and treat him/her accordingly.

5. Do speak to your manager when in doubt about what to do.

6. Don't make excuses like "we're short." This does not help solve the problem or make the guest feel better.

7. Don't blame anyone. This also does not help solve the problem, and it reflects poorly on the restaurant and you.

8. Don't ask for sympathy or understanding. Remember, it's the guest who has the problem.

9. Don't argue. Nobody ever wins an argument with a guest. Keep in mind that the guest may not always be right, but he/she is never wrong.

10. Don't get defensive. If you remember not to take a guest's comments personally, you won't get defensive.

- **TIME REQUIRED:** 30–45 minutes
- **MATERIALS NEEDED:** Employee Guide, Teaching Aids, Board or easel pad
- **LEARNING GOALS:**

The employee will be able to:

1. list two effects of alcohol, describe blood alcohol concentration, and recognize factors affecting it.

2. explain the techniques for preventing a guest from becoming intoxicated.

3. recognize and react to the stages of intoxication.

KEY CONCEPTS	TRAINER'S DIRECTIONS

INTRODUCTION

	Method: Guided Discussion
What might happen if you let an intoxicated guest drive him/herself home?	• Ask employees the question at left and write down their responses on a board or pad.
1. Possible car accident	
2. Possible injuries	• Explain that in many states, the restaurant and server can be held liable for damages caused by the intoxicated guest, and that it is illegal to serve alcohol to minors or to intoxicated guests.
3. Possible death	
4. Possible lawsuit against restaurant	
	• Hand out Employee Guide.
	• Explain learning goals.

LEARNING GOAL 1

The employee will be able to list two effects of alcohol, describe blood alcohol concentration, and recognize factors affecting it.	

	Method: Guided Discussion
Effects of Alcohol	
• Slows down the nervous system	• Explain that alcohol is a depressant drug. Then, using Teaching Aid 8-1, explain

- Loss of inhibition
- Slurred speech
- Loss of some muscle coordination
- Aggressiveness

Blood Alcohol Concentration (BAC)

- BAC is an indicator of how much alcohol is in the blood.
- At 0.10 level, a guest is legally intoxicated in most states and driving ability is impaired.
- At 0.20, a guest is a 100-times-greater traffic risk.

Factors Affecting Absorption of Alcohol into Blood

- Amount of alcohol consumed
- How quickly the alcohol is consumed
- The guest's weight

- The guest's sex

- Whether the guest eats before or while drinking

some of its effects, which will vary depending on how much alcohol was consumed.

- Explain that alcohol is absorbed directly into the bloodstream from the stomach and intestine. Use Teaching Aid 8-2 to discuss BAC.

- Using Teaching Aid 8-3, explain the factors affecting how quickly alcohol is absorbed.

- Ask employees whose BAC will be lower after drinking the same amount of alcohol: a man who weighs 250 pounds or a man who weighs 150 pounds (Answer: 250-pound) man. Alcohol generally affects small people more intensely than heavier people.

- Ask employees whose BAC will be lower after drinking the same amount of alcohol: a man or a woman of the same weight (Answer: the man). Explain that alcohol is absorbed more quickly in women.

- Ask employees whether eating slows down or speeds up the absorption of alcohol into the blood (Answer: slows down).

LEARNING GOAL 2

The employee will be able to explain the techniques for preventing a guest from becoming intoxicated.

How to Prevent a Guest from Becoming Intoxicated

1. First, make sure the guest is old enough to drink.

    When to ask.

    Type of proof required.

    If proof appears forged or tampered, see manager.

2. Measure drinks according to rules.

3. Do not serve a guest more than one drink at a time.

4. Do not serve several drinks to a guest within a short period of time.

5. Offer guests food when they are having a drink.

6. Have an idea of how many drinks guests are consuming.

7. Know the stages of intoxication, which are discussed next.

Method: Guided Discussion

- Ask employees what techniques they can use to prevent a guest from becoming intoxicated. Write on a board or easel pad and cover all Key Concepts.

- Review your policy on when to ask for proof of age, and what type of proof (such as a driver's license with photo) is required.

LEARNING GOAL 3

The employee will be able to recognize and react to the stages of intoxication.

Yellow Zone Signs:

- Guest gets noticeably louder or more quiet.

- Guest becomes overly friendly with others.

- Guest complains about weak drinks and slow service.

Method: Exercise

- Ask employees to work in groups of two or three and complete the Stages of Intoxication Exercise.

- Ask employees for their answers and write on a board or easel pad.

What to Do:

- Keep an eye on guest.

- Keep count of the number of drinks served and the time span in which they are served.

- Recommend food.

- Serve drinks at a slower rate.

Red Zone Signs:

- Guest has trouble walking and may fall or stumble.

- Guest asks for doubles.

- Guest has slurred speech and may be incoherent.

- Guest has hard time picking up change.

- Guest starts arguing with others.

What to Do:

- Tactfully, but firmly, inform guest that no more alcoholic drinks will be served.

- Offer nonalcoholic drinks and food.

- If guest is planning on driving home, offer a ride either in a taxi or company car or offer to call another party. Take guest's car keys if necessary (in a reasonable manner).

- If an intoxicated guest leaves in his or her car, get license plate number and notify police.

- Review your policy here.

SUMMARY

Method: Guided Discussion

- To reinforce the importance of serving alcohol responsibly, ask employees to guess how much an average liquor liability suit costs a bar or restaurant ($500,000).

- Ask employees to complete Responsible Alcohol Service Quiz and review the following answers.

Responsible Alcohol Service Quiz Answer Key

Directions: *Circle the appropriate answer.*

1. Alcohol is a:
   A. Stimulant
   B. Depressant
   C. Muscle relaxant
   Correct answer: B

2. In most states, you are legally intoxicated when your blood alcohol concentration is:
   A. 0.05
   B. 0.10
   C. 0.20
   D. 1.00
   Correct answer: B

3. Alcohol is absorbed faster in:
   A. Men
   B. Women
   C. Neither, there is no difference
   Correct answer: B

4. Having food in your stomach while drinking alcohol:
   A. Slows down the rate of alcohol absorption
   B. Speeds up the rate of alcohol absorption
   C. Has no effect
   Correct answer: A

5. To prevent a guest from becoming intoxicated, you can:
   A. Serve only one drink at a time
   B. Slow down how quickly you serve drinks
   C. Offer food
   D. Offer nonalcoholic beverages
   E. All of the above
   Correct answer: E

6. If you question whether a guest's proof of age is authentic, you should:
   A. Ask the guest to leave
   B. Have a bouncer escort him or her out

C. Speak to the manager

D. None of the above

Correct answer: C

7. A given amount of alcohol affects small people more intensely than heavier people.

A. True

B. False

Correct answer: A

8. It is against the law to serve alcohol to a minor.

A. True

B. False

Correct answer: A

9. If an intoxicated individual comes into your restaurant, you can't refuse to serve him/her a drink.

A. True

B. False

Correct answer: B

10. Offer an intoxicated guest an alternative ride home.

A. True

B. False

Correct answer: A

11. If you notice that a guest has slurred speech and a difficult time walking, what would you do? Explain your house policy.

■ INTRODUCTION

Today's training covers how to serve alcohol responsibly in order that guests do not leave our restaurant in an intoxicated state and possibly hurt themselves and others. Under laws in many states, a server who sells alcoholic beverages to an intoxicated person or a minor can be held liable for damages caused by that person's drunkenness. By the end of today's training, you should be able to:

1. explain the techniques for preventing a guest from becoming intoxicated.
2. list two effects of alcohol, describe blood alcohol concentration, and recognize factors affecting it.
3. recognize and react to the stages of intoxication.

■ STAGES OF INTOXICATION EXERCISE

Directions: *You can classify your guests who are drinking alcoholic beverages into any one of three categories, or zones, as follows.*

Green Zone: There are no noticeable behavior changes in the guest so drinks can continue to be served.

Yellow Zone: There are some noticeable behavior changes so you need to monitor the guest.

Red Zone: The guest is intoxicated and must be handled accordingly.

Directions: *In the spaces provided below, write down the signs of guests who are in the Yellow and Red Zones, and also what you think you should do as a server when you notice a guest has entered these zones.*

Yellow Zone

SIGNS	SERVER ACTIONS

EMPLOYEE GUIDE *(continued)*

Red Zone

SIGNS	SERVER ACTIONS

■ KEY POINTS TO REMEMBER

Alcohol is a depressant drug that slows down the nervous system. Its effects may include, depending on the level of alcohol consumed, the following.

Loss of inhibition

Slurred speech

Loss of some muscle coordination

Aggressiveness

Too much alcohol will culminate in unconsciousness.

When you drink alcoholic beverages, the alcohol passes from the stomach and intestine into the blood where it travels all around the body. An accurate way to determine how much alcohol has been consumed is through a Blood Alcohol Concentration (BAC) test. At 0.10 level, a guest is legally intoxicated in most states and driving ability is impaired. At 0.20, a guest is a 100-times-greater traffic risk.

There are many factors affecting the absorption of alcohol into the blood.

The amount of alcohol consumed.

How quickly the alcohol is consumed.

The guest's weight: Alcohol generally affects small people more intensely than heavier people.

The guest's sex: Alcohol is absorbed quicker in women than men.

Whether the guest eats before or while drinking: Eating slows down the absorption of alcohol into the blood.

EMPLOYEE GUIDE *(continued)*

How to Prevent Guests from Getting Intoxicated

Your first defense in serving alcohol responsibly is to prevent guests from getting intoxicated. The following suggestions can help.

1. First, make sure the guest is old enough to drink.

   When to ask.

   Type of proof required.

   If proof appears forged or tampered, see manager.
2. Measure drinks according to rules.
3. Do not serve a guest more than one drink at a time.
4. Do not serve several drinks to a guest within a short period of time.
5. Offer guests food when they are having a drink.
6. Have an idea of how many drinks guests are consuming.
7. Know the stages of intoxication, which are discussed next.

The Stages of Intoxication

You can classify your guests who are drinking alcoholic beverages into any one of three categories, or zones, as follows.

Green Zone: There are no noticeable behavior changes in the guest so drinks can continue to be served.

Yellow Zone: There are some noticeable behavior changes so you need to monitor the guest.

Red Zone: The guest is intoxicated and must be handled accordingly.

Following are specific signs you can recognize and actions you should take when guests are in the yellow or red zones.

Yellow Zone

SIGNS	SERVER ACTIONS
• Guest gets noticeably louder or more quiet.	• Keep an eye on the guest.
• Guest becomes overly friendly with others.	• Keep count of the number of drinks served and the time span in which they are served.
• Guest complains about weak drinks and slow service.	• Recommend food.
	• Serve drinks at a slower rate.

EMPLOYEE GUIDE (continued)

Red Zone

SIGNS	SERVER ACTIONS
• Guest has trouble walking and may fall or stumble.	• Tactfully, but firmly, inform guest that no more alcoholic drinks will be served.
• Guest asks for doubles.	• Offer nonalcoholic drinks and food.
• Guest has slurred speech and may be incoherent.	• If guest is planning on driving home, offer a ride either in a taxi or company car or offer to call another party. Take guest's car keys if necessary (in a reasonable manner).
• Guest has hard time picking up change.	
• Guest starts arguing with others.	• If an intoxicated guest leaves in his or her car, get license plate number and notify police.

HOUSE POLICY
_____

_____

_____

_____

_____

RESPONSIBLE ALCOHOL SERVICE QUIZ

Name: _____

Date: _____

Trainer: _____

Directions: *Circle the appropriate answer.*

1. Alcohol is a:
   A. Stimulant
   B. Depressant
   C. Muscle relaxant
   _____ Correct Answer

2. In most states, you are legally intoxicated when your blood alcohol concentration is:
   A. 0.05
   B. 0.10
   C. 0.20
   D. 1.00
   _____ Correct Answer

3. Alcohol is absorbed faster in:
   A. Men
   B. Women
   C. Neither, there is no difference
   _____ Correct Answer

4. Having food in your stomach while drinking alcohol:
   A. Slows down the rate of alcohol absorption
   B. Speeds up the rate of alcohol absorption
   C. Has no effect
   _____ Correct Answer

5. To prevent a guest from becoming intoxicated, you can:
   A. Serve only one drink at a time
   B. Slow down how quickly you serve drinks
   C. Offer food
   D. Offer nonalcoholic beverages
   E. All of the above
   _____ Correct Answer

6. If you question whether a guest's proof of age is authentic, you should:

    A. Ask the guest to leave

    B. Have a bouncer escort him or her out

    C. Speak to the manager

    D. None of the above

    _____ Correct Answer

7. Alcohol generally affects small people more intensely than heavier people.

    A. True

    B. False

    _____ Correct Answer

8. It is against the law to serve alcohol to a minor.

    A. True

    B. False

    _____ Correct Answer

9. If an intoxicated individual comes into your restaurant, you can't refuse to serve him/her a drink.

    A. True

    B. False

    _____ Correct Answer

10. Offer an intoxicated guest an alternative ride home.

    A. True

    B. False

    _____ Correct Answer

11. If you notice that a guest has slurred speech and a difficult time walking, what would you do?

12. If you notice that one of your guests is getting noticeably louder and very friendly with anyone near her, what would you do?

- Slows down the nervous system
- Loss of inhibition
- Slurred speech
- Loss of some muscle coordination
- Aggressiveness

- BAC is an indicator of how much alcohol is in the blood.

- At 0.10 level, guest is legally intoxicated in most states and driving ability is impaired.

- At 0.20, a guest is a 100-times-greater traffic risk.

- Amount of alcohol consumed
- How quickly the alcohol is consumed
- The guest's weight
- The guest's sex
- Whether the guest eats before or while drinking

Training Resources

Advantage Media

21601 Marilla Avenue
Chatsworth, CA
818-700-0504

Their videotape catalog has several videos on foodservice sanitation and safety.

Brittanica Training and Development

310 South Michigan Avenue
Chicago, IL 60604
312-347-7903

Brittanica Training and Development sells video programs formerly developed by National Educational Media. Their catalog includes a wide selection of foodservice programs, most designed for commercial foodservices.

Channing L. Bete Co.

200 State Road
South Deerfield, MA 01373
800-628-7733

The Channing Bete Co. produces short booklets for employees on a wide variety of foodservice topics, such as keeping food safe and infection control.

Learning Resource Center

The Culinary Institute of America
Hyde Park, NY 12538

The Learning Resource Center produces videotape programs mainly in the area of cooking and food production.

Mark-Maris

2280 Main Street
Buffalo, NY 14214
716-837-7555

Mark-Maris produces a number of videotape programs on hospital foodservice topics.

National Restaurant Association

The Educational Foundation
250 South Wacker Drive, Suite 1400
Chicago, IL 60606
800-765-2122

The Educational Foundation's (formerly NIFI) *Excel* catalog contains training and resource materials for foodservice operators. They include video training in areas such as sanitation, textbooks, and other foodservice programs and services.

National Restaurant Association

Publications Department
1200 Seventeenth Street, N.W.
Washington, DC 20036
800-424-5156

The National Restaurant Association's yearly catalog contains many practical and useful publications on topics such as sanitation, safety, hospitality, food preparation, management, and marketing. In the area of sanitation and safety they also have employee handout materials and wall posters.

Vocational Media Associates

Box 1050
Mount Kisco, NY 10549-9989
800-431-1242

Vocational Media produces relatively inexpensive and good-quality videotapes on many foodservice topics.

Training Forms

CLASS EVALUATION FORM

Name of Class: _____

Name of Instructor: _____

Today's Date: _____

Directions: *Do not sign this form. This is your opportunity to tell us your thoughts about this training session. Please check the response that most accurately reflects your evaluation.*

1. Amount of material

    _____ Adequate _____ Too much _____ Too little

2. Level of class

    _____ Appropriate _____ Too easy _____ Too advanced

3. Length of class

    _____ Appropriate _____ Too long _____ Too short

4. Opportunity to participate in class

    _____ Adequate _____ Much opportunity _____ Too little

5. Presentation of class

    _____ Interesting _____ Very interesting _____ Boring

6. Helpfulness of trainer

    _____ Appropriate _____ Very helpful _____ Not very helpful

7. Overall rating of class

    _____ Excellent _____ Good _____ Adequate _____ Poor

Additional Comments:

Employee Training Record for 19___

Employee Name: _____

Title: _____

Date of Hire: _____

DATE OF TRAINING	TRAINING DESCRIPTION

Certificate of Training

_____

Has Completed
the Required Course of Training For

_____

And Is Awarded This Certificate By

_____

This _____ Day of _____ 19 _____